Praise for *The Lost Gutenberg*

"A lively tale of historical innovation, the thrill of the bibliophile's hunt, greed, and betrayal."

—*The New York Times Book Review*

"[E]ngrossing reading . . . a fascinating story that touches on the origin of books, the passion of collectors, the unseen world of rare-book dealers, and the lives of the super-rich, past and present. A great read for any book lover."

—*Kirkus Reviews* (starred review)

"A gripping, well-researched account of the importance of books as cultural artifacts and of one particular work that transformed the world, as well as the lives of those who owned a copy, that will appeal especially to bibliophiles."

—*Library Journal*

"The depth of Davis's research cannot be understated. The writing in this book is straightforward and, at times, even heartbreaking, but outstanding reporting lies at its core. . . . *The Lost Gutenberg* pulls readers into a five-century saga, plunging them into the minds of those who desired the Bible and the prestige that came with it. This makes it a book about not only Number 45 and its owners but also a narrative that explores our collective obsession with art, technology, change, and history."

—*NPR*

"You don't need to be a bibliophile to relish this history of how one particular copy of the Gutenberg Bible—known as No. 45—passed from owner to owner in the 19th and 20th centuries before being acquired by Estelle Doheny. . . . Margaret Leslie Davis not only explains how Gutenberg printed his Bible but also details its afterlife in various private libraries and sale rooms. Though one of America's preeminent collectors, Doheny still needed three chances before she was able to acquire her own Gutenberg. When she finally did in 1950, she was virtually blind."

—*The Washington Post*

"An addictive and engaging look at the 'competitive, catty, and slightly angst-ridden' heart of the world of book collecting . . . *The Lost Gutenberg* reads like a comedy of manners starring the cast of an Ayn Rand novel. . . . It's improbable and riveting."

—*Houston Chronicle*

"A fascinating read for anyone who cares about books."

—Minneapolis *Star Tribune*

T0200790

"Book collecting might seem a preoccupation of a limited cadre of obsessive, pedantic academic wannabes, but Davis makes bibliographic history utterly page-turning and absorbing, with intrigues, devastating tragedies, vast fortunes, embezzlement, a seductively voiced telephone operator, the Teapot Dome scandal, murder-suicide, earthquake, and even Worcestershire sauce. Davis's brilliantly told story features outsize characters but focuses primarily on Estelle Doheny, the Los Angeles purchaser of Number 45, who, in one further irony, held in her hands this long-sought volume only after she had turned nearly blind."

—*Booklist* (starred review)

"Heartbreak of the $100 million blockbuster: Six centuries old, it's the best-preserved Gutenberg Bible in the world. And its extraordinary history is a thrilling page-turner."

—*Daily Mail* (UK)

"What's truly surprising about *The Lost Gutenberg* is that Davis makes the 500-year journey of this one book more exciting than any spy novel. For the imaginative Hollywood producer, this book's life story could provide the basis for a richly enjoyable big-budget blockbuster. The action travels across centuries and moves from England to Los Angeles to Tokyo, bringing together the avaricious, duplicitous and deeply religious, all driven by the same desire: to own a copy of one of the most famous books in the world."

—*Catholic Herald* (UK)

"A fluently told, well-executed history . . . This is, at heart, and with heart, an entertaining and insightful human story of obsession about books, and a telling examination of what inspires those who catch the collecting bug."

—*The Daily Telegraph* (UK)

"Stories about rare objects changing hands among collectors have become a distinct subgenre of historical nonfiction. . . . But it'll be a challenge to find a better example this year than this riveting story about a single copy of the Gutenberg Bible, one of the most valuable books on earth."

—*The Week*

"[Take] a break from politics and war this year with this fascinating story tracing a rare copy of the Gutenberg Bible on its unlikely journey around the world."

—*New York* magazine

"Gutenberg Number 45 is a historical artefact of great interest and monetary value. It is a souvenir from a crucial turning point in the history of the human family."

—*The Sydney Morning Herald*

"*The Lost Gutenberg* by Margaret Leslie Davis weaves a fascinating tale of the 500-year journey of one of these Bibles from owner to owner, including Estelle Doheny of Los Angeles, widow of an oil tycoon who achieved her lifelong dream of owning a Gutenberg Bible in 1950. The book reads like a detective novel, but is really a love story professing the far-reaching and personal impact of the Bible."

—*The Book Minute*, Museum of the Bible

"*The Lost Gutenberg* is a riveting account of a book, the people who had to own it, the history of printing, and the history of book collecting. In Margaret Leslie Davis's careful hands, it is also a wonderful read, informative and exciting."

—*Scintilla*

"Davis records the history of this book with enthusiasm and attention to detail— qualities that can also be attributed to many of the book's hunters and custodians over the years. 'Hunter' is a particularly apt term here since, as Davis shows, this Gutenberg Bible and its surviving siblings have become some of the most sought-after books produced in the West, inspiring lifelong searches and intense rivalries and commanding eye-watering prices at auction. . . . The value of rare books—personal, cultural, and financial—are recurring themes. Davis reminds us that books have long been objects of desire but shows that their perceived value is connected to a constantly shifting social and economic context. The tales of frenzied aristocratic bibliomania occur during what she calls the 'Imperial Century,' when the prices were high and the reputational stakes higher."

—*History Today*

"A gripping exploration of the life of the world's oldest and most famous printed book, the Gutenberg Bible . . . The real talent of Davis is in producing a detailed, highly readable narrative which places this incredibly rare book within its cultural and historical context and in melding this with the lives of its owners which has resulted in a fascinating narrative where we can vicariously experience the thrill of the hunt and the obsession of collectors."

—*Glam Adelaide* (Australia)

"This is an absolutely fascinating book, beautifully and engagingly narrated and populated with marvelous eccentric characters who thought nothing of spending a fortune on a book. It is also the story of how rare books have now become extremely valuable commodities but, thanks to modern technology, their secrets and beauty are readily available to us all."

—*Good Reading Magazine* (Australia)

"Author Margaret Leslie Davis has struck upon a fantastic idea: tracing one copy of the Gutenberg Bible through its various owners, with some wonderfully bizarre tales involving Worcestershire sauce and plutonium isolation thrown in for good measure. Hers is a tale of triumph and betrayal; as a profile of Doheny alone, Davis's book is worth the price of admission. . . . Her reporting is spot-on, and her style is lively and engaging. . . . An admirable achievement."

—*Fine Books & Collections*

"Bibliophiles love books, and none more than the book collector's dream of dreams, a Gutenberg Bible. Davis tells not just with skill but also with sympathy and even love. A richly informative but finally a deeply moving story."

—Jack Miles, Pulitzer Prize–winning author of *God: A Biography*

"Margaret Leslie Davis's *The Lost Gutenberg* is a fascinating and apt successor to her *Mona Lisa in Camelot*, for the Gutenberg Bible is to the book arts what the Mona Lisa is to painting—a Holy Grail and epitome of the art it embodies. Davis writes of the succession of owners of a particular copy of Gutenberg's masterpiece, Number 45. She gives a haunting and at times heartbreaking account of the way a material object can acquire a mystical resonance and affect different people and lives across centuries."

—Victoria Steele, former Brooke Russell Astor Director
of Collections, New York Public Library

"The fascinating story of how one Gutenberg Bible traveled through two centuries and how one woman, the legendary Los Angeles book collector Estelle Doheny, pursued, purchased, and cherished it. This tale, written for both ardent bibliophiles and those seeking an engaging historical narrative, includes a sad episode of betrayal, exciting nuclear discoveries, and the arrival of Gutenberg into the digital age."

—Alan Jutzi, former Avery Curator of Rare Books, The Huntington Library,
Art Museum, and Botanical Gardens

"*The Lost Gutenberg* has two protagonists: a singularly beautiful copy of the Gutenberg Bible—known as #45—and the California heiress who emerged from scandal to chase it. Along the way, Davis takes in the larger-than-life stories of the aristocrats, libertines, billionaires, and bibliomaniacs who all competed to own this unique piece of literary history. A fascinating exploration of the shifting value we place on rare books, and the shifting wealth and power of those who hunt them."

—Michael Blanding, *New York Times* bestselling author
of *The Map Thief: The Gripping Story of an Esteemed Rare-Map Dealer
Who Made Millions Stealing Priceless Maps*

THE Lost Gutenberg

The Astounding Story of One Book's
Five-Hundred-Year Odyssey

• • •

MARGARET LESLIE DAVIS

A TarcherPerigee Book

tarcherperigee

An imprint of Penguin Random House LLC
penguinrandomhouse.com

First trade paperback edition 2021
Copyright © 2019 by Margaret Leslie Davis
Photos on pp. x, 86, 97, 98, 100, 132, 134, 136, 137 reproduced with the permission
of the Archivist of the Roman Catholic Archdiocese of Los Angeles, on behalf
of the copyright holder, The Roman Catholic Archbishop of Los Angeles, a
corporation sole.
Photos on pp. 8, 164 courtesy Thomas A. Cahill.
Photos on pp. 15, 24, 33, 39, 43, 51, 58, 59, 71, 86, 108, 140, 142, 157, 158, 168, 179,
181, 183, 186, 208, 215, 227, 236, 238 courtesy Rita S. Faulders.
Photos on pp. 22 and 62 courtesy National Portrait Gallery, London.
Photo on p. 188 courtesy Richard N. Schwab and Thomas A. Cahill.
Photos on p. 246 courtesy Keio University.

TarcherPerigee with tp colophon is a registered trademark of Penguin Random
House LLC.

Most TarcherPerigee books are available at special quantity discounts for
bulk purchase for sales promotions, premiums, fund-raising, and educational
needs. Special books or book excerpts also can be created to fit specific needs.
For details, write: SpecialMarkets@penguinrandomhouse.com.

LIBRARY OF CONGRESS CATALOGING-IN-PUBLICATION DATA
Names: Davis, Margaret Leslie, author.
Title: The lost Gutenberg : the astounding story of one book's
    five-hundred-year odyssey / Margaret Leslie Davis.
Description: New York : TarcherPerigee, 2019. | Includes bibliographical
    references and index.
Identifiers: LCCN 2018049581 | ISBN 9781592408672 (hardback) |
    ISBN 9780698409804 (ebook)
Subjects: LCSH: Gutenberg Bible. | Books—Provenance. | Doheny,
    Estelle, 1875–1958. | Book collectors—Biography | BISAC: HISTORY /
    Europe / Western. | BIOGRAPHY & AUTOBIOGRAPHY / Historical. |
    RELIGION / History.
Classification: LCC Z241.B58 D39 2019 | DDC 093—dc23 LC record available
    at https://lccn.loc.gov/2018049581
p.   cm.

ISBN (paperback) 9780399573361

Printed in the United States of America
1st Printing

Book design by Tiffany Estreicher

CONTENTS

THE LOST
Gutenberg

Estelle Doheny soon after her marriage to oil tycoon Edward Doheny, circa 1900. She was the unseen telephone operator connecting his calls to oil investors and Doheny claimed he was entranced by her voice. They married after a short courtship.

PART I

THE IMPERIAL CENTURY

The Gutenberg Bible is a masterpiece of world culture. Only forty-eight or forty-nine copies of this landmark work survive, and of those, only one has been owned by a woman collector. This is the true story of that book, the copy designated as Number 45, printed by Johann Gutenberg sometime before August 15, 1456.

CHAPTER ONE

Million-Dollar Bookshelf

A WOODEN BOX CONTAINING one of the most valuable books in the world arrives in Los Angeles on October 14, 1950, with little more fanfare—or security—than a Sears catalog. Code-named "the commode," it was flown from London via regular parcel post, and while it is being delivered locally by Tice and Lynch, a high-end customs broker and shipping company, its agents have no idea what they are carrying and take no special precautions.

The widow of one of the wealthiest men in America, Estelle Betzold Doheny, is among a handful of women who collect rare books, and she has amassed one of the most spectacular libraries in the West. Acquisition of the Gutenberg Bible, universally acknowledged as the most important of all printed books, will push her into the ranks of the greatest book collectors of the era. Its arrival is the culmination of a forty-year hunt, and she treasures the moment as much as the treasure.

Estelle's pursuit of a Gutenberg began in 1911, when she was a wasp-waisted, dark-haired beauty, half of a firebrand couple reshaping the American West with a fortune built from oil. Now seventy-five, she is a soft, matronly figure with waves of gray hair. The auspicious occasion brings a flash of youth to her face, and she is all smiles. But she resists the impulse to rip into the box, leaving it untouched overnight so she can open it with appropriate ceremony the next day.

Estelle has invited one of her confidants, Robert Oliver Schad, the curator of rare books at the Henry E. Huntington Library, to see her purchase, and at noon he arrives with his wife, Frances, and their eighteen-year-old son, Jasper. Estelle's secretary, Lucille Miller, escorts the family through the mansion's Great Hall to the library, and with a sweep of her hand invites the group to sit at the oblong wood table in the center. The Book Room, as Estelle affectionately calls it, is finished in rich redwood and had been her husband's billiard parlor. Its walls had once featured paintings related to Edward Doheny's petroleum empire, murals commissioned by the onetime prospector who drilled some of the biggest gushers in the history of oil. Today the room is lined with custom-built shelves for Estelle's beloved books—her own personal empire, worth as much as Edward's oil.

Her collection began almost as a lark, sparked by popular lists of books that everyone should own, but now contains nearly ten thousand exceedingly rare volumes available only to the fabulously wealthy and culturally ambitious—gilded illuminated manuscripts glowing with saints and mythical creatures; medieval encyclopedias; and the earliest examples of Western printing, 135 incunabula—books printed before the year 1501. Such seminal works of Western culture as Cicero's *De officiis* and Saint Thomas Aquinas's *Summa Theologicae* rub shoulders with a sumptuous 1477 copy of *The Canterbury Tales*. This is the million-dollar company the Gutenberg Bible will keep on its shelf.

The two-by-three-foot crate waits at the center of the table, spotlighted by a bronze-and-glass billiard lamp. When Estelle enters the room, accompanied by her companion and nurse, Rose Kelly, the group stands silent. Lucille takes out a pair of scissors and passes it around. Estelle, dressed for the occasion in a pale blue printed silk dress, a gem-studded comb at her right temple, wants everyone to take part, so each person makes a cut in the knotted cord that winds the package.

It's an emotional occasion for Lucille, too, a slim, long-limbed woman with center-parted, brown hair that curls up around her cheeks. Never without a pencil tucked behind her ear, she has a subdued beauty that's easy to miss, a pale, symmetrical face hidden behind her glasses. Lucille has been Estelle's steady partner in the quest for the Gutenberg, party to every promise, hope, and near miss for nearly twenty years. She almost allows herself to smile as she pulls away the box's coverings and lifts the lid, but then she sees the shabby mess inside. "I could hardly believe my eyes," she said later. "It just looked like a bundle of old tattered, torn papers. It was the most carelessly wrapped thing I ever saw."[1] The precious book has been enclosed without padding, wrapped in thin cardboard and then in dark corrugated paper tied with a heavy cord. Lucille mentally chastises the customs officials in New York who had opened the parcel for inspection and then shoved it back in the box "any old way, and tied a string or two here or there and along it came."[2]

It will be a miracle if the book is not damaged.

But as she lifts it out of the last of the wrappings, the Bible appears to be fine. For an expert like Robert Schad, there is no mistaking the original fifteenth-century binding of age-darkened brown calfskin stretched over heavy wood boards. The copy now in Estelle Doheny's possession is the first issue of the first edition of the first book printed with movable metal type, in near-pristine condition, its pages fresh and clean. The lozenge and floweret patterns stamped into the leather cover are still sharp and firm to the touch. Five raised metal bosses protect the covers, one ornament in the center and one set in an inch from each of the four corners. Two broken leather-edge clasps are the only reminders that this book, which has presented the Living Word for nearly five centuries, has been opened and closed often enough to wear down the heavy straps.[3]

Lucille moves close to her employer, standing on her left and tucking her arm under the spine of the heavy book so that Mrs. Doheny can more easily examine it. Estelle reaches out to touch the fine old leather and slowly lifts the cover and opens the enormous volume. With her gold-framed glasses perched on the edge of her nose, she glides her right hand softly over the edges of the book's rippling leaves, taking special care not to touch the print. As she turns the crackling pages one by one, she is overcome with quiet joy. Her pursuit of this object of Western invention had begun long ago, during happier days, before her husband was embroiled in scandal. She feels the smoothness of the heavy rag paper under her fingers and strains to focus her gaze on the black Gothic letters, but the Latin text is lost in a cloudy blur and she can't make out the printed lines. A hemorrhage in one eye and glaucoma in the other have left Estelle almost completely blind at the age of seventy-five.

Still, she knows well what she possesses, and just to be in its presence would be stirring to anyone who understands its significance. The European advancement of printing with movable metal type transformed every aspect of human civilization, and Johann Gutenberg's execution of the work set a standard that few would match.

As Estelle runs her hands over the book, Schad, a poised man of medium build who's dressed today in a black suit and tie with a crisp white shirt, points out a few of the qualities that make it unique. Every Gutenberg Bible is somewhat different from every other because while Gutenberg's workshop printed the pages of each massive volume, the printers left it to the purchaser to have them bound and decorated. Guided by the owner's taste and budget, a whole team of artisans might step in to customize the book—illuminators would be hired to paint the highly pictorial ornamental letters, and specialists known as rubricators added chapter titles and headings separate from the text.

The first owner of this Bible had not scrimped on ornamentation. The volume is filled with elaborate, richly colored illuminations and enlarged capital letters. In the upper left corner of the first page, a large capital letter *F* is painted in bright green and gold with ornaments of green leafy vines and tiny, bell-shaped flowers that trace the outer margin. The intricate foliage sweeps down the page and across the bottom, where in the far right corner the artist added a white-bellied blue bird with a bright yellow beak.

Such imagery stands in delicate contrast to the enduring richness of Gutenberg's type. Jet-black and lustrous, the ink shimmers as if the pages were just recently printed, a quality that was long one of the great mysteries of Gutenberg's art, a hallmark of the Bibles he printed in Mainz, Germany, before August 15, 1456.

Incipit epistola sancti iheronimi ad
paulinum presbiterum de omnibus
diuine historie libris·capitulu prim.

RAter ambrosius
tua michi munus-
cula pferens·detulit
sit et suauissimas
litas·q a principio
amicicias·fide pba-
te iam fidei et veteris amicicie noua:
pferebant. Era eni illa necessitudo e-
t xpi glutino copulata·qua non vtili-
tas rei familiaris·non pncia tantum
corpo·non sbdola et palpans adulaco·
sed dei timor·et diuinaz scripturaru
studia conciliant. Legim in veterib
historiis·quosda lustrasse·puincias·
nouos adiisse pplos·maria transisse·
ut eos quos ex libris nouerant: cora
q videret. Sicut pitagoras memphi-
ticos vates·sic plato egiptu·et archita
tarentinu·eandemq oram ytalie·que
quonda magna grecia dicebat·labo-
riosissime peragrauit·et ut qui athenis
mgr erat·et potens·cuiusq doctrinas
achademie gignasia psonabant·fieret
peginus atq discipulus·malens aliena
verecude discere·qui sua ipudent ingere·
Denicz cu litras quasi toto orbe fugien-
tes psequit·capt a piratis et venundat-
us·tiranno crudelissimo paruit·duct
captiuus vinct et seruus. Tame quia
pfius maior emente se fuit·ad tytum
liuium·lacteo eloquencie fonte manante·
de vltimis hispanie galliarucz finibz
quosdam venisse nobiles legimus·et
quos ad contemplacione sui roma no
traxerat·unius hois fama pduxit. Ha-
buit illa etas inaudiu omnibz seculis·
celebrandumq miraclu·ut urbe tanta

ingressi·aliud extra urbem quererent.
Apollonius siue ille magus ut vulgus
loquitur·siue pfius·ut pitagorici tra-
dunt·intrauit psas·ptransiuit caucasu·
albanos·scithas·massagetas·opule-
tissima indie regna penetrauit·et ad
extremum latissimo physon amne
transmisso puenit ad bragmanas·ut
hyarcam in throno sedente aureo et de
tantali fonte potantem·inter paucos
discipulos·de natura·de morib·ac de
cursu dierum et siderum audiret docentem.
Inde p elamitas·babilonios·chalde-
os·medos·assyrios·parthos·syros·
phenices·arabes·palestinos·reuisus
ad alexandria·perexit ad ethiopia·
ut gignosophistas et famosissimam
solis mensam videret in sabulo. In-
uenit ille vir ubiqz qd disceret·et semp
proficiens·semp se melior fieret. Scrip-
sit super hoc plenissime octo volumi-
nibus·philostratus.

Quid loquar de seculi hominibz·
cum apostolus paulus·vas electionis·
et magister gencium·qui de consciencia
tanti se hospitis loquebat·dicens. An
experimentum queritis eius qui in me
loquitur xps. Post damasci arabiacz
lustrata·ascedit iherosolima ut videret
petru et masit apud eu diebz quindeci.
Hoc eni misterio ebdomadis et ogdo-
adis·futur genciu pdicator instruen-
dus erat. Rursusq post annos quatuor-
decim assumpto barnaba et tyto·expo-
suit cu aplis euangeliu·ne forte in vacuum curreret aut cucurrisset. Habet
nescio qd latentis energie·viue vocis
actus·et in aures discipli de auctoris
ore transfusa·fortius sonat. Unde et
eschineus cu rodi exularet·et legeretur

*A striking green F and delicately drawn foliage distinguish the first page of
the Doheny Gutenberg Bible, printed in Mainz, Germany, sometime before
August 15, 1456.*

Most scholars believe that Gutenberg produced about 180 copies, and among these, most likely 150 were printed on paper and 30 on animal skin known as vellum. The price of the book when it left the printer's workshop was believed to be about thirty florins, equivalent to a clerk's wages for three years. The vellum versions were priced higher, since they were more labor-intensive and expensive to produce—a single copy required the skin of 170 calves.[4]

Estelle's copy is one of the forty-five known to exist in 1950. They're in various conditions, scattered around the world in private libraries and museums: twelve in America, eleven in Germany, nine in Great Britain, four in France, two in Italy, two in Spain, and one each in Austria, Denmark, Poland, Portugal, and Switzerland.[5] Fewer than half have all their original pages, a precondition of being designated "perfect."

Hers is perhaps the most beautiful of the surviving paper copies. Despite its age, this volume lacks no pages and has no serious damage. Designated as Number 45 in a definitive list compiled by Hungarian book authority Ilona Hubay, this Bible has clearly received special care through the centuries, or at least supremely benign neglect.

Gutenberg's printed pages were usually bound in two volumes, and nearly half of the known copies are considered "incomplete" because the second volume has been lost. That is the case with Number 45, which contains the Old Testament from Genesis through the Psalms. But it is one of the few to retain its original binding, created in Mainz contemporaneously with its printing. The calfskin cover is decorated in a distinctive pattern of impressions. A lattice motif of small diamonds, known by bookmen as a "lozenge diaper," surrounds six different stamps: an eagle, a trefoil, a fleur-de-lis, and a seven-pointed star. Those details, and the cover as a whole, are in exceptional condition.

Lucille steps aside so that Schad can gently steady the fifteen-pound volume for Estelle. Of all the bookmen who have come and gone during her decades of zealous acquisitions, none have meant more to her than Robert O. Schad, a trusted adviser in her quest, who for the past twenty years has hand-selected the items purchased to strengthen the magnificent "collection of collections" at the Huntington Library.[6] Like Estelle, he is completely self-taught, educated through decades of direct contact with the world's most important books and the famous dealers who trade them. He has always treated her with respect, and always welcomed her questions, no matter how unsophisticated.

Schad signals his son to pick up the Kodak Duaflex twin-lens camera they've brought. Jasper rapidly snaps a half-dozen photographs, covering the bulb with a white handkerchief to protect Mrs. Doheny's sensitive eyes. In one frame, Estelle holds the Bible, gazing down at its pages. As far as Schad knows, this is only the second time a Gutenberg Bible and its owner have been photographed together.

The day has become "boiling hot,"[7] and the party retires to the mansion's Pompeian Room. Beneath a twenty-four-foot-wide Favrile glass dome ceiling attributed to Louis Comfort Tiffany, the group fetes the Gutenberg Bible's arrival with a luncheon whose menu Lucille saves for the ages: jellied consommé madrilene with crackers and relishes; fried chicken with hominy and hot biscuits; mixed-green salad and a platter of fresh peaches, pears, and persimmons; and a dessert of cream puffs and cookies, with tea served in glasses chilled with an abundance of ice.

According to Lucille's daybook, the luncheon ends promptly at 2:30 p.m., when she returns to the Book Room to put the Bible back in its shipping box, preserving the tattered wrapping. As she tucks it away, she notices a stiff white card that reads simply: "Customs Officer: Please handle with GREAT CARE and repack in same manner. Thank you." Below the handwritten note is printed, "With the COMPLIMENTS OF MAGGS BROS. LTD."

"I am keeping the book," Estelle hurriedly writes Ernest Maggs, one of London's revered book dealers, early the following morning. She dispatches a check for twenty-five thousand pounds sterling, the equivalent then of $70,093.[8]

It is a check that she is delighted to sign. Thanks to a strong US dollar and the recent devaluation of the British pound sterling, she has managed to secure one of Western civilization's great artifacts at a bargain price. With payment tendered, Estelle Betzold Doheny becomes the first and only woman to purchase a Gutenberg Bible as a private collector.[9] Her deep need to own this holy book not only reflects her faith as a devout Catholic but also reveals her shrewd mind for the bottom line.

She tells Lucille she has never felt richer or more content. The book is a panacea for the deep personal losses she has faced, and, she believes, it is a gift from God. It not only lifts her heart, it changes her very image of herself.

◆ ◆ ◆

AT 8:15 THE next morning, Lucille pulls into the circular driveway of the Doheny mansion in her black Ford Model A. Her first job is to catalog the newest addition to the library, as she's done since the summer of 1931, when she answered an ad in the newspaper for a temporary typist and signed on, not knowing "a rare book from a pulp novel."[10] Slipping an unruled, white, three-by-five-inch card into her charcoal-gray Royal Aristocrat manual typewriter, she begins: "BIBLIA LATINA [Mainz: Johann Gutenberg, before 15 August, 1456]." In the right-hand corner, she adds the book's acquisition number, 6979, and underlines it. Then she fills in details of its format and binding, using information sent from Ernest Maggs:

> On paper; Gothic type; 324 I. [through the Book of Psalms]; 15 ⅞ in. x 11 ½ in.; double columns of 40–41–42 lines; contemporary stamped calf over wooden boards rebacked, 5 metal bosses on each cover, remains of clasps

She wants to make sure that the news about the purchase doesn't leak. She's nervous about keeping the book on the premises, certain that it is "only a matter of time before the secret got out," and reporters and lookie-loos will be on the front lawn demanding to take pictures.[11] Still haunted by the spectacle of the Teapot Dome scandal, when there was no escape from paparazzi and the lurking press, she and Estelle do all they can to avoid bringing attention to the Doheny residence at 8 Chester Place. No one outside the household is told about the book, including the guards posted at the entrance of the gated residential compound in the West Adams neighborhood of Los Angeles.

Lucille is hypervigilant. Each night before she drives home, she checks and double-checks to be sure that Number 45 is safely locked inside the vault that's hidden behind the thick velvet drapery in the Book Room. She obsesses about making sure the lock is really locked, and more than once she walks back to the Book Room to check it again. "It was up to me to keep the Bible in the book library safe," Miller said later. "I've never been so scared in my life."[12]

She is used to handling incunabula, but taking responsibility for a book this significant rattles her. Over the next few days, she calls a handful of experts, saying obliquely that she is seeking advice on how best to preserve a fragile, folio-size, leather-bound book printed on paper from the fifteenth century. The name Gutenberg is never mentioned.

Cautions abound. The book, she is told, must be kept in darkness most of the day because exposure to light could cause ink and pigments to fade, and anytime it is open for display, light levels must be measured and controlled. Inside the vault, it must be securely positioned on a shelf to avoid any accidental damage by bumping. She's advised to keep the vault as cool as possible, and to watch the relative humidity—if it's too high, mold could grow; too low and the pages could become desiccated and brittle. Fluctuating levels would be a horror, causing the book to expand and contract, which might lead paper to cockle, ink to flake, and covers to warp.

Ideally, she'll keep the book between 55 and 68 degrees Fahrenheit, with 35 percent to 60 percent relative humidity. But that's a fantasy. Los Angeles is in the midst of a mid-October heat wave, and the Doheny mansion isn't air-conditioned. They'd unpacked the Bible on the hottest day 1950 had seen, and even opening every window of the three-story, 24,000-square-foot residence hadn't been enough to keep the mid-morning indoor temperature from reaching one hundred sweltering degrees. Somehow, though, the Bible must be kept bone-dry, cool, and stable. Lucille's great fear, which leaves her "positively terrified,"[13] is that the book will develop what she calls "rabbit back," a badly warped spine caused by a drastic change in the elements.

As the experts talk on, the perils seem endless: insects, including a category known as booklice, or *Liposcelis divinatorius*,[14] and book-worms, which apparently love incunabula's ancient rag paper.[15] Dust, dirt, smoke, or soot, which could absorb and hold moisture, can accelerate deterioration through acid hydrolysis (the chemical decomposition of paper). And there's no consensus on how much the book can safely be handled. Some advisers suggest turning the pages as little as possible to avoid any damage to the spine, while others insist that paging through it at regular intervals will allow it to "breathe."

Lucille's head spins. "It was like having a new baby,"[16] she re-called, saying that she was gobsmacked by the weight of the re-sponsibility. She is somewhat relieved when Robert Schad laughs and tries to talk her down, telling her not to fret. He says that al-most any librarian can attest that incunabula were built to last in a way that modern books are not. Books printed on the acidic wood-pulp paper used during the late nineteenth and early twen-tieth centuries are likely to disintegrate within a hundred years. But paper made from linen rags in the fifteenth century can easily last one thousand years or more. The paper found in the Guten-berg Bible is far more stable than that found in any current dime-store novel.

"Not to worry," he tells Lucille. The Gutenberg Bible will likely reach its one thousandth anniversary. "The book will take care of itself," he says. He cautions, however, to dust it only once every six months.

The Doheny Gutenberg Bible as it appeared soon after its arrival in Los Angeles in October 1950. The dark spots on the left and right edges of the book are knots of vellum that served as a primitive index system marking different sections of the book.

Alone with the Bible, Lucille begins her inspection. It is larger and heavier than she had imagined. The finished pages measure about sixteen inches tall and twelve inches wide, a size known by experts as a "royal folio." Even without a magnifying glass she can see that the paper has the watermarks of three different papermakers—a stag or bull's head with a cross-like star; a bunch of grapes, which falls between the columns of type; and a simple line drawing of a sprig or branch from a tree, which appears on the inner margins. These marks and their variants are found in all the existing paper copies of the Gutenberg Bible[17] and can be traced to manufacturers in the town of Piedmont, a region in northwest Italy.[18]

Every great beauty has a flaw, and Number 45 is no different. Lucille dislikes the three "hideous little knots"[19] of vellum that hang along the pages of the Bible's fore edge. She has never seen anything like them before. In fact, they are a primitive index system, used as thumb markers to identify different sections of the Bible. Such knots are exceedingly rare, and no other Gutenberg

Bible is known to have them. She can only guess that in the fifteenth century there had been dozens more attached to the book. Over the decades most had fallen away until now only three remain.

Lucille lingers over the leaves. The first printed page is a universe of its own in terms of sheer beauty. Two dark columns of letters float on a creamy field of paper, perfectly squared. The margins are clean and even with no ragged edges. It is a "miracle of pure mechanics," Lucille says. She can't read the Latin of the thirteenth-century text, the so-called Paris version of Saint Jerome's translation, which was the definitive Bible of the Middle Ages. But she is moved by its careful balance, its presence.

◆ ◆ ◆

TO APPRECIATE THE "miracle" that captivated Lucille and set so many in pursuit of Number 45, it helps to imagine the conditions that produced those pages sometime before August 1456, in the Rhine River town of Mainz, Germany. Imagination is key, because the story of Johann Gutenberg and his Bible is dominated by ellipses, with unknowns and conjecture far outpacing any certainty. Gutenberg, wittingly or not, wrapped himself in anonymity. Each of his Bibles has more than a thousand pages, but not one is signed, dated, or marked with the place it was printed. No notes about his process, if he made any, survive. And there lies the paradox at the heart of any attempt to understand the history of a Gutenberg Bible. This most famous of books has origins we know very little about. The stories we tell about the man, and how the Bibles came to be, have been cobbled together from a fistful of legal and financial records, and centuries' worth of dogged scholarly fill-in-the-blank.

The well-accepted version goes something like this: Johann Gensfleischzur Laden zum Gutenberg was born into a patrician family in Mainz around 1400. His father held a position at a local mint, and scholars guess that Gutenberg came in contact with the art of casting gold coins and may have been skilled in goldsmithing and other forms of metalwork.

The leap from there to printing is shorter than it may seem. Goldsmiths were at the center of a creative surge in the early 1430s, and German craftsmen, likely using modified goldsmiths' tools, were developing techniques for carving images into metal plates, creating a new form of engraving. Like artisans across Europe, they were also searching for ways to create what was known as "artificial script," a vehicle for producing written text that didn't rely on the slow, steady, trained hand of the scribe.

Gutenberg was likely part of that search. In 1439, he formed a partnership with three men, promising to teach them proprietary techniques, ostensibly experiments for creating artificial script. Legal papers that document the breakup of the partnership make reference to "formes" and "presses" and "a secret art," noting that the partners agreed to pay Gutenberg to train them and took an oath promising not to disclose what they learned. There are no records of that time, and nothing documenting what he did afterward. But when he resurfaced four years later, he seems to have been fully prepared to begin printing in a way that represented a striking departure from the past.

Single-page printing had existed for centuries, with the text of whole pages carved into wood, inked, and pressed onto paper. But what Gutenberg developed was a sophisticated process based on the use of single metal letters, which could be combined and recombined to create an ever-changing stream of words. The underlying idea of movable type wasn't new. It had been tried in eleventh-century China but proved to be unwieldy, given the written language's thousands of distinct ideograms. The more contained Western alphabet finally made it feasible to consider using single letters, not pages, as the building blocks of mechanical printing.

Gutenberg's contemporaries had already begun to puzzle out how to make that work, experimenting with carving letters from wood or metal and arranging them into words to be stamped on parchment. The problem was that carving, and re-carving, hundreds or thousands of letters one at a time to produce a book would be extremely time-consuming, and the letters would be subtly different from each other. A scribe could probably go faster and do a better job.

The key was to design and fabricate attractive type that could be produced easily and yield armies of durable letters. That's what Gutenberg was prepared to do by the time he set up shop in Mainz. His innovation involved carving individual raised letters, or components of them, from metal, punching them into a softer material to create a mold, then pouring in molten metal that would, when it hardened, produce an identical replica. That process, and the fast-hardening alloy of tin, lead, and antimony he developed, would allow practiced fabricators to expediently cast type, which they could melt down and recast as needed.

Printing meant arranging the letters into words, the words into perfectly straight lines, and the lines into even blocks of text to be inked and pressed onto paper or vellum. And each small step of the process, which sounds so mundane today, required invention.

Gutenberg created frames to hold the type in place and fashioned presses from those traditionally used to press olives or grapes. He designed Gothic-looking letters to mimic the calligraphy of the scribes and refined techniques to ensure that even pressure would be applied to blank sheets placed atop the inked, raised type. As well, he located paper that would absorb ink readily and formulated deeply pigmented, varnish-based metallic inks that wouldn't smear or fade. His ingenious assembly of these elements, and processes for using them, would allow him to create a book that could be re-printed comparatively quickly, easily, and accurately.

His first projects were modest. Several single-leaf papal indulgences—widely used church documents that offered the for-giveness of sins, often in exchange for a "donation"—have been attributed to Gutenberg's workshop, along with a short Latin gram-mar book and a lunar calendar.

It is incredible that (as far as we know) just those few initial tri-als made Gutenberg feel that he was ready to attempt a complete Bible. But a burgeoning market may have pushed him to try. The German cardinal Nicholas of Cusa had recently insisted that all monastic libraries should have a consistent and accurate copy of the Bible, and Gutenberg could likely count on substantial orders from churches, convents, and monasteries. A single handwritten Bible could take as much as two years to produce. Even squadrons of scribes couldn't hope to satisfy the increasing demand.

Gutenberg's highly ambitious, learn-on-the-fly project would be a work of 1,200-plus pages using 270 different characters—punctuation as well as upper- and lowercase letters and letter combinations and variations, all designed to mimic the script and space-saving shorthand developed by scribes over centuries. Stephan Füssell, director of the Institute of Book Studies at Johannes Gutenberg University Mainz, has estimated that the complete printing of the Bible required the casting of an astonishing one hundred thousand individual pieces of type.[20]

To use them, and turn his press into an assembly line, his workers had to master an array of skills—reading the Latin of the source Bible; rapidly and accurately arranging the type, upside down and backward, in frames to duplicate the text for printing; spacing type line by line and employing the scribe's art of using hyphenation and abbreviations to ensure that it lined up perfectly in two columns of equal width. Not to mention learning to ink the type, work the presses, and pull clear, unblemished pages, tens of thousands of times.

Number 45 was proof of the workshop's unlikely success. The artistry that still floated from the page didn't look like the haphazard work of beginners who would set things right next time. It was uncannily precise, thoughtful in its detail, and beautifully executed. For Estelle and Lucille, the printed pages seem emblematic of the hand of God.

CHAPTER TWO

Treasure Neglected

B UT REVERENCE IS never a given. The four owners Number 45 meets before it makes its way to Estelle's Book Room are all men of significant means, often with wealth comparable to hers. But the sheen of their libraries sometimes glows brighter than their regard for the ancient texts themselves. Just because they can afford a Gutenberg doesn't mean they love or understand it. That's especially true of the first known owner, an Irish-born aristocrat, Archibald Acheson, 3rd Earl of Gosford, who buys the book in 1836.

Gosford lives in an imposing castle, which is the centerpiece of a village known as Markethill in Northern Ireland, and though he is a fanatical collector whose acquisitions fill shelves that reach to a fifty-foot ceiling, he has a curious lack of regard for the Gutenberg Bible, progenitor of the works he vacuums up at auction. Where Estelle Doheny sees a divine hand in its craftsmanship and story, he sees a rather disappointing old book. For him, it is an afterthought, an awkward fit in a collection built around a nineteenth-century sensibility inclined to judge a book in no small measure by its cover.

In an early portrait, Gosford's intelligent eyes gaze out from a placid face framed by chin whiskers and parted hair that brushes a broad forehead. The son of an Irish Protestant lord whose ancestors are said to have helped James VI of Scotland secure the throne of England in 1603, he is born into a family drawn to talk of literature, often with literary stars of the day. But he sets aside any fascination with character or story when he begins collecting in the 1820s.

Books like Number 45, which had been secreted in the libraries of European aristocrats and monasteries for centuries, have been shaken loose by the French Revolution and Napoleon's occupying forces, licensed to "requisition" them for the French national library. The chaos of war has allowed tens of thousands of illuminated manuscripts and early printed books—including nine of

Archibald Acheson, 3rd Earl of Gosford, purchased the Gutenberg Bible in 1836. He was swept into a British craze for rare books but wasted no love on his Bible.

Gutenberg's Bibles—to make their way to Britain for the first time. It's a looking-glass time when Britain's men of means are buying rare books for sport, going after them with the unhinged intensity that the Dutch once aimed at tulip bulbs.

They measure themselves by the size of their libraries, spawning a fashion for ever-bigger, ever-more-beautiful collections and rooms to house them. The ranks of collectors had once been thick with book lovers and scholars. But now, as Britain's elites and merchant classes extract wealth from the nation's thrumming industries and trade routes, men like Gosford often enter the market with a different stance. They regard books as trophies. Status symbols. Decor. There's a fad for fancy hand-tooled bindings, colored leather that looks good on the shelf.

Gosford says that the craze for books entered his bones when he was nine, as he pulled the illustrated volumes off the shelf in the family library. An introverted and awkward boy, he often retreated there with his mother, Mary Sparrow, listening to her read poetry, losing himself in adventure stories, and perhaps lingering at the edge of the conversation when her friend Lady Byron, wife of the famed poet, came to visit. This is where Gosford's grandmother Anne Acheson once entertained Jonathan Swift, the author of *Gulliver's Travels*, who flirtatiously made her the center of a risqué one-hundred-line rhyme.

The library became a refuge when Gosford was thirteen and his father, a politician embroiled in battles between Catholics and Protestants and mistrusted by both, sought legitimacy and status through an audacious project: replacing the family home with a 242-room Norman Revival castle. The all-consuming, fortune-guzzling folly, complete with Romanesque turrets and a central

Early drawing of Gosford Castle, the largest castle in Northern Ireland, designed by British architect Thomas Hopper in the 1820s. A never-ending construction project and family folly, it was never completed.

keep, demanded armies of workers, and construction chaos would bang around Gosford for the next forty years.[1]

Given the two strands of Gosford's DNA—a mother's love of books and a father's obsession for endless construction—it hardly seems surprising that bibliomania engulfs the son soon after he leaves home in 1824 to attend Oxford University's Christ Church. Gosford is, by then, a reserved and shy odd young man with a slight facial tic and stutter. But he finds a welcoming home when Beriah Botfield, an outgoing botany student and book lover, pulls him into the rowdy theater of London's crowded book scene.

Bookshops and auctions throw together men of different classes, with the tradesmen and paper mongers who find and sell books mixing, not always comfortably, with the elites. That democratizing ground serves Gosford and Botfield well. Despite differences in temperament and social standing, they become companions, making the rounds of auction houses and enjoying the hush of presale viewing days when they can inspect and compare rare volumes at their leisure.

Gosford may not have walked in with a clear desire to build the largest and finest library in Ireland, but he's quickly overtaken by the quest. The potent blend of money, adrenaline, aesthetics, and high-status bidders draws him in, and bibliomania sets its hook. Gosford has money to spend, and Botfield has the taste and knowledge to guide him, astutely showing his friend what to buy, and when.

The ultimate prizes are the works of the great Venetian printer of the Italian Renaissance Aldus Pius Manutius, whose books are known as Aldines. A humanist scholar, Aldus was the first to print Aristotle, Thucydides, Herodotus, and Sophocles (among others in the Greek canon) and was likely the first printer to compare manuscripts to derive the most accurate version.[2] The handsome volumes were designed for learning and pleasure, some small enough to be held in a reader's hand. Reflecting the refinements that catapulted typography forward from the medieval style of Gutenberg, the Aldines were svelte and elegant, the embodiment of an idealized classical world.

In 1501, Aldus printed the first of his octavo editions of the classics, a format based on a sheet of paper folded three times. He called these books, which could be tucked in a pocket, *libri portatiles*, or "portable books." Early precursors of the cheap and popular volumes just beginning to roll off England's new steam-powered presses, the Aldines helped spark the concept of personal reading, the prototype of today's ubiquitous paperback.[3]

Gosford is attracted to the handheld Aldines for one simple reason: he fancies the way they look. The highly legible and elegant typography captivate him. The Aldine Press was the first to use a roman typeface, the inspiration for the modern Bembo, praised for its simplicity and readability. The earliest printed works, like Gutenberg's, were designed to economically squeeze words onto expensive paper or vellum. But the type produced by the Aldine Press with "pure Renaissance inspiration and design" focuses on the ease of the reader. This is the aesthetic that would dominate European typography for the next two centuries,[4] and Aldus's work becomes not only the centerpiece of the massive new library going up at Gosford Castle but the engine driving Gosford's obsession.

Gosford buys a copy of the definitive catalog of the Aldines, Renouard's *Annales de l'imprimerie des Alde,* published sixteen years earlier, and makes it his scorecard. His desk is crowded with towering piles of auction catalogs that he fills with scribbled notes and repeated calculations. He quickly masters the specialized vocabulary that describes a book's condition and binding, symbols like *c.m.,* meaning *charta maxima* (large paper) or *c.t.* for *corio Turcico* (Turkish leather).[5] Focused on the particulars of size and shape, the color and texture of a binding, he can fall in love with a volume knowing little about its substance, the way a person might collect train tickets without ever thinking to take a ride. But because the books he seeks are so rare, he fits easily among the elite book hunters who desire the earliest printed works from the fifteenth and early sixteenth centuries, men who will soon be nicknamed "The Fifteeners."

◆ ◆ ◆

GOSFORD PREFERS TO enjoy his books in secret, "fondling his treasures alone."[6] He pursues collecting with the same drive as an addict. He is a voracious consumer of thousands of rare volumes he will never read and never share. Similarly obsessive collectors are pushing prices to unprecedented heights, but the Gutenberg Bible is not on the most wanted list. Not yet known as the most celebrated book in the world, it was given only "scant" attention for three centuries until[7] Britain's most distinguished book collectors finally begin to take notice.

Young bibliomaniacs like Gosford revere collectors like George John, the 2nd Earl of Spencer, patriarch, five generations back, of the clan that would produce Princess Diana. In 1789, Spencer had felt the irresistible pull of London's book row, which was just then absorbing waves of freshly dislodged incunabula and other early volumes. A naval officer, Spencer had shown little prior interest in collecting but found himself intrigued by black-letter books—volumes printed in heavy Gothic lettering like that used by Gutenberg and others, including William Caxton, who learned the art of printing in Bruges and brought it to England in the 1470s.

Lord Spencer's interest in the Gutenberg Bible materialized as the scattered dots of its origin were being connected, triggering interest in a book that had largely been forgotten.[8] In 1763, French book authority Guillaume-François de Bure recognized its importance when he discovered a copy in the library of Cardinal Mazarin, the chief minister to the king of France. He quickly cited it as the earliest substantial book printed with movable metal type. "We do not hesitate for a single moment, in according it the highest rank," De Bure wrote in an influential guidebook, "not only above all other editions of the Bible but above all other printed books whatsoever."[9] (For all that, though, he christened the books Mazarin Bibles, in honor of the owner, not the printer.)

In 1790, Spencer purchases a Gutenberg Bible from London bookseller Thomas Payne II and carries it home to the family library at Althorp. The price is reportedly £80 (adjusted for inflation about $14,000).[10] That single purchase produces a ripple effect, piquing interest in other Gutenbergs, helping to lay a foundation in the marketplace. Four years later, the first Gutenberg Bible auctioned in London sells for the steep sum of £126,[11] demonstrating its budding desirability.

By 1809, the Reverend Thomas Frognall Dibdin, who worked as chief cataloger and book scout for Spencer, first coins the term *bibliomania* to describe the "disease" that produces wildly inflated prices, and the book lust that would inflame legions of individual collectors like Gosford.

Dibdin believed that coolheaded scholarship was bibliomania's cure, but as Spencer would soon prove, even that didn't guarantee immunity from the *mania* of bibliomania. The disease consumes him completely in 1812, when the king-size library of the Duke of Roxburghe comes up for auction. Spencer and his cousin bid up the price of the only known 1471 first edition of Boccaccio's *Decameron*, taking it to an astronomical £2,260—$192,968 in today's dollars.[12]

The British press covered the auction details with breathless prose, and the dueling cousins were described as "book maniacs" of the highest order. The battle over one book "astonished the whole book world," noted Dibdin at the time. "Not a living creature could have anticipated it: but this might be called the grand era of Bibliomania."[13] The Roxburghe sale was a watershed moment, the first time a four-figure number is reached in an auction for a printed book. Set against the continuing wars with France, which had so recently dispatched its aristocrats, and the working-class squalor at home that Charles Dickens would soon describe, the spectacle of seeing such money thrown at one rare book might have left some hearing echoes of "Let them eat cake." But what it mostly seems to fuel over time is envy, fashion, and a desire to join in.

By Gosford's time, printers are designing inexpensive editions that emulate the volumes showing up at auction. Newly minted library furniture is available to house such books in the homes of gentlemen or well-to-do tradesmen who clamor for libraries of their own. And extremely wealthy, newly intoxicated bibliophiles like Gosford keep lining up to throw themselves full throttle into the bidding.

◆ ◆ ◆

GOSFORD HAS THE misfortune of finding his passion just as the market crests, and the young earl rarely has a chance to pay prices that are less than exorbitant. Collecting practices at this stage of the game are quirky, reflecting bibliomania's high regard for surfaces over almost anything else. It is common for collectors to seek out the finest paper copies available or the "tallest" copies printed on vellum, and to tear off the original covers of books that are centuries old, spending huge sums on luxurious custom bindings in a wide array of leathers (crushed morocco, turkey, scored calf leather), or forel (parchment), often emblazoned with a family crest. Some of the earliest books, medieval volumes whose covers or pages have darkened with time, are prime candidates not just for rebinding but also for bleaching to lighten the paper or remove marginalia left by centuries' worth of previous owners. The pages might be "enhanced" with illuminations or illustrations designed to show off an owner's coat of arms or taste in art. It is also common to remove pages from one book to "complete" another or to break up volumes and sell or collect single leaves. Even curious and informed collectors like Spencer see no need to hold back from tearing apart their treasures to make them more "perfect."

Newly collectible books also risk being sold for scrap before they reach booksellers. Some of the same vendors who source the rare-book trade sell their "ugly old books" to shopkeepers and fishmongers who need paper for wrapping their wares. There are still disconnects in the valuing of these medieval relics, which are entering the world of commerce at the dawn of the Industrial Age.

Gosford mostly ignores books he doesn't crave. Those he does, though, he pursues single-mindedly, and over the next twenty years, he acquires dozens of Aldines. He marks up his Renouard catalog, noting items he has purchased and correcting or supplementing Renouard on points of pedigree or description.

His collecting companion, Beriah Botfield, is pulled by the desire to handle the first books that made classic works available to eager Renaissance minds. But Gosford is purely interested in the details of their production, rooting out peculiarities that distinguish one volume from any other, obsessing over issue dates, binding variants, misprints, and textual snafus. Dealers regard him as a "point maniac," a collector who loves a book's "points," or attributes, to excess.[14] He studies his purchases the way an entomologist catalogs the wings of insects. There's a calming order in classification that is lacking at the perpetual construction site that is his family home.

Once he moves back to the castle in Markethill, Gosford returns as frequently as possible to London, where he engages in extravagant buying sprees in competition with reserved aristocrats and vulgar American tycoons. During the last three months of the year, known as "the season," he goes from auction to auction, hauling in new specimens. When he takes them home, he meticulously examines each page to verify the number and order of the printed sheets. Assured that his purchase is fully intact, he pencils on the endpaper *collated and perfect* or simply *c & p*. A book thus cataloged and shelved might not be taken down again, unless he needs to compare some aspect of it to a new acquisition.

Then, as fast as the frenzy had materialized, it vanishes. In 1829, the rare-books bubble spectacularly pops. Prices that had seemed to defy the laws of economics and logic reenter the realm of more ordinary merchandise. Bibliomania is replaced by a new era of temperance that Dibdin labels "Bibliophobia."

"Fear is the order of the day," he writes. "To those very natural and long-established fears of bailiffs and tax-gatherers, must now be added the fear of reform, of cholera, *and of books.*"

The market lull lasts fifteen years and overlaps with changes in Gosford's personal life that significantly curb his ability to keep up his pace, even with lower prices. In June of 1832, he marries Lady Theodosia Brabazon, the only daughter of John Chambré Brabazon, 10th Earl of Meath, and a book lover. The awkward collector looks up from his acquisitions long enough to father seven children, and soon, between household expenses, continuing construction costs on the castle, and unpaid taxes, he is forced to slash his expenditures. His correspondence becomes filled with agonies of remorse.

But in 1836, he sees an opportunity. Though he is no fan of black-letter printing, an intriguing volume comes on the market at a hard-to-resist price. It is Number 45.

As a neighbor writes to a mutual friend, "Lord Gosford told me yesterday that he has one volume of the Mazarin Bible, the first book ever printed, for which he gave £45." The price is small, about $6,000 in today's dollars. The number is less than half of what Spencer had spent, and a fraction of the £504 a collector named Henry Perkins had given for both volumes of the Bible at the market's peak in 1825.

The book has retained enough of its cachet to be attractive to Gosford, but he takes no particular pleasure in it. He carries it back to Markethill wrapped in old sheets of newspaper tied with string. In letters to peers he hardly mentions the acquisition, commenting simply that he has obtained "an old Bible." He is disappointed that he owns only one of the two volumes, telling his neighbor William Reeves, that if he had the second in "like condition [it] would make the lot worth £1,000."[15]

The troubled construction of Gosford Castle is still under way, but some of its grand rooms are finally habitable. Number 45 joins Gosford's other trophies in the castle's immense library, which looks like something out of a fairy tale, with fantastic painted ceilings, an enormous stone fireplace, and bookshelves decorated in elaborate Byzantine designs. Flanking the grilled hearth are towering shelves that shoot upward almost fifty feet. Displayed in majestic order on bookcases framed by intricately carved plaster[16] are Gosford's thousands of books, each with its spine delicately touching a shelf's outer edge. Some are suspended at such a height that it requires two men and a forty-foot ladder to retrieve a single volume. The room is a bibliomaniac's, if not a reader's, dream.

Gosford doesn't bother giving Number 45 his custom ex libris, the bookplate he adds to the volumes he loves. He simply makes his permanent mark at the top left corner of the blank front paste-down page, his surname in strong black strokes underlined with a bold flourish. Then he exiles the Bible to the outer reaches of his shelves.

Though the book holds scant interest for him, his purchase may have caught the eye of others who know its true worth. In a neat bit of symmetry, the same year he buys it, he is invited to join the Roxburghe Club, the circle of elite collectors that traces its origins to Lord Spencer, who had been so instrumental in establishing the

The Gutenberg Bible was shelved and largely forgotten in Gosford Castle's fairy-tale library from 1836 until 1884.

Gutenberg Bible's value in Britain. Capping their collecting careers, Gosford and Beriah Botfield are inducted together. It is the kind of honor that makes a man permanently relevant—but it doesn't seem to broaden Gosford's world. He stays holed up at Markethill.

While some collectors eagerly open their libraries to visitors, Gosford rarely allows anyone in, not even his wife, though he spends most of his time there. Over the ensuing years, members of the large Gosford clan resent the earl's single-minded attachment to his book collection and estrange themselves from him. Theodosia, too, begins complaining bitterly that he is more interested in his library than in her. Gosford becomes even more reclusive and moody, rarely venturing outside the grounds of the castle except to buy books.

Subsequent years are full of tragedy. Theodosia dies unexpectedly in 1841. Four years later, the devastation of the Great Famine sweeps across Ireland. Then, on March 27, 1849, Gosford's father, the 2nd Earl of Gosford, dies in his bedroom, leaving Gosford a crippling debt shackled to an unfinished castle that stands amid piles of soggy debris. A "byzantine process of debt rescheduling"[17] absorbs much of Gosford's energy and talent for the rest of his life. According to reports, he and his agents are remarkably adept at juggling accounts to keep the estate solvent, and Gosford dutifully continues work on the castle, though on a far smaller scale than originally planned.

Once he is able to buy books again, he purchases the one volume he truly loves: a First Folio of Shakespeare. The First Folio is considered "the book that gave us Shakespeare," preserving the Bard's plays because no manuscripts survive.[18] After paying the enormous sum of 157 guineas,[19] he treats the book as if it were his favorite pet, stroking its fine crimson morocco binding. He values it for its size and reported perfection, scarcely seeming to care about its considerable historic value.[20]

◆ ◆ ◆

GOSFORD'S EFFORTS TO save the castle eventually cripple him. He locks the library door and spends the majority of his time alone at his London townhouse, taking no comfort in his books, abandoning even his First Folio. He is only fifty-seven years old when he dies, after what the *Armagh Guardian* describes as "an attack of gout in the head, which terminated fatally." His title, castle, and collection go to his eldest son, Sir Archibald Acheson Brabazon Sparrow, who becomes the 4th Earl of Gosford.[21]

The new earl, who is nineteen, is nothing like his father. He had been a headstrong child, robust and handsome, and visits the castle only in August or September for grouse shooting. Otherwise, he has fashioned a city life of gambling, heavy drinking, and mingling with London's royals, playing backgammon. He quickly racks up debts that far exceed his annual allowance. The estate is doomed, one of his agents concludes, "unless his lordship can find a good wife with a large fortune" or sell one or more parcels of land.

First, though, the Gosford heir liquidates his father's library. The Aldines go in 1878 and 1884 to settle a gambling debt. As expenses mount and cash runs scarce, the 4th Earl of Gosford abruptly puts the rest of his father's collection on the auction block. This is the modus operandi of the Gosford clan—one generation's obsessions dissolving another's.

At ten minutes past one p.m. on April 21, the auctioneers at Put-tick and Simpson launch the sale of the remaining "fine, extensive and valuable library of the Rt. Hon. Earl of Gosford." The high point of the auction, expected to last ten days, is advertised as "A Perfect Copy of the First Folio Shakespeare, clean and sound, with title and verses mounted, in crimson-hued morocco." Though prices for rare books have somewhat recovered from the crash, there are low ex-pectations for the Gutenberg Bible, listed simply as Item 339, "Vol-ume One of the Famous Mazarin Bible." But Number 45 turns out to be the auction's sleeper, fetching a price that shocks collectors, dealers, and the public, making headlines in British newspapers:[22] "£500 to book dealer James Toovey."

Eight days later, Lord Gosford's favorite volume, the Shake-speare folio, has its turn on the block. Lot 2673, William Shake-speare's *Comedies, Histories, and Tragedies*, published by Isaac Jaggard and Edward Blount in London in 1623, sells for £470, £30 less than its German elder. The hammer price reflects an evolving under-standing of the *book of books*. Gosford's Shakespeare sold for three times the price he paid; his Gutenberg increased by a thou-sand percent.

CHAPTER THREE

The Bibliophile

Didlington Hall, the Gutenberg Bible's new home, is a grand country house in the wooded Norfolk countryside, one hundred miles north of London. Even the simplest description of its spaces reads like a catalog of wealth: forty-six bedrooms (including one reserved for visiting royalty), twelve reception rooms, a grand ballroom, a small museum brimming with Egyptian antiquities, and a library with a secret vault. Its grounds, 7,105 manicured acres that border an estate of the Prince of Wales, feature stables, kennels, greenhouses, tennis courts, a falconer's hut, and sixty acres of tended gardens. Far from Gosford's muddy Irish castle, the book has entered the domain of a man who embodies Queen Victoria's Britain and the aristocracy at the height of its wealth and power.

Lord William Tyssen-Amherst has a connoisseur's eye, a great love for books, and a bottomless hunger for the best the world has to offer. Number 45 will cap a carefully curated library that traces the history of printed books that sit amid rare and precious objects that include stringed instruments by Stradivarius, fine silver and Limoges china, Persian carpets, tapestries, stone capitals from the Alhambra in Granada, and the bells of old Worcester Cathedral. Amherst, as one observer puts it, is a man "unable to deny himself for too long when confronted with beautiful objects."[1] The year Number 45 enters Didlington Hall, the mansion's doors are flanked by seven towering, two-ton statues of the lion-headed Egyptian goddess Sekhmet—the same statues that sit today near the Temple of Dendur at the Metropolitan Museum of Art.

Amherst's rarefied world reflects three decades of collecting. He came into the fortune that would sate his taste for beauty in 1855, when he was only twenty, midway through his studies at Oxford's Christ Church. He lost his mother, then his father, and suddenly the student who had recently been writing home from his Grand Tour of Europe to reassure his family that he'd stopped "talking as wild" as before and "would not run my head needlessly into danger" was left to make arrangements for his three teenage siblings—and to manage a massive inheritance. The wealth that passed to him includes a family trust, thousands of acres of land, several fine small estates, and Didlington Hall, which his father had recently purchased and begun to expand.

A few months after he buried his father, Amherst celebrated his coming-of-age with a lavish birthday party that involved 700 pounds of plum pudding, a whole roasted 1,100-pound bull, and immense quantities of other food and drink for the 550-plus guests who filled three long, white tents that covered the lawn. A newspaper story noted that the crowd toasted Amherst's fiancée, Margaret Susan Mitford, an admiral's only child, whom he would soon wed.

British bibliophile Lord William Tyssen-Amherst had a connoisseur's eye, a great love for books, and a bottomless hunger for the best the world had to offer. He acquired the Gutenberg Bible in 1884.

Margaret, an exuberant woman known for her singing voice and her dexterity as a fine woodworker, married into wealth, and Amherst into worldliness. Margaret's father, Robert Mitford, was a sailor, naturalist, artist, and military man whose ship had ranged the southern Mediterranean during the Napoleonic Wars. A stop in Egypt had left him with a passion for Egyptian culture that he'd passed to his daughter, along with taste for sailing and travel—all of which would soon pervade Amherst's life as well.

The Amhersts' first desire, though, seemed to be to fill Didlington Hall with children. Their daughter Mary Rothes Margaret was born the day Amherst turned twenty-two, and over the next eleven years, there would be six more girls, all with *Margaret* in their names.

As Margaret runs the household, Amherst begins to focus seriously on collecting. When he was three, his mother had read him *The Adventures of Philip Quarle,* and he was mesmerized by its illustrations of the shipwrecked mariner pulling a huge codfish out of the sea. As a schoolboy, he'd spent his pocket money in bookshops and made his own bookplate, and in college he had wandered the ornate halls of the Bodleian Library at Oxford. A man who always has a book in his hand or tucked in his coat pocket, he firmly believes that a person is not well-bred unless he knows and loves books. Amherst had picked up his first incunabulum in Arles during his Grand Tour. Now he'll roam the rare-book dens of London.

It doesn't take long for a young man of Amherst's means to meet Bernard Quaritch, a dealer whose ambitions are shaping the book world. Prussian-born Quaritch is a veteran of the trade at thirty-nine, apprenticed to it in Berlin at age fourteen. He'd come to London vowing to push himself to the top of the heap, and in 1858, the year Amherst walks into his shop, he is poised to become the greatest bookseller of his era. Quaritch has been studying the history of printing in Europe at least since the age of nineteen, when he picked up an early German text on typefaces and printers, and he now has the chutzpah, if not always the wherewithal, to buy up premier examples of the art. He has just purchased his first Gutenberg Bible for £595, and also put together his first complete catalog of his stock, logging an inventory of five thousand items. As the book market rebounds, his aggressive presence at auctions will help drive prices to new heights.

Shrewd, unyielding, and irascible,[2] Quaritch butts heads with Amherst in their very first transaction, when the aristocrat, then twenty-three years old, decides that he is unhappy with a rare medieval manuscript he has purchased. Amherst writes the dealer saying that the book, for which he paid £50, is in inferior condition, and he wants to return it for full credit. Quaritch refuses, and in a flurry of letters, he schools his new client in the realities of the business: Every transaction has costs, and even Amherst isn't exempt from paying them. The refund will be £42. Period.

Once Quaritch has marked his territory, the relationship dramatically improves,[3] and years of regular contact establish a firm bond between dealer and collector. While Amherst will buy books from many dealers, the bulk of his significant purchases will come from Quaritch.

They meet most often at No. 15 Piccadilly, where the dealer moved his shop in 1860 and rules from the back office, a dark, cramped room dominated by a table and chairs, several portraits of himself, and a handful of glass-fronted cases, which hold the pick of his lot, several thousand pounds' worth of rare finds. At Piccadilly, he has begun producing text-rich auction catalogs that take on increasing degrees of sophistication, offering detailed entries that could serve as a guide to the history of books and their provenance as they offer his own pithy opinions. He hires a bibliographer to advise him and compile his listings and begins issuing themed specialist catalogs, leading with *Bibliotheca Xylographica, Typographica et Palaeographica*, "Early Productions of the Printing Press."

Quaritch grooms his young client to appreciate valuable books, sharing an expertise that looks beyond surface beauty to see both their place in history and the layers of typographical and production detail that make each one unique. Amherst begins to fashion a select and expensive collection that will create what his daughter Sybil describes as "a continuous chain" of history illustrating themes that interest him. Perhaps not surprisingly, given the opportunities in Quaritch's stock, Amherst focuses intently on the history of printing and bookbinding, and the history of the

Reformation and the Anglican Church, seeing each tract, book, or Bible he purchases as a link in the chain.[4]

Unlike Gosford, whose library was an elegant warehouse for volumes he often seemed to lose in the aeries of his shelves, Amherst builds a library that both crystallizes his intellectual curiosity and becomes the spiritual heart of his home. Despite being humongous (some reports indicate it was 1,200 square feet), with a hidden door behind one bookcase, the room is surprisingly cozy.[5] Expensive volumes line the walls, and the nine Muses gaze down from a vivid pastel mural that covers the ceiling, but this is a *working* space where Amherst's daughters, autodidacts schooled at home, spread out at tables placed on the room-size Persian carpet, reading, sketching, and working on their many projects. As the girls grow, the family's collection of references on botany and English gardening, and on railroads and Egyptology, share space with needlework, painting supplies, microscopes, foreign-language dictionaries, magazines, newspapers—and rare books. Amherst's desk sits in front of a fireplace at one end of the room, where he can survey the activity from his straight-backed chair.

The library brings the world to the family, but young Lord and Lady Amherst crave seeing it firsthand. They adventure their way through Egypt and Syria in elaborate caravans and return frequently to the Middle East, sometimes staying for months at a time, acquiring souvenirs and antiquities on each visit. Amherst has a yacht, *The Dream*, built to carry the family around the Mediterranean, specifying that it must easily accommodate the nine Amhersts with guests, and that the shelves of the ship's bookcases must be tall enough to accommodate his copy of *Gulliver's Travels*. They winter in the Middle East or Spain, visit Denmark, and sum-

Lord Amherst pored over the Gutenberg Bible in the grand library at Didlington Hall, the book's home from 1884 to 1908.

mer on the French Riviera, where Amherst builds a villa called Lou Casteou. He develops luxurious resort properties and dines with German Kaiser Wilhelm I aboard *The Dream*. Back at Didlington Hall, the family keeps their staff humming to accommodate their active social life. Newspapers of the day fully chronicle their comings and goings as they host balls, dinners, and shooting parties that exceed the fictional grandeur of Julian Fellowes's *Downton Abbey*. Amherst also owns an elegant London townhouse at 88 Brook Street, Grosvenor Square, where he sleeps during his many book-buying sprees.

This lavish life floats on a fast stream of cash. According to financial records kept by Amherst's solicitor, in 1883, the family properties in Norfolk, Yorkshire, Lent, and Middlesex alone produce more than £7,000 (about $772,000 in today's dollars) in annual rents.

Antiques, artifacts, and collectibles flow in from around Europe and the Middle East as Amherst and his wife strike up international friendships with experts and vendors who share their enthusiasms. Amherst's family fortune was built with globalization, when a Dutchman on his mother's side, Francis Tissen, entered Britain's lucrative trade in sugar, gold, and humans. With positions in the East India Company and the Royal Africa Company and leased-out sugar plantations in Antigua, Tissen minted wealth, brought it to Britain, and plowed it into real estate. Generations later, such fortunes are vast enough to pull in the world's cultural riches, and in an expansive, seemingly invulnerable moment between wars, Amherst and his peers bring "home" to Britain the Rosetta stone, the Elgin Marbles, burial objects, bodies and goddesses from the ancient tombs of Egypt, and some of Europe's and the West's earliest books and manuscripts, burnishing their trophies with scholarship and inserting themselves in the narrative.

Quaritch styles himself a servant of that process. Staying in frequent touch with his client, he jockeys for Amherst's attention and urges him to think about the importance of the books he seeks, favoring significance over cost as he builds his collection. The dealer himself is paying the highest prices for the finest volumes as major libraries come to market, and he needs clients who can support his high-rolling business strategy and the bold statement his auction bids make about the value of what he buys. In February of 1870 he writes Amherst to say: "A wealthy connoisseur like yourself, ought to buy my whole collection of rarities. By spending about £10,000, you would get a collection of first class rarities only rivaled by the Libraries of Earl Crawford, of the Earl of Ashburnham, and of the Spencer Collection. . . . I have never been afraid of the price, when I had the opportunity of getting a first class book."[6] As American financiers and oilmen gain ground after the Civil War, Quaritch continuously reminds his aristocratic clients that the newly moneyed Yanks will soon be nipping at their heels, stealing Britain's cultural entitlement from under their noses. "Nearly half of my business is now with the U.S. of America and the colonies," he cautions. "Do not hope for better times for collecting books, as America further develops itself English books will get scarcer and dearer."[7]

Quaritch urges Amherst to invest in a Gutenberg Bible, pushing hard when two copies suddenly appear on the market in 1873. The auction catalog boasts: "It is unquestionably the first time, as it may with almost absolute certainty be said that it will be the last, that two copies of this book are sold in one day." Quaritch implores Amherst to bid on both books, estimating that the complete vellum copy is worth at least £2,000, "but could fetch as much as £3,300" (more than $299,000 in today's dollars). He values the two-volume paper copy at £1,200 but thinks the price might go as high as £1,600 (more than $145,000 today).

Amherst resists, believing the price will climb higher and bidding is too risky. And he may have other reasons for holding back. *The Dream* is undergoing extensive repairs, and he is thinking of adding a museum at Didlington Hall to house the Egyptian antiquities he is rapidly accumulating. Dumbfounded, Quaritch writes urgently to say, "What are a thousand pounds to a very rich man, if he sets his mind upon having an article?"

He describes the upcoming auction to Lord Amherst in feudal

terms: "The sale is to a certain extent a Tournament for the great book collectors—they are the knights, we booksellers are the horses. A good horse and a good servant are naturally desirous that their masters should win. It is for this reason that I lowered the charge of my commission, to the great annoyance of other booksellers."[8] The dealer adds that he will cut his usual fee to only 5 percent and just 1 percent for any items in excess of £250. But even with that handsome offer, Amherst won't budge.[9]

Quaritch winds up buying the paper copy of the Gutenberg Bible for himself—for £2,690 ($244,000 in today's dollars), more than twice his estimate—though he candidly admits he cannot afford it. "This is the finest copy I ever beheld, or anybody else," he inscribes inside the book, which he later sells, at a profit to famed collector Henry Huth. (Today the Gutenberg designated Number 38 is in the Morgan Library and Museum and valued in excess of $50 million.)[10] The vellum copy goes to Frederick Ellis, a longtime rival of Quaritch's, for £3,400 on behalf of the Earl of Ashburnham, toppling the sixty-one-year-old record for a printed book set at the Roxburghe sale of 1812. Just as Quaritch predicts, missing this chance will turn out to be the worst mistake of Lord Amherst's book-hunting career.

The close relationship between Amherst and his hard-charging mentor and dealer couldn't be rightly called a friendship. Both the droopy-eyed aristocrat and the bald, barrel-chested tradesman, whose "grating voice and sardonic humor"[11] are said to have unnerved some of his customers, know their places in the hierarchy, and Quaritch takes pains to show it. "Respect for the aristocracy is nowhere more firmly established than in England," he writes Amherst in 1858, "and I am an ardent upholder of this sentiment. For your patronage we tradesmen are bound to render you faithful service—and that I shall continue to do to the last day of my life.”[12] He courts, cajoles, and carefully stays on his side of the line as he guides his client's methodical collecting.

If anything underscores the underlying distance between them, it is the way Amherst finally acquires his Gutenberg, Estelle's Number 45, in 1884, more than ten years after he'd passed on the first two. He buys it not at auction, and not from Quaritch, but in a private, unpublicized transaction with book dealer James Toovey, following the final auction of the Gosford library. Toovey, another Quaritch rival, lets Amherst have the book for £600. Toovey makes a nice profit, pocketing £100, and Amherst gets an unmatched bargain.

If Quaritch knows, he doesn't let on, and Amherst never tells him. The book is Amherst's secret—even though it's the keystone of his collection. He has worked over decades to construct a three-dimensional history of printed books that embodies the knowledge, passions, and hostilities of the people who created and used them, and this single volume fits into that scheme not only as the fountainhead of modern printing but also as the origin point for his collection of first editions of the books of the Reformation.

Thanks to the efforts of Quaritch and others, the book is increasingly being attributed to Gutenberg. In 1877, a London dealer, an American expat named Henry Stevens, had argued that it was time to stop calling it the Mazarin Bible: “The honour of producing the first, and as many think, the most perfect book, is now ascribed to Gutenberg alone . . .” he wrote in the catalog for a display of historic Bibles. “We call it, therefore, the Gutenberg Bible, and have no sympathy for any French name . . .” Other dealers have begun using the quote in their catalogs, too, and Quaritch continues to hammer home the point. No longer referred to as the *Mazarin* Bible, the book Amherst now owns has become the *Gutenberg* Bible for posterity.

◆ ◆ ◆

WHERE GOSFORD SIMPLY cataloged the Bible and forgot it, Amherst revels in it, leaving the heavy book on his desk and sitting with his daughter Sybil, to answer her questions. Father and daughter discover peculiarities on each page. This version of the Bible, the official text in use in Gutenberg's time, is a translation by Saint Jerome that begins with a prologue, a letter to Bishop Paulinus, who had commissioned the work. Jerome begins it with the Latin for "Our brother Ambrose"—*Frater Ambrosius tua mihi*—and a vibrant green, intricately decorated Lombard capital of the letter *F* leaps from the top left corner of the first page (recto).[13]

Sybil and her father use a magnifying glass to examine the register marks used to position the books' leaves on Gutenberg's press. Amherst explains that large sheets of paper were moistened before printing so they would better hold ink, and once that was done, each was folded and pierced at points around the edges with a needle or an awl, providing guides so that the print would be impressed at exactly the same place on the front—and back—of every page. Gutenberg printed his Bible double sided, and the holes were one solution to the problems that process created.[14] The first pages of the book were marked with ten holes per page, four each at the top and bottom and two at the outer edge. But farther back, there were only six pinholes per page—the two innermost pricks at the top and bottom were missing—suggesting that the printers had adjusted their technique midstream.[15]

Lord Amherst points out to Sybil one of Number 45's most intriguing aspects: the number of lines per page. While Gutenberg's glossy, even type is precisely aligned, the columns on some pages contain more printed lines than others. There are three different settings. Pages 1 to 9 and pages 256 to 265 have forty lines each. On page 10, forty-one lines are set. Yet the rest of the pages contain forty-two-line columns.

Historians surmise that the printers had started by setting forty lines per column, but as the project progressed, they experimented with squeezing more lines onto the page, most likely to make the most of costly paper. After about one-eighth of the Bible had been printed, they decided to increase the size of the edition. But by that point, the type they had set for the first pages had been melted down and the metal reused, so Gutenberg's workers had to re-set the first pages before they could print more, and they followed the later format of forty-two lines.[16] Later, in collating the sets of pages, Gutenberg and his crew used everything they'd already printed, regardless of how many lines were on a page.[17] Consequently, some finished copies of the Gutenberg Bible have pages that are all forty-two lines, but others, like Number 45, have a mix of line settings. Amherst proudly points out that they have some of the first pages Gutenberg printed, with their forty-line count.

Despite the variations, each page has the same amount of space devoted to type, so the difference is at first glance completely unnoticeable. This is another of Gutenberg's technical accomplishments, achieved by decreasing the space between the lines on pages with forty-one or forty-two lines. Today, anyone could do that with a few keystrokes or mouse clicks, but for Gutenberg, it meant either finding a mechanical means to close up the space or changing the dimensions of the type by rough calculation and trial and error, and adjusting until the depth of the type block on one page matched that of the previous. The Bibles with forty-two-line pages are designated as B42s, to distinguish them from another Bible of the time, thought to have been printed by a Gutenberg contemporary (or, as has sometimes been argued, Gutenberg himself), who set the book in a similar typeface on thirty-six-line pages. Those are known as B36s.

Another surprise catches Sybil's attention. In the upper right-hand corner of the inside cover plain as day are written in pencil the words: BEFORE 15 AUGUST 1456.[18] The strokes are strong and fluid, as if the writer had no qualms about adding the notation to such an important book. It was undoubtedly the handwriting of a dealer or cataloger, most likely added during the presale days of the Gosford library auction. "Why?" Sybil asks.

Amherst explains that the date is critical to identifying an authentic Gutenberg and is one of the few tangible clues surrounding the book's date of origin. It comes from an inscription made by an illuminator in the back of a two-volume forty-two-line Bible discovered at the Bibliothéque nationale de France in Paris. The artist took credit for his work, as Gutenberg had not, and fortuitously added the date:

> This book was illuminated, bound and perfected by Henry Cremer, vicar of the Collegiate Church of Saint Stephen in Mainz, on the feast of the Assumption of the Blessed Virgin [August 15] in the year of our Lord 1456. Thanks be to God.[19]

Cremer's note leaves little doubt that Gutenberg had completed the printing of his work sometime before August 1456.

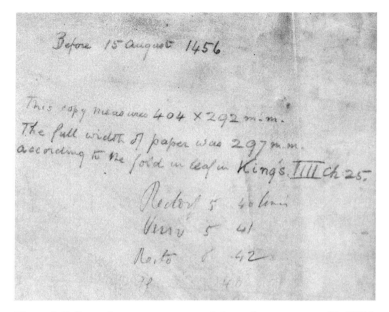

The words Before 15 August 1456 *were penciled onto the upper corner of the Bible's inside cover, probably by a book dealer, and which identified the book as a Gutenberg.*

Sybil, who was twenty-six when the Bible came to Didlington Hall, recalls her father's excitement at turning up an anomaly as they studied the text. The last three words on page 129, *autem non errant*, are duplicated at the beginning of page 130, and the mistake is indicated by minuscule red dots added on page 129, below the first instance of the words.[20] Someone in the chain of production had flagged the spot for correction, but the flag had gone unnoticed. This printer's error—a beauty mark of sorts—exists only in Number 45.

Once he has absorbed his new purchase, Amherst builds a fireproof vault in a small room adjacent to his library to safeguard the Bible, which he keeps locked inside what looks like a child-size casket made of steel and shows only to visiting royalty or trusted intimates. The rest of the time, unless it calls to him, the precious book rests in darkness. The hidden vault houses just one other book: King Charles the I's own copy of the celebrated Cambridge Bible. Bound in boarded red velvet whose back and sides are richly embroidered in gold and silver thread, this edition has front panels displaying the royal arms in heraldic colors with lion and unicorn, a crowned knight's helmet and mantle, above which are carved the initials *C.R.*, for "Carolus Rex."[21]

Quaritch, who is oblivious to the fact that Number 45 is at Didlington Hall, never stops urging Amherst to seize the opportunity to build his collection and bring home a Gutenberg Bible. The dealer sometimes lays on the persuasion, warmly affirming that all this book hunting is an elixir in itself: "Your love of books is not only making you happy, it also prolongs your life. It is much better for you to enjoy the pleasures of bibliophily than to be the victim of physicians."[22]

Amherst often shows his appreciation, and perhaps his unease about his secret, by overpaying Quaritch's standard commission, sometimes handsomely, a bonus Quaritch divides with his staff. And each Christmas, Amherst sends his workers to Quaritch's bookshop to deliver baskets heaping with game killed on his estate, a tradition that delights the dealer.

In turn, Quaritch pledges—and delivers—gifts of his own. The most significant is the bookseller's decades-long effort to help Amherst secure the finest specimens of William Caxton, Britain's first printer and the object of enduring attention among British collectors. There are thought to be fewer than six hundred Caxtons, and

Quaritch is certain that by the end of the century they will become impossible to obtain. He helps Amherst buy seventeen volumes. The jewel of the glittering set is billed as the "only genuine perfect copy known" of *Recuyell of the Historyes of Troye*, a French history of Troy that Caxton translated and printed—the first book printed in the English language about 1474.[23]

Quaritch had steadily deepened Amherst's knowledge and love of books. They had been his solace in the dark days of 1880, when he lost his twelve-year-old daughter, Bee—Beatrice—who contracted typhus on a trip to Cannes. His younger brother Francis had died at sea earlier that year, returning home from his sugar plantation in the Solomon Islands. Quaritch's bibliographer, Michael Kerney, gave the grieving Amherst a copy of a 1568 Spanish manuscript called *The Discovery of the Solomon Islands*, and with the help of his daughters, he retreated into the lengthy task of translating it.

Bernard Quaritch dies in London on December 17, 1899, at the age of eighty. In one of his last letters to Lord Amherst, the dealer expresses his pleasure in having lived long enough to see the library at Didlington Hall nearly complete: "You are now so rich in early printed books," he told his longtime client, "that your Library has become the rival of Lord Spencer's at Althorp."[24]

It was the ultimate validation from the "Titan of the auction room."[25]

As the century nears its end, Amherst's collection reflects a thousand Quaritch campaigns, including 1,103 rare printed books and 71 manuscripts, nearly all produced before 1700 and each with a distinguished pedigree. Elevated to the peerage in 1892, the lord of the manor is now 1st Baron Amherst of Hackney,[26] one of the great bibliophiles of his generation.[27]

His collection of Egyptian artifacts, too, has gained surpassing breadth and importance. With the purchase of several Egyptian collections and the many objects gathered during his travels, his private museum at Didlington is stacked high with antiquities that draw a steady stream of scholars—and have a deep impact on the imagination of Howard Carter, the archaeologist who will create an international sensation when he unearths the golden tomb of Tutankhamen in 1923. As a child, Carter, the son of a local artist the Amhersts had hired to paint murals on the walls at Didlington Hall, roamed amid Amherst's vividly painted Egyptian coffins, statues, and funerary figurines while his father worked. Amherst even arranged an apprenticeship at the British Museum, launching Carter's career as an archaeologist.

The Greek and Egyptian papyri Amherst brought home are opening new understandings of early Christianity and Egyptian beliefs on tomb robbing and the afterlife, and the collector contributes to papers on both. And in the late 1890s, he will make a purchase that brings his seemingly disparate interests together: a collection of Mesopotamian clay tablets that used cuneiform printing and can be seen as a link in the chain between Near Eastern culture and the mechanically printed word.

Arrayed around Amherst and his many daughters are the fruits of nearly a half century of collecting and connoisseurship—a cultivated, well-ordered empire.

◆ ◆ ◆

BUT IN MAY of 1906, all order dissolves. Amherst's longtime solicitor, Charles Cheston, is found dead, an apparent suicide. Cheston, sixty-three, had been a senior partner at Cheston and Sons, one of London's most respected firms, with full responsibility for managing Amherst's considerable assets, and it is soon discovered that he has embezzled the lion's share of the Amherst family fortune. Local newspapers speculate that the lawyer feared he'd been discovered and had killed himself with a shotgun to avoid arrest.

Investigators find that the lawyer had been engaged in a "long and continued fraud" that drained Amherst's bank accounts, diverted rents from his land holdings, and sold off properties. Initial estimates are that he defrauded Amherst of at least £250,000.[28] It emerges that Cheston had been "gambling wildly on the stock exchange," mainly in mining shares, and had squandered the funds of his clients. In the end, investigators believe he may have lost as much as $2 million of his client's money. (The final figure turns out to be much higher, and when adjusted for inflation totals $32 million.) "Broke and unable to face Lord Amherst," one writer says, "Cheston took the coward's way out."[29]

On August 3, 1906, a Friday afternoon, Amherst gives a short, emotional speech at a public luncheon in Marham. "I wish to take this opportunity which you kindly have given me by inviting me here of thanking my friends from the bottom of my heart for the very great sympathy which you have shown us in this cruel financial trouble which has so suddenly come upon us in our old age," he says. The gathered crowd cheers loudly and Amherst waves his hand. "We thought we should have been spared to see the completion of fifty years of wedded life happily spent among you; and we have, I can assure you, appreciated all the many kindnesses which we have received from all our friends, so many of whom I see around me. The trouble is, indeed, a cruel and heavy one."[30]

Amherst feels duty bound to make full restitution, and that will require drastic action. He first finds a tenant for Didlington Hall—and all too soon he realizes he must also sell his books. He had hired noted bibliographer Seymour de Ricci to produce a catalogue raisonné, a comprehensive description of each item in his collection, but now the task, which would have taken several years, is scuttled in favor of a quick inventory. De Ricci laments, "Sad circumstances, already well known to the British public, have compelled the owner of this library to issue a catalogue at a few weeks' notice, and to reduce the proposed publication to the proportions of a mere hand list."

Copies of that list are circulated to dealers, collectors, leading librarians, and museum curators, in hopes that a single buyer might be found. Eventually, Amherst negotiates a bank loan with the London Joint Stock Bank, putting up his books and manuscripts as collateral. The bank insists that the books be taken from Didlington Hall for safekeeping, and they are moved to the bank's vault in Chancery Lane. The thousand-plus volumes that form the heart of his collection, including the Gutenberg Bible and the precious seventeen Caxtons, are carefully packed and sent on their way.[31]

Sybil is stricken over the possible dissolution of what her father has built. It was unthinkable, she wrote later, that "this chain may be broken and its links scattered, as if a necklace of many rows of faultless pearls were divided . . . never to look the same exquisite ornament again." Amherst retreats to his bedchamber and spends his days speaking with his advisers in a last-ditch effort to hold on to his books.

Howard Carter hopes to assist his benefactor, but there is little he can do. They discuss the possibility of selling the giant Sekhmet statues if a buyer can be found, but Carter can't make a match. After a somber visit with Amherst as more treasures are packed, Carter tells colleagues that the family's living conditions are poor. "Didlington is in brown paper parcels," he says, "and Lady Amherst is saving odd bits of string."[32]

Amherst begs Bernard Alfred Quaritch, his longtime dealer's son and successor, to see if the collection can be sold en bloc to a prestigious institutional library or a wealthy American collector. J. P. Morgan has already declined, so Quaritch sails for New York to approach John D. Rockefeller, who also politely refuses. The library can't be saved.

A poignant photograph of Amherst holding his most precious Caxton, the *Recuyell of the Historyes of Troye*, appears in the 1908 Christmas issue of *Pall Mall Magazine* alongside Sybil's nuanced description of her father's collection. He appears a broken man, his face hollow and lifeless.

Amherst represents the last of a British breed, writes the *Times of London*, eulogizing his collection before the sale. It describes Amherst as a bookman who hunted rare books before American competition arrived, "when it was still possible for an English collector with money, taste, and energy to buy the finest books of all epochs."[33]

On December 4, 1908, Lord Amherst watches as his Gutenberg Bible, Item 78, sells at auction for £2,050 (about $256,000 in today's dollars). Three days later, the book that had rested beside it in the library vault for nearly twenty-five years reaches the block. The Cambridge Bible, with its elaborate cover and the initials *C.R.*, sells to J. P. Morgan.[34] The monarch's personal Bible now belongs to the king of American finance.

*Defrauded by his solicitor, Lord Amherst of Hackney
lost his fortune and was forced to sell his Gutenberg
Bible at auction. He was photographed in his library
chair in 1908, just weeks before the sale.*

Amherst never recovers. The master of Didlington Hall dies just six weeks after Number 45 is sold. On the final morning of his life, William Tyssen-Amherst appears to be in good health at breakfast but suddenly becomes ill and falls unconscious. Doctors are summoned but can't revive him. His death at age seventy-three is described as painless, but the anguish he has suffered is lost on no one.

"When the auctioneer's hammer fell on the last lot," the *London Sunday Times* declares, "all reason for living ceased for Lord Amherst of Hackney."[35]

The funeral takes place at Didlington Church, Norfolk, and a

The personal bookplate Lord Amherst affixed inside the Gutenberg Bible depicts two great white egrets, beak to beak, with the words Victoria Concordia Crescit *(Victory Comes from Harmony) woven into a trellis below.*

memorial attended by many of his bibliophile friends is held in London at St. George's, Hanover Square. When his will is brought to probate, his gross assets are calculated at £67,457 and his net at just £341. The scales have been nearly balanced, the ruinous debt repaid.

Lord Amherst has been described as one of the greatest nineteenth-century collectors, but because his library was scattered so frantically, he rarely appears on lists of Britain's great book figures. His collection seems lost even to memory. But he left his mark on Number 45. His elaborate family bookplate, pasted inside, depicts two great white egrets, beak to beak, with the words *Victoria Concordia Crescit* ("Victory Grows by Harmony")[36] woven into a trellis below.

His signature, in black ink, is smooth with a slight flair, as if its author couldn't have a care in the world.

CHAPTER FOUR

The Patriot

IN SOME HANDS, books are little more than inert props. Number 45's first two owners had added it to extensive libraries, briefly studying, cataloging, and at least in Amherst's case, carefully admiring it, before locking it away. The treasure, most often, was a closed book—protected from the overhandling that could shorten its life, more symbol than object.

For a brief time, though, Number 45 enters a small, precious cache of illuminated manuscripts and early printed books that might spend significant time off the shelf. Their owner, Charles William Dyson Perrins (or Dyson, as he prefers to be called), is heir to a vast fortune being actively fed by the Lea & Perrins Worcestershire Sauce empire, and for him, books create an intimate connection with the arts they embody and are meant to be studied, shared, and enjoyed—no matter how rare the volume.

Charles William Dyson Perrins, heir to the Lea &
Perrins Worcestershire Sauce empire, brought the Bi-
ble into a small, select collection of rare books.

His philosophy is clear to those who frequent his home on the outskirts of Malvern, a town in the English midlands eight miles from Worcester, where Lea & Perrins and Dyson's other business interest, the Royal Worcester Porcelain factory, operate. His entire library sits on a handful of shelves in a strong room next to a study comfortably set up for research, with a high center table broad enough to allow manuscripts to be examined side by side. Window seats overlook the lush symmetry of well-tended grounds and the lambent Malvern Hills.[1]

Dyson is not a particularly religious man, and it is the brilliant craft of a book that seems to move him. Though he never pretends to be a scholar, he absorbs the work, the names of illuminators and engravers. He spends hours with his invalid wife, poring over the details of some of the rarest and most beautiful art in the world, radiant scenes of gardens and angels that fill ancient books of psalms and prayers, all intimately gathered in the 150 volumes of his library. And now he has a Gutenberg.

◆ ◆ ◆

LITTLE IN DYSON's background would suggest an interest in such books. His father, James Perrins, was a chemist and local politician who assumed control of the family's share of the booming sauce business eight years before Dyson was born and sat on the board of the china company, a leading Worcester employer through the nineteenth century. Perrins collected contemporary paintings by the likes of Turner, Rossetti, and William Etty, the first significant painter of English nudes, expanding a gallery at the family's Malvern home, called Davenham, to display them. Dyson's mother, Frances, was an active patron of charitable works.

Dyson entered Queen's College at Oxford at eighteen to study law, but he struggled from the beginning, failing the school's basic freshman exam in ancient Greek, Latin, geometry, and logic several times before he finally passed. After similar difficulties on his sophomore exam, he dropped out. Plan B was military service, for which twenty-one-year-old Dyson headed to Scotland,[2] drawn by the opportunities for fishing, hunting, and adventures—far from family scrutiny.

His Glasgow-centric regiment, the Highland Light Infantry,

was one of six Scottish units of the British Army, and the only one to put its soldiers in trousers instead of kilts. In the relative peace between 1885 and 1889, Dyson's Fourth Battalion of the HLI ("Hell's Last Issue") was a part-time reserve militia, and between duty stints, he made the 350-mile trip home to learn the ropes at the Lea & Perrins factory.

The sauce that brewed the family fortune had been pouring out of Worcester since the mid-1830s, when Dyson's grandfather, pharmacist William Henry Perrins, and his partner, John Wheeley Lea, hit on the winning recipe at their chemists' shop on Broad Street. An oft-repeated legend had it that around 1835, Lord Marcus Sandys, a onetime governor of Bengal, walked into the shop and asked the partners to re-create a recipe he'd encountered in India. The chemists stirred up Lord Sandys's recipe using the foodstuffs and imported herbs and spices the store stocked, and pronounced the resulting mixture revolting. But rather than throwing it out, they poured it into a stoneware jug and stuck it in the cellar. Months later, they came across the jug and braved a second taste. Magically, the sauce's ingredients had mellowed into "something delectable."[3]

The most colorful elements of the story were largely fiction and may simply have been a brilliant early marketing trick.[4] No one has been able to identify a Lord Sandys who lived in Bengal, much less served as its governor. But a certain exotic mystique clung to the sauce and helped fan intense devotion to a singularly British product with a flavor profile from the distant reaches of the empire. From the beginning, the piquant combination of fermented anchovies, pickled garlic, and onions, along with cloves, tamarind, and a list of other ingredients, was a hit. With the help of savvy promotion—getting their product onto ocean liners[5] and paying stewards to introduce it to passengers—the condiment went global. And in just a few years, the partners went from selling fewer than seven hundred bottles a year to selling thirty thousand, the numbers steadily climbing.

By Dyson's time, Lea & Perrins is a money machine, available not only in Britain but across Europe, the US, Australia, and such unlikely points as El Salvador, Tibet, and South Africa. Fifty to sixty people handle production in the Worcester factory, much of the work devoted to tending and turning hundreds of oak barrels of aging, fermenting ingredients, whose precise proportions are a closely guarded secret to this day.[6]

How much of the nuts and bolts of the operation the young militiaman takes in, or cares about, is hard to know. The trim soldier with neatly combed hair and a fashionable mustache is caught up in his life in Scotland, and neither his father nor his father's partner Charles Wheeley Lea has immediate plans to retire. But in early 1887, while attending a meeting, James Perrins loses consciousness, and by nightfall he is dead. As the only male among Perrins's five children, Dyson, at age twenty-three, inherits his father's golden share of the sauce operation—and with it, all the expectations that go with being a Perrins in Worcester, a city that leans heavily on the success of the family's businesses and their generosity.

At times, it seems as though ownership of Number 45 requires prepayment in tragedy. Near bankruptcy, public humiliation, and the early loss of parents, spouses, and children all seem to wind through the stories of the individuals who've bought the Bible. Not a curse exactly, but a pulse of sudden, dark shocks. The loss of his father is Dyson's first jolt.

With Lea & Perrins under the steady hand of Charles Lea, Dyson delays moving home, remaining in the military for three more years. He falls in love with Scotland and with Catherine "Kate" Christina Gregory, a Scottish corn merchant's daughter, and they marry at St. Giles' Cathedral in Edinburgh in October 1889, a month after he's made captain in the Fourth Brigade. James Allan Dyson, their first child, arrives in 1890, followed by two more sons and two daughters.

◆ ◆ ◆

THE PERRINS ENTERPRISES begin to exert an insistent pull in 1891, when Dyson is voted onto the board of Royal Worcester Porcelain, a post his father had held for eighteen years. Lea & Perrins is the financial driver of the family holdings, but china—at least for Dyson—is the soul. When he enters the life of Royal Worcester's porcelain works, he finds himself at the center of a community of craftsmen and artisans that has been continually refining the art for almost a century and a half. For Dyson, it is a short path from witnessing the company's contemporary operation to becoming fascinated with its historic work, then seeking out rare Worcester porcelain. The exposure to painting and printing processes he gains in the world of china making becomes a bridge to an interest in early printing and book illumination.

The Royal Worcester operation, so thick with buildings it is almost a town within a town, sprawls over five acres along the

Severn River. Its painting, shaping, and glazing facilities wind through a two-story flared U of a building, whose window-lined halls stretch the length of multiple city blocks. The plant's fifteen multistory brick kilns dominate the landscape with their Chianti-bottle shape and the smoke of their wood and coal fires. By the end of the nineteenth century, forty thousand people live in Worcester, and some seven hundred of them—men, women, and children—work at the factory.[7]

The company began in 1751, when Dr. John Wall, an inventor and entrepreneur, put together a partnership to bring porcelain to Worcester. The exquisite strength and luminescence of eggshell-thin Chinese porcelain had created a heavy demand for imported "china" and set off a hunt for ways to re-create it with local materials. Early experiments yielded teacups that tended to shatter on contact with boiling water and glazes that cracked and crazed. But around 1748, a Quaker merchant named Benjamin Lund, working from notes made by a Jesuit priest in China, mixed white British clay with the pivotal ingredient—soapstone from Cornwall—to create a product that equaled its inspiration. Worcester wasn't in England's pottery belt, with close-by sources of raw materials and coal, but the partners *did* have Lund, whose operation they bought out to begin an enterprise that incorporated the ideas of the best porcelain makers and painters through time, whether local or from abroad.[8]

Royal Worcester's early pieces mimicked blue-and-white Chinese designs, with pagodas, boats, foliage, and slim Chinese figures in conical hats, but its painters, who included Dr. Wall, steadily broadened their repertoire as they came in contact with more varied work over time—naturalistic birds from German potters, trellis patterns from France, sheaves of wheat and flowers from Japan.[9] British aristocrats began loaning paintings to the factory for the artists to use as inspiration, and replicas of Old Master still lifes and portraits appeared on lines of dinnerware. In Dyson's time, the factory's artisans are known for their depictions of luscious fruit and flowers, and for the spectacular honeycombed pierced work painstakingly created by an artist named George Owen. But Dyson is particularly drawn to the blue-and-white pieces of the earliest years, when the factory's work was markedly uneven, and he begins to collect it.

"A collection of the early experimental work of an old factory must necessarily be interesting," he writes in a 1902 *Connoisseur* magazine essay. "Mine, I think, certainly is so. For in it one can read as in a printed book the story of the experiments, leading at one time to comparative failure, at another to success, until at last we come to those much appreciated specimens," the more showy pieces others prefer.[10]

On the factory floor,[11] he can watch as the experiments continue. While Dyson isn't yet in a library or showroom studying ancient books, he is regularly part of a creative workshop and printing operation that gives him an intimate view of the kinds of accidents and artistry—and even some of the techniques—it might take to produce an illuminated manuscript or Gutenberg's Bible.

Parts of the production process are largely unchanged from the factory's earliest days. Grinding stones in ten-foot wooden tubs still crush the components of the porcelain—soapstone, white clay, feldspar, quartz, and the ash of animal bones (part of a formulation that created a resilient bone china). Those are mixed with water and processed into workable clay—both solid and liquid (slip) in the vats and clay cellar of the slip house. At long workbenches that line each side of the windowed production floors, scores of workers press clay or pour slip into molds to shape plates or cups or pitchers, while others apply handles and shape surface details, or fit together intricately sculpted pieces produced from multiple molds. Their fragile output piles up on shelves and tables, hauled in and out on trays to the high, packed kilns, from which it emerges glassy and translucent.

The most dramatic transformations unfold in the decorating department, which has thirty painters of varying ages, most male and most of whom have been refining their art since apprenticing in this factory or another at age fourteen. Lined up at desks along the windows, where the light is best, they stand or sit bent over bare porcelain pieces, painting swans and perfect English roses, butterflies and feathers, flamingos, cows, interiors, and copies of well-known paintings. Their mix of art and craft involves not just producing lifelike images but imagining how the layers of dull metallic glazes they use will bloom into full color after firing. Year by year, the apprentices learn to copy, to glaze, to keep sticky porcelain surfaces free of dust and fingerprints,[12] and to curb the urge to start a cricket match in the wide, china-lined aisles (though a cricket ball does come out at least once, with predictable results.)[13] A painter could spend a lifetime there.

The place is immersive, and Dyson wades in.

The factory was at a peak just before he arrived, marking its first five-figure profits[14] and winning acclaim with the spectacular pieces it took to exhibitions in Melbourne, Manchester, and Chicago. But it overreached, absorbing artisans from two local porcelain operations that it overtook just as demand fell for Royal Worcester's most carefully wrought pieces. The painters have taken a cut in pay, and more work goes to the craftspeople who work on lower-priced lines that use a transfer printing process pioneered by the company. Designs are engraved on metal plates that are then inked with ceramic color and printed onto paper that is pressed to fired porcelain. The ink designs stick, the paper is lifted away, and the outlines are filled in by a team of female colorists.

There is ample work for them, and for the printers through the slowdown, as well as for the factory's gilders, who paint dull brown washes of gold onto the rims and designs of nearly every piece, and the burnishers, who rub the brown to brightness. Even stripped-down artistry calls for at least that touch of illumination.

◆ ◆ ◆

WHEN CHARLES LEA retires in 1892, Dyson takes the lead at Lea & Perrins. He is twenty-eight by then, and he becomes a full partner two years later. When new rail yards come to town in the mid-1890s, he builds a modernized sauce plant adjacent to the tracks. And when US import duties threaten profits from the lucrative American leg of the business, he okays a New York factory that will make the sauce from start to finish instead of using components skipped in from Worcester.

Global business is good, and he buys Ardross estate, "complete with castle," 550 miles to the north in Scotland, not far from Kate's hometown of Inverness.

The fortune generated by global sales of the popular sauce supported a porcelain factory and allowed Dyson Perrins to chase some of the rarest books in the world.

Just a year later, though, Royal Worcester is in crisis. Demand is stagnant, and competitors are slapping the Worcester name on lower-quality goods. Some of the plant's most skilled artists are sidelined after the company's traveling salesman comes back with few or no orders for their specialties. The factory needs a cash infusion to stay afloat, and Dyson begins making loans that will total £20,000.

Then Kate becomes gravely ill with influenza and pneumonia. Seeing her struggle for every breath, Dyson and the doctors aren't sure she will pull through, and when she does, it seems like a miracle. Though she never fully regains her health, the next years are filled with gratitude. The Perrinses put up the funds for a nondenominational chapel for the community near Ardross, and later they build a hospital in Malvern and pay for a public library there. Dyson buys Dibidale and Kildermorie Forest to expand the Ardross estate to 42,000 acres and adds a personal railroad siding to the Worcester station for the use of a private train that will take his Scottish bride, and their friends, family, and household staff, north to the property for holidays. He also begins to buy illuminated manuscripts.

◆ ◆ ◆

IN JUST A decade, Dyson amasses one of the finest private collections in Britain, but he always talks about his books in a self-effacing way, with little of the authoritative tone that appears when he is around rare porcelain. His interest in rare books and manuscripts seems tied to personal curiosity and pleasure, and he downplays any perception of himself as scholar or aspiring expert, though he does build a deep expertise, the kind that comes from traveling widely to unearth new acquisitions and view his rarities side by side with similar works.

It's unclear what first piques his interest. Maybe someone in his circle takes him to an auction preview where something on a gilded leaf—a landscape or figure or perfectly curved vine—recalls the labors of his own porcelain illuminators. Whatever the catalyst, he begins buying in the early 1900s. He likes to tell the story of how he made a rushed stop at Sotheran's bookshop in London in 1904 to find something to read on the train and was presented with a boldly illuminated fourteenth-century British Psalter, which he was persuaded to take home on approval for ten days.[15] He was struck by the manuscript and liked the price—£5,250—but needed a second opinion. So he asked Sydney Cockerell, something of a book maven for hire, to come up to Malvern to take a look.[16] With that invitation, he gained a friend, adviser, and direct route into the competitive, catty, and slightly angst-ridden heart of the new century's book scene.

Cockerell is a richly self-educated bibliophile who is continually extending his network and knowledge through his work for the most prominent collectors of the day, and his travels with the literary world figures he counts as friends. He'd been William Morris's assistant, cataloging and helping him acquire the vaunted library of medieval manuscripts and early printed books Morris used for inspiration, and coming to know an ever-widening circle of painters, poets, bookmen, and scholars. He visited Tolstoy with one set of friends, spent time with John Ruskin and Henry James and George Bernard Shaw. In short, he is "a welcome guest at the dinner tables of half the millionaires of England,"[17] who records every day of his life in diaries he keeps in a minute hand. He is working half-time for Henry Yates Thompson, who has built one of the country's great libraries, and work for Dyson will soon begin to fill the other half of his schedule.

Cockerell tells Dyson that the book he has borrowed is an unquestionable "yes," a manuscript whose history he'd like to plumb, and Dyson adds it to his shelf. (Cockerell later recalls that "a single glance was enough for me to recommend its purchase at any price.")[18] Over the next three years, they travel with the manuscript, putting it next to Psalters of the period from Yates Thompson's library, the British Museum, Oxford's Bodleian Library, and even a fine French work they cross the channel to see. Cockerell's research on Dyson's purchase, which he studies for extended periods, connects it to a manuscript workshop in Gorleston, a small town on the border of Suffolk and Norwich. The monograph he produces establishes the book—which he christens the Gorleston Psalter—as a premier example of the work of the East Anglican School of Manuscript Illumination, the most distinctive workshop of its time.

Between 1905 and 1910, these social interactions add a new dimension to Dyson's life. A reserved and modest man, he delights in stepping through the many doors Cockerell opens.[19] Cockerell seems to have a mental index of where the choice fourteenth-century psalters and books of hours reside, along with the ability to help pry them loose, and the two men go calling in the countryside, smoking cigars as they're chauffeured about in one of Dyson's beloved motorcars. Piece by piece, Dyson's collection grows. They go to Paris and bring back a book of hours with art, and the only known signature, by the celebrated thirteenth-century illuminator William de Brailes. Dealers like Bernard Alfred Quaritch offer their best. An abbot shows up at Malvern to offer Dyson an unknown manuscript from the tenth century. Discoveries squirm out of hiding.

By the end of 1905, Dyson has a museum-worthy collection of thirty manuscripts, and in another five years he'll have more than one hundred. He makes an offer on a number of items from the celebrated library of Charles Fairfax Murray, the noted painter and intimate of William Morris. Cockerell steers his friend toward the cream. "Enclosed, please find my cheque for £3,200 for the M.S.S.," Dyson writes Fairfax Murray, "and allow me to thank you for the opportunity of adding such treasures to my collection." He flatters the collector and invites him to Davenham, saying, "I think you would feel rewarded for the journey by the [Gorleston] Psalter which I acquired from Lord Braybrooke . . ."[20]

Those pieces are his gateway purchases. He doubles the size of his collection the next year by adding thirty-four more Fairfax

Murray treasures, the best of the lot. Cockerell advises him on some of the selections, and Dyson lets his own taste lead him toward the rest.[21] (Cockerell is generally critical of pieces Dyson chooses himself, pronouncing one masterpiece, the Wenceslas Psalter—now in the Getty—"showy" and another "rather ugly."[22] But Dyson pleases himself.)

His eye next lands on the library of R. C. Fisher, a collection built over two generations, as the auction catalog notes, "for the purpose of illustrating the development of the art of engraving in its connection with literature, chiefly in Italy, France and Germany."[23] "All the best Italian Woodcut books are included," the introduction tantalizes, from the Aesops of 1485 and Apocalypse of 1515 to the 1495 *Epistole et Evangelii*, along with a whole series of "Books of Hours, Offices and other Devotional Works of the Late XVth and Early XVIth Century." Lot 596 is William Morris's copy of a 1508 *Spirito della Perusia*, with "woodcuts consisting of wheels of fortune, figures of kings, signs of the Zodiac" and so on, which the catalog labels a "very rare edition of this remarkable book on fortune-telling." Hundreds more pieces, including a first edition of Martin Luther tracts and a host of early German illustrated books, crowd the catalog's 109 pages.

But it is the mention of *Epistole et Evangelii* that snares Dyson's attention. The book of Gospels and lessons features more than 150 woodcuts illustrating the masterpieces of fifteenth-century Florentine wood engraving.[24] This volume, one of two known copies, will be expensive, and Dyson, who wants it badly, decides to circumvent the bidding by making an offer for *all* of Fisher's books. He has the means—why not?

"This was obviously an opportunity to be made the most of,"

Dyson later writes, with some understatement, "and I was fortunate enough to rescue them at the eleventh hour from the perils of the auction by persuading the owner to sell them to me *en bloc*—a proceeding which I fear was not very pleasing to other collectors,"[25] notably US bidders who had crossed the Atlantic to find the promised four-day sale over before it began.

Dyson then borrows an idea from Henry Yates Thompson, who has one of the only private British collections that rival what the sauce king now owns. Yates Thompson, former publisher of the *Pall Mall Gazette*, had plowed his profits from the sale of the paper into illuminated manuscripts and, years earlier, had found himself in a position similar to the one Dyson now faces. Yates Thompson had bought the library of the Earl of Ashburnham, some 250 manuscripts, and famously declared that rather than letting the acquisition swamp him, he would keep only the best and limit his entire collection to just one hundred books of the highest value and quality that he'd come to know extremely well. He would continue to collect but would sell lesser items when he bought something new. To make his works more accessible to scholars and bibliophiles, he published a series of catalogs detailing his collection, with entries by M. R. James, head of the Fitzwilliam Museum, and Cockerell, among others.

Dyson follows suit, hiring Cockerell to help him cull and write descriptions of his cache, and later bringing on James; Sir George F. Warner, the British Museum's retired Keeper of Manuscripts; and Alfred W. Pollard, the museum's Keeper of Printed Books—all of whom he now counts as friends and consults on purchases—to catalog his library. Cockerell spends weeks at a time with Dyson's books at Malvern or Ardross Castle, where he studies, composes entries for the catalog, and roams in the beauty of the deer forest. A Sotheby's sale the next year, labeled only as items "from the library of a gentleman," cashes in Dyson's stellar discards and duplicates and brings his collection down to around 150.

Critics have puzzled over some of the books he chose to keep. "Far too many cripples, soiled, washed and mended copies bear [his] illustrious bookplate," writes one.[26] A scholar who visits to see a sixteenth-century volume in Dyson's collection describes finding that "the text has often been rendered difficult to read by the pages having been gummed together, and part of one leaf having come off on to the one opposite."[27] As happy as Dyson is to have copies of important books represented in his library, condition isn't his first criterion. The many fifteenth-century books of hours and "the more romantic collection of charming and precious bibelots"[28] on his shelves are also unlikely choices, and even questionable. But his selections reflect the dual facets of his taste, shaped both by scholars and by his wife, Kate, who sometimes joins him as he visits fellow collectors to share his finds.

When Kate suffers a stroke in 1908 that leaves her partially paralyzed, the visits cease, but now there is reason to spend even more time with his books. The couple can lose themselves in the illuminations of Dyson's "charming bibelots" more easily than in the less winsome woodcuts of some of his "more important" early printed books. Dyson often says that he collects illuminated manuscripts so he can sit by the fire with Kate after dinner and roam through them with her. Angels and Annunciations. Gardens and Apocalypse.

One book of hours from the fifteenth century, previously owned by the Duke of Warwick, presents an intricately patterned scene of the Annunciation, with a pink-robed and pink-winged Angel Gabriel unfurling his announcement on a white, snakelike banner.[29] The moment depicted is dreamlike, with the tiny dove of the Holy Spirit approaching Mary's haloed head, and a small, outstretched figure of the Christ Child flying toward her on the dove's gilded path. A short prayer in Latin is below the image, and a wide border, rich with interlaced foliage, winds around the page.

Kate's stroke is only the latest jolt for the family. A few years before, a fire started at Davenham when a candle in a servant's room blew into a linen drawer. The blaze tore through the whole north wing of the house, and only chance saved the children, who slept directly below the servants' quarters. The fire was stopped just one room away from the gallery that housed the family paintings and Dyson's rare china collection.

The book world, especially now, is a respite for Dyson, and even a source of acclaim. Sydney Cockerell uses every contact he has to mount a landmark 1908 exhibition of 270 illuminated manuscripts at the Burlington Fine Arts Club (the modern insurance value of the collected works, one scholar estimates, might be almost half a billion pounds).[30] Dyson is highly visible as the leading contributor, loaning fifty pieces, and that year, he is invited to join the exclusive bibliophile society the Roxburghe Club. Cockerell, for his part, wins the directorship of the Fitzwilliam Museum.

There is one more significant prize that year to come.

◆ ◆ ◆

R. C. FISHER'S COLLECTION, with its many examples of early woodcuts, had focused Dyson's attention once more on the kinds of accidents and experiments that push an art form forward. "The illustration of the printed book by means of the printed picture—the grafting of an old art upon the new—has always appealed to me with especial force," Dyson writes in the catalog he produced of the woodcuts in his 135 Italian illustrated manuscripts. "It is more than interesting to observe the points of resemblance and of difference between the new form of book and the old, and to see how the limited skill of the artisan, the wood-block cutter, fettered and bound the efforts of the book-artist who had long before come to the height of his powers in the Illuminated Manuscript." Gutenberg's Bible, that first grand experiment printed mechanically but illuminated by hand, sits at the cusp of old and new, preceding the volumes that will be illustrated with woodcuts and engraving, opening the door for them. That makes the book a fit for his shelf.

Number 45's illuminations are one of its distinguishing features, as it is one of the few Gutenberg Bibles illustrated in Mainz, where it was printed. Its floral motifs are naturalistic, its lines elongated and slender, and the range of color is narrow—bright green and a light pink contrasting with pale gray, red, and, rarely, blue. The overall feeling is restrained, unlike the rougher and more colorful borders created in Germany during the same period. There is only one similar example of illumination from this time, a Bible made around 1472 in Heidelberg in southern Germany that seems to have been decorated by the same hand, though some years later. Number 45's floral illustrations have extensive leaves and round bulbs, a style common in painting in northern Germany at the time, particularly in Cologne. These are the clues that come into play as experts triangulate the details—Mainz sits between

Heidelberg and Cologne—and place Number 45's illuminator in Gutenberg's hometown.

None of this was known to Dyson, but it's easy to imagine how, sitting with Kate, or bent over the Gutenberg in his study, he might have noticed the same sorts of variations in the work—"Look at the way the leaves change!"—that contemporary incunabula scholar Eberhard König does, studying Number 45's opening page:

> The frontispiece page contains an elaborate border of curly acanthus leaves, forming an initial F of a kind not found elsewhere in the copy. But this first style changes on the page itself: in the bottom margin, more natural leaves in bright green and pink colors . . . replace the dark acanthus border. One might think of this simply as an altera- tion of pattern, were it not that the pen work itself also changes, from red lines (acanthus) to brown lines (quasi-natural leaves).[31]

König's conclusion: the book was illustrated by two different art- ists. His guess is that a backlog of Bibles produced by Gutenberg's technology was the reason. Quite suddenly, an unusually large number of copies of a very extensive book presented themselves, all requiring hand completion by rubricators who added decorative lettering and illumination. No artists' workshop in Mainz seemed to be capable of handling the task efficiently. The traditional craftsman whose work appears on the first page of the Dyson copy apparently took on a share of the job but could not finish it, and he may have hired other artists to help him as undecorated manuscripts stacked up like pale pieces of porcelain, waiting for color from a brush.

The £2,058 pounds that Bernard Alfred Quaritch bids to win

Number 45 for Dyson at the Amherst sale is a trifle compared with the sum it must've taken to land the Fisher library. But the book is not yet a star in its own right, in part because it contains only half the Bible. In the news articles leading up to the auction, Gutenberg's work is only fleetingly mentioned, after detailed descriptions of the Amherst Caxtons, its most sought-after pieces. It gets the briefest nod in a long list of auction items in the London *Times* story, and *The Nation*'s sale preview gives it just two sentences, one of them comparing it to the two-volume vellum copy from Lord Ashburnham's library that was sold to American Robert Hoe for £4,000 in 1897. Reporting on Dyson's purchase is similarly muted.

Just a few years later, though, popular awareness of Number 45 and its siblings heightens in Britain. When Robert Hoe's collection goes on the block in New York in April 1911, his two-volume vellum Gutenberg, the same one Bernard Quaritch (the father) had begged Amherst to buy, sells to tycoon Henry Huntington for $50,000. Bernard Alfred Quaritch (the son) takes part in the intense bidding, but simply can't keep up.

The sale of a Gutenberg Bible for that price is a headline grabber in an auction that is all over the news, dispersing 16,000 lots and bringing in the highest total of any collection ever put on the block, "not only in America, but in the world," according to the *New York Times*.[32] Reading the coverage, many British collectors suddenly wake to a reality that some claim has long been obvious—bibliographical treasures are streaming to America in a "sad blow to British pride." The "Rip Van Winkles of the British press," as one reporter called them, blast the exodus as a threat to England's cultural heritage. As early as 1902, the *Times* had noted that "throughout Great Britain there is now widespread feeling of concern—one might say of jealousy, so bitter are the printed comments,"[33] about American buyers in the British auction rooms. Now the murmuring is a loud, angry howl as the American Century emerges on the scene, usurping Britain's bookish patrimony.

◆ ◆ ◆

THE CONCERN ISN'T misplaced. Even Dyson, the only private owner of a Gutenberg Bible in Britain and one of the last with the resources to compete with institutions and voracious American moguls like Henry Huntington, won't be active much longer. He continues to add choice works to his shelves over the next five or six years, especially when notable libraries come up for sale, and has a sharp enough eye to cable for a thirteenth-century Bible he spots in an Italian catalog because he thinks its art looks "Brailes-ish." (Indeed it is the work of the noted illuminator.[34]) But some of his most trusted guides are gone—Cockerell is busy at the Fitzwilliam, and Bernard Alfred Quaritch died at age forty-two, not long after the Hoe sale—and there is much else to command his attention. Dyson's fourteen-year-old son, John Stewart, the youngest, dies of pneumonia in 1914, and soon after, Dyson has to send two others, James Allan and Charles Francis, into the carnage of the Great War.

Worcester, like the rest of the country, mobilizes all its men under a certain age and rallies itself for victory but struggles through onslaughts of loss. The Worcestershire Regiment sends 130,000 from Dyson's region[35] and loses 9,000 of them, with countless more wounded. A thousand are killed or missing in the horrific 141-day Battle of the Somme in 1916, which leaves more than a million from all sides dead, injured, or unaccounted for.

Royal Worcester Porcelain retools for the war effort, trading its tea services for industrial porcelain used in hospitals, laboratories, and schools. And Lea & Perrins, through it all, continues to produce its quintessentially British sauce. Advertisements in a short-lived 1915 campaign show two British soldiers in a trench with a bottle of Lea & Perrins from a nearby open box. "A Gift of Sure Appreciation," the ad reads. "Your soldier friends will appreciate the gift of a few bottles of Lea & Perrins Sauce to use with their War Rations. It makes Bully Beef appetizing, and when mixed with jam is an excellent substitute for chutnee." The ad offers to send a dozen half-size bottles "direct to any member of the Expeditionary Force on the Western Front Carriage Paid, for 5s." (A follow-up public notice withdraws the offer, "owing to a Postal Regulation that parcels containing bottles cannot in the future be accepted for dispatch by Parcel Post" to the front.)

Dyson makes numerous contributions to the war effort, the most notable coming when he agrees to house a small selection of the British Museum's most valuable printed books, which are secretly evacuated from air-raid-threatened London and transported to Malvern for safekeeping. These rare books will wait out the war alongside Dyson's Gutenberg Bible.

As the war closes, with his sons safely home, Dyson makes one last dramatic bid to expand his collection, offering £100,000 to Henry Yates Thompson, who is selling his carefully curated one hundred illuminated manuscripts[36]—exquisite books of hours, Greek classics, treatises on love and philosophy—because cataracts have left him unable to enjoy them. Yates Thompson, whom Dyson considers to be his chief rival, says no, and Dyson comes away with just a handful of purchases.

That proves to be fortuitous. Royal Worcestershire is struggling mightily. A national labor strike in 1926 dramatically slows the public's spending, especially for nonessentials like fancy porcelain. The company ventures into earthenware and female nude figurines in an attempt to broaden its appeal,[37] but the experiments fall flat. Dyson begins paying his painters a minimal five shillings per piece from his own funds to keep them at the plant. He plumps the balance sheet by buying (at far above market value) the company's collection of its lines across time, an invaluable reference for its artists and a record of its history. Along with his own porcelain pieces, it will remain at the factory, he stipulates, preserved for future generations.

The company staggers into receivership, closing briefly in 1929, and Dyson marshals his resources to reopen the works, selling Lea & Perrins to Birmingham-based HP Foods, and buying the china works outright. Letting Royal Worcester fail would mean dispersing generations' worth of skill and knowledge, he knows, and it would be nearly impossible to reassemble a group with that level of mastery. Putting his artisans out of work is out of the question, so he rallies new management and looks for a way forward.

In the scramble for business, Royal Worcester converts some of its older buildings to tearooms, where a shilling will buy a "Chamberlain" tea of assorted sandwiches, a slice of fruit cake, and a pot of tea, all served on the company's wares, which he hopes visitors will be enticed to buy. The Great Depression decimates Royal Worcester's US sales, and by 1934, china orders are down by

50 percent. Though Dyson and company receive a welcome royal citation from King George V the next year, such honors don't pay the rent. The porcelain works is bleeding money, and Dyson sells his 53,000-acre Ardross estate to help cover the costs.

During World War II, production of ornamental china largely stops in Britain, and Royal Worcester begins producing insulators for use in aircraft radios and radar gear, as well as resistors for wireless equipment. Later in the war, the factory churns out spark plugs. It experiments with a smattering of figurines during the war, but few of them sell. Through the struggles, Dyson expresses no regrets. "It is true that I have lost a very large sum of money in my efforts to keep the works going," he says, "but I feel more than repaid by the knowledge that I have at least succeeded in that objective and by the fact that those whose interests were my chief consideration realize and appreciate what I have done."[38]

As soldiers finally trickle home, the works begins to gear up for normal production. A wave of apprentices come on board with an infusion of energy. But to keep running, some parts of the aging plant need extensive rebuilding. Dyson, now a widower in his early eighties, decides to make one last investment in the art he loves and the workers who depend on him. This time, it will cost him his books.

Bibliographer Seymour de Ricci once talked about the role collectors like Dyson play in the cultural life of the country: "Public institutions have done their best, but, in nearly every instance, private initiative has shown them the way," he wrote. "Personal vanity, the mainspring of collecting, has continually given way to local and national pride. In England, to be a collector has nearly always meant—to be a patriot."[39] To De Ricci, that meant building and

C. W. Dyson Perrins sold the Gutenberg Bible to help save his floundering porcelain business but left his signature, and a bookplate, inside the book's front cover.

holding on to collections as an expression of British cultural dominance, its genteel "ownership" and stewardship of the past. But Dyson, faced with a choice between historic treasures and the living ones, chooses the living, a different, harder sort of patriotism, and perhaps a more meaningful one, after the trauma of two long wars.

◆ ◆ ◆

WHEN IT COMES time to decide which of his books will go, Dyson singles out his early printed book collection. The Gorleston Psalter and the other priceless illuminated manuscripts he had begun rounding up with Cockerell, as well as the precious bibelots he'd pored over with Kate, stay with him to the end of his life. The rest, including the fifteenth-century *Epistole et Evangelii* that had originally drawn him toward the first fruits of the printing press, will be sold on four dates between 1947 and 1948 in what is described as the first big-time book auction of the postwar period. The collection will bring £147,627, more than half a million dollars, and set the china factory, one of the last remaining British companies from the beginning of the Industrial Revolution, on course to last into the twenty-first century.

The most significant price for a single item in the Dyson sales is reached on March 11, 1947, when lot 564—Number 45—goes on the block. This time, the first volume of Gutenberg's Bible is no longer a bullet point buried in a long list of treasures. It is the inescapable star. And its surprise return to the marketplace gives the book-collecting world—especially in America—a towering thrill.

PART II

THE AMERICAN CENTURY

CHAPTER FIVE

The Mighty Woman
Book Hunter

I T IS IMPOSSIBLE to miss Number 45 in the royal-blue catalog that Sotheby's issues for the sale of Dyson's collection. The frontispiece folds open to reveal a two-page color photo of the Bible, showing Jerome's Epistle, with its subdued acanthus vines winding the margins and the signature flourish of its first initial *F*, green and trimmed in gold leaf. The statement made by the size and placement of that photograph is more emphatic than any catalog copy, and the anticipation it fuels for the auction is intense. In the four decades since Number 45 last appeared on the market, it has worked its way to the head of the pack of early printing's coveted treasures, and now it is undeniably revered.

That shift, and the avid international attention focused on the Dyson sale, reflect a reconfigured world whose order has once more been shattered by war, and whose new design is being pieced together in an age being shaped by transatlantic communication, airplane travel, early television, and American bravado. Gutenberg's Bibles might seem to have little place in this ever more modern era, but they have long been kingmakers in their way, conferring on their owners a cultural importance and legitimacy that money alone can't buy.

Tracking the whereabouts of the Bibles over time produces a heat map of shifting influence, as the books move from the confines of the Catholic Church and into the libraries of Europe's aristocrats, and then flow to Britain's empire builders, embellishing the reputations of each successive set of owners. With Dyson, the merchant class showed its rise, and now the red-hot center of power is the US, where mogul/collectors like J. P. Morgan and Henry Huntington have been flexing their New World muscle and, like the British aristocrats before them, providing a ready market for the libraries being sold to finance escapes and recovery from the hardships of war, or a better path through them. The new kings want Gutenbergs. And by force of personality and bottomless wallets, they get them. Prices shoot upward, as does the book's cachet, now trumpeted through American megaphones.

The posturing begins early for the auction. American collector Lessing J. Rosenwald (son of Julius Rosenwald, former co-owner of Sears, Roebuck and Company) announces that he plans to buy eighty-four titles in the Dyson catalog, and he has staked out the Gutenberg Bible among them.[1]

Also watching alertly, excitedly, is Estelle Doheny, the American heiress, businesswoman, and elite collector who, by the time of the bidding, will be in the thick of a pursuit whose only allowable conclusion is possession of the book. Eleven years younger than Dyson, she had been drawn into collecting much as he had been, with no previous exposure, and like him, she has grown into a deep love for illuminated manuscripts.

Her desire for a Gutenberg Bible, and the decades-long quest it will bring, flickers into view for the first time in 1911, just after Dyson's collecting flurry has, perhaps unknown to him, peaked. At that moment, hers is about to begin.

◆ ◆ ◆

ESTELLE'S HUSBAND IS an oilman, a self-made multimillionaire from an immigrant Irish Catholic family. Wealth shoots from the derricks Edward Doheny hoisted in Los Angeles and from the wells he's wildcatted in Mexico's jungles; his fortune could fill tankers. Photos of Estelle from later in their marriage, dressed primly for tea or standing at a garden party, show a rich man's society wife. But the independent spirit and grit that will propel her flash from a photograph taken on her wedding day in 1900. The new Mrs. Doheny stands, the only woman in a clutch of men and boys, at the back of the private railcar that will function as wedding chapel, honeymoon suite, and home for the next three months as her husband roams the Southwest, inspecting his oil fields and scratching up the money to develop them. Estelle is twenty-five, the vibrant figure behind the telephone operator's voice that beguiled Edward just months before. In a dark dress tightly cinched at her narrow waist—no white for this bride—she leans out from the edge of the car, hand on hip. Though one elbow is locked through Edward's, she expands into her own space on the other side. Her gaze at the camera is direct. It holds a challenge, softness but also steel. Now she is stepmother to Edward's young son, Ned, manager of stateside dealings, keeper of the idea of home for a man who lives his rough business mostly on the road. She's no "Madam" or "Missus." She's a woman of the frontier, and later she wants to be called Ma Dee.

Edward and Estelle Doheny on their wedding day, August 22, 1900. Doheny's private Pullman car, later christened the Estelle, *stopped in New Mexico Territory long enough for a justice of the peace to preside over the ceremony. Left to right: Carrie Estelle Betzold, Edward L. Doheny, Albert Canfield, and Edward "Ned" Doheny Jr.*

In the spring of 1911, she's thirty-five, and Edward, at age fifty-four, is worth an estimated $75 million,[2] $1.8 billion in today's dollars. Travel and entertaining are constants as they work to weave the connections that will provide the steady stream of favors and capital that the international oil business requires. They divide their time among a lavish apartment in Midtown Manhattan; hotel suites in Washington, DC; and a showplace mansion in the exclusive West Adams neighborhood of Los Angeles. Soon there will be a 411-acre Beverly Hills ranch and more properties up the coast as well.[3]

Estelle has filled their Los Angeles home with art that reflects Edward's love of the American West, the wellspring of their fortune and the place they think of as home. Neither of them collects books, but that March, it's hard to miss the news of the grand cultural circus surrounding the sale of Robert Hoe's library in New York, and like everyone else, Estelle is intrigued. The papers are full of news stories anticipating astronomical prices. "Hoe Library Sale May Break Records," the *New York Times* headline blares. "Gutenberg Bible, Which Last Sold for $20,000, to be Offered on First Day . . . Many Books Worth $10,000 Each."[4]

A breathless front-page story then reports the results: "Gutenberg Bible Sold for $50,000. Buyer for Henry E. Huntington Gets It at the Highest Price Ever Paid for a Book." The bidding had advanced in $1,000 increments, leaving Bernard Alfred Quaritch behind at $30,000, and finally stopping twenty bids later. "There were cries of 'Who is the buyer?' from all over the room," the *Times* reports, and at a nod from bookseller George Smith, who had been bidding for Huntington, his identity was dramatically revealed.[5]

Follow-up profiles try to get inside "The Man Who Paid $50,000 for the Gutenberg Bible." If Huntington had wanted or needed the approbation such publicity brings, now he has it. "Mr. Huntington does not like yachting as do so many other men of wealth. The possession of fleet racehorses holds no charms for him. He neither drinks nor smokes, and eats very sparingly," the *Times* writes. "All the enormous energy which made him in his business days a genuine hustler is now concentrated on his collections."[6] Why? The takeaway quote says nothing of his deep seriousness or philanthropic intent. It is wildly, quotably American. He's made his money, he says. "Now I want some fun."

That sale captures Estelle's imagination. Huntington has a home just across town. He inherited a railway fortune and expanded it exponentially by building an interurban rail system that crisscrosses the Los Angeles basin. If circumstances had been different, Estelle and Edward might have moved in the same social circles—their wealth, their drive, even their teetotal ways give them much in common. But Catholics and Jews aren't particularly welcome in Pasadena society, and newly minted millions don't ease the way into a Southern California elite that privileges older money, even if it's just a generation old. The Dohenys' colorful backgrounds—he spent years as a prospector traveling with pack and mule before striking oil; she was a telephone operator with scant education—don't confer status either, even in a town raised around the myth of reinvention. Edward and Estelle are constructing their own circle, outside the orbit of the Henry Huntingtons and within the community that invites their contributions most warmly, the Catholic Church. Perhaps, though, there are ways to level the polo field.

Edward and Estelle Doheny early in their marriage, photographed at the Doheny Mansion in Los Angeles.

Estelle looks up from her papers and turns to Edward. "Will you, someday, buy me a Gutenberg Bible, dear?" she asks.

Yes, he replies. "I promise you I will."

As the years pass, she never lets go of that answer.

♦ ♦ ♦

EVEN AS EUROPE moves toward and through the Great War, the Mexican wells keep producing, and the Dohenys' home on 8 Chester Place becomes a reflection of their success. They begin to buy other properties on the street, gradually turning the grounds into a hub for entertaining financiers and oilmen, visiting aristocrats, musicians and notables (Einstein, Madame Curie), and colorful

Hollywood neighbors like film femme fatale Theda Bara, Fatty Arbuckle, and Douglas Fairbanks. Old money may be discreet, but new money, at least in Edward's case, bangs around with cymbals. Edward declares his intent to transform all of Chester Place into a "magnificent park, right in the heart of the most expensive and exclusive residence section of the city, with fountains, secluded walks and all that practically unlimited means can procure."[7] They build a deer park and raise a massive glass-and-steel conservatory— the Palm House—that's two-thirds the size of a football field and fifty feet high, importing towering palms from Mexico and Venezuela along with thousands of rare orchids that surround a heated swimming pool big enough to have its own canoe. The architects

Edward and Estelle Doheny's home, 8 Chester Place, Los Angeles, circa 1910.

are noted for their work around the city, but Doheny, a difficult customer, brings a shock of oil-world rough-and-tumble to the process. When he gets an answer he doesn't like from one of them, he punches him in the face and breaks his nose.

One way or the other, he *will* get what he wants. When bankers and real estate investors have conventions in town, the Dohenys court them, giving dinners for one or two hundred, and they join the Rockefeller crowd in the exclusive parade of vessels trailing the America's Cup, entertaining friends and potential clients on their steam-powered yacht, the *Casiana*, with its crew of forty. They take an ocean liner across the U-boat-infested Atlantic on the eve of World War I (passing the sunk *Titanic*) to set in motion deals to convert coal-powered steamships to oil and establish the British Mexican Petroleum Co., creating global distribution for Edward's oil.

In 1914, Edward stops briefly in New York at the Fifth Avenue art galleries of Knoedler & Company, where Wall Street tycoons buy their Old Masters, saying he wants to see eight paintings from the Barbizon school, those lush French landscapes by the likes of Corot and Rousseau, whose skies and even cattle seem slightly reminiscent of the West. He walks out having paid more than $150,000 for twenty-two pieces, including two by Frederic Remington, a romanticizer of cowboys and Indians.

This is the point in the oil-sheened narrative where we might see such a man enjoying the cachet that cultural recognition brings and asking his wife, "And what would you like, dear? Didn't you mention something about a Gutenberg Bible? I'm going to *find* you one."

But the path to fulfilling his casual promise to Estelle begins in a darker way—as all roads approaching Number 45 seem to—with a sudden and dramatic reversal of fortune ten years later.

◆ ◆ ◆

THE DARKNESS COMES in June 1924, when father and son are accused of bribing the US secretary of the interior, Edward's friend Albert B. Fall, to get favorable terms on drilling rights on federal land. Spun one way, Edward Doheny's gifts to Fall, including a $100,000 no-interest loan delivered by Ned in cash, look like graft. Spun another way, they're simply expressions of a wealthy man's generosity to a longtime friend. The case bleeds into the most notorious political scandal the country has yet known—Teapot Dome. The Doheny men each face federal bribery and conspiracy charges and lengthy, overlapping civil and criminal trials that drag on for nearly a decade. The looming threat is not just financial

Edward Doheny in 1923 at the peak of his power and prestige, before the oil scandals known as "Teapot Dome" erupted.

ruin. Edward could be sentenced to spend the rest of his life in prison.

Every twist and turn is covered in the press, and cascading events keep Estelle in daily contact with Edward's larger-than-life criminal defense attorney, Frank J. Hogan, who sets up a headquarters in the area of the Doheny mansion that was once Estelle's bowling alley. "The best client," Hogan tells friends, "is a rich man who is scared." Doheny, very rich and very scared, is the best of the best. Hogan is fabulously charismatic despite a slight speech impediment that turns his *r*'s into *w*'s, and he can seize authority in a room with his darting eyes and sharp mind. He practically lives with the Dohenys during stretches of the trial years, and spends long days with Estelle in the winter of 1926 as she prepares to take the stand in her husband's defense.

Expertly coached by Hogan, Estelle is calm and convincing in court, delivering a detailed account of how the money changed hands and offering a careful rationale for what looks like a cover-up.[8] Her testimony is printed nearly verbatim on the front page of the *New York Times* and in papers around the world, and news accounts describe her as forthright, clear, and unembarrassed. The jury believes, and Edward is acquitted.

But soon there is another trial, this time for conspiracy, and as it progresses, tension builds to an almost unbearable level. Estelle and Hogan begin to talk about books. Rare books. Expensive books. Books suddenly serve as a welcome distraction as their usual social activities dry up and disappear. Estelle and Edward have been pariahs since the criminal accusations surfaced, and real friends are few and far between. Yet a tight circle of trust pulls around them and manages to hold firm. Their priests. Family. Their closest business partners, lawyers, and associates, many of whom live in the Chester Place compound with their families, part of the tribe. There are also true friends with nothing to lose by association, like the famed Irish tenor John McCormack.

Leila Wellborn, a neighbor, and wife of one of Edward's civil lawyers, has been close to Estelle since she moved to Chester Place, and she gives her friend a life raft in a copy of *High Spots of American Literature,* a popular new book that lists some two hundred "outstanding American books," from *Moby-Dick* to *Rebecca of Sunnybrook Farm,* that might form the collectible core of a library. Estelle is captured by the idea of owning them all and decides she'll distract herself by finding as many as she can in first editions. She makes her desire known to the dealers at Dawson's, a downtown antiquarian bookstore, and books begin to stream in, with packages arriving almost daily. Soon, Hogan joins the game, and a rivalry builds as they defuse the trial's intensity by working their way through the list.

At the same time, the Gutenberg Bible reappears in the news. With inflation rampant in Europe, and postwar politics becoming ever more turbulent, long-hidden Bibles have been resurfacing, and one of them has just become national property—by act of the United States Congress. Dr. Otto Vollbehr, a German industrialist (and Nazi apologist), had plumped up his rare-book collection after World War I, acquiring a three-volume vellum Gutenberg from a Benedictine abbey in Austria. He arrived in the US in 1926 with more than three thousand fifteenth-century books valued at $3 million and, after displaying one hundred of them at the Library of Congress, offered that if someone would come up with the funds to buy half the collection, he would donate the other half.

Miraculously, in the crush of the Great Depression, a Mississippi congressman, Ross Alexander Collins, rallied support for the purchase, especially the Gutenberg Bible, which he called, with Barnum-like enthusiasm, "the greatest book on Earth." Congress embraced the proposal, allocating $1.5 million to expand the rare-books holdings at the Library of Congress, and just as Estelle's interest in collecting takes off, President Herbert Hoover makes the purchase official, signing the authorization into law.

The story feeds Estelle's fantasy, but first, she'll have to survive the overlapping criminal and civil trials. At last, after five years of torture, there's a verdict.[9] Jurors believe the rationale Hogan expertly sells, and they acquit Edward. But his codefendant is not as fortunate. Fall is sent to federal prison, the first cabinet officer in US history jailed as a result of misconduct in office, convicted of receiving the very bribe Doheny is acquitted of giving. (The bitter sting of that twist lives on in the term it gave currency: "fall guy.")

The contradictory verdicts make Frank Hogan famous, landing him on the cover of *Time* magazine. "In court, if occasion demands, he will start a fight with a witness, leap in the air, howl, weep, do anything to distract or sway a jury," *Time* says of his unconventional, if highly effective, courtroom style.[10] Hogan is now not only the best-known trial attorney in America, he's also very wealthy. According to news accounts, his fees for his labors in the Teapot Dome debacle total more than $1 million, and the day after the acquittal, a new Rolls-Royce appears at his Sheridan Circle town home in Washington, DC, a gesture of thanks from Doheny.

The victory is sweet, but there is tremendous psychic and physical rebuilding to do. Four years into the draining courtroom

drama, in February 1929, the Dohenys were blindsided by an un-
fathomable tragedy that the verdict can't erase. Ned, Edward's
only child, was shot in the head at close range in his bedroom by
a longtime family employee in what appeared to be a murder-
suicide. The assailant, a man named Hugh Plunkett, had been
swept up in the pending criminal trial as a possible witness. The
loss was shattering, but with the nonstop onslaught of the trial
there was little time to grieve. In the quiet of the aftermath, the
couple feel the trauma reverberating more loudly than ever. Estelle is racked with grief, and Edward is still inconsolable, a "broken and changed man" who no longer cares about the affairs of the
world.[11]

Estelle works to create a sanctuary. She escapes with Edward
to their Ferndale Ranch in Santa Paula, a scenic area in Ventura
County where he can rest in seclusion. The property, set in the
rugged beauty of the chaparral, has commanding views of the
Topa Mountains, and a silence that gently mutes the lingering
pain. Estelle bought the property and urgently set architect Wallace Neff to work on it after Ned's death, and it has become a place
of rejuvenation, a hacienda with orchards, a nine-hole golf course,
and a stream flowing into three trout ponds set so Edward, increasingly infirm, can fish from a wheelchair—all completed in
just six weeks. Neff has also designed a memorial for Ned, a thirty-
two-seat chapel with a stone grotto displaying a statue of our Lady
of Guadalupe, the Virgin of Mexico. Each morning they're at the
ranch, Estelle and Edward attend a private Mass inside the elegant
chapel to pray for Ned's soul.

Frank Hogan returns home to the East Coast but stays in touch
with Estelle. He's taken to book collecting with the same energy

he brings to the courtroom, and even before the end of the trial he had made the leap from the *High Spots* list to a fascination with the treasures that began to emerge as Los Angeles booksellers directed him toward their more expensive shelves. His first big purchase was a "not quite so perfect" Shakespeare Second Folio. Now, famous and flush with funds, he begins to receive the hopeful solicitations of those with wares aimed at a moneyed clientele. A rare-books catalog appears in the mail, and, because he can, he carries it all the way to Philadelphia to see an item that has been enticingly described, a copy of Ellen Terry's *The Story of My Life* filled with pithy margin notes by its previous owner, George Bernard Shaw.[12] That visit introduces him, and by extension Estelle, to a realm of the book-collecting world neither of them had yet experienced. He walks out of the store carrying not just the Shaw copy but also an Oscar Wilde presentation copy that had been given to the author, and first editions of *Tom Jones* and *A Sentimental Journey*. The $10,000 he spends that day buys him the effusive attention of the shop's legendary owner, A. S. W. Rosenbach.

Abraham Simon Wolf Rosenbach, known as "the Doctor" for his degree in literature, is, by all appearances, a reincarnation of Bernard Quaritch on American soil, even taking on the Quaritch mantle of the "Napoleon of the auction room." From his Philadelphia office, he has been more responsible than any other single buyer for the steady exodus of rare items from the British market.[13] He was one of Henry Huntington's primary dealers, and he was the bidder who secured one of the two Gutenberg Bibles at the Hoe sale, as well as another that came to the market more recently, an Austrian Gutenberg that belonged to the Benedictine monks in Melk. That sale, in 1926, was dramatically staged with the book's two leather-bound volumes kept behind maroon curtains until the auction, their crisp pages then revealed under brilliant lights. Belle da Costa Greene of the Morgan Library opened the bidding at five figures, but when the gavel fell, it was Rosenbach's £9,800 (with the British pound at $4.87; about $48,000) offer that prevailed. "It was fun to pay through the nose," he laughed in the front-page accounts.[14]

Just a few years later, very few buyers have money like that, and Rosenbach greets Hogan, who does, eagerly, with an invitation to spend the night at his home and see the collection of a legend. The two outsize personalities take to each other immediately, with the DC lawyer quickly becoming not just one of Rosenbach's valued sources of funds in the dry Depression days, but also a friend and champion. During their first visit, Hogan suggests that Rosenbach send his memoir *Books and Bidders* to Estelle, and the dealer dispatches it with a note reading, "If I can be of any assistance to you in forming your collection, do not hesitate to let me know."

Estelle reads every word of the book, which is chock-full of Rosenbach's escapades with the nation's most distinguished collectors, and she pores over stories about the dealer from the *New York Times*, *Life*, and *Fortune*. She is charmed, intrigued. She writes back modestly: "I am such a novice that when anyone feels he could mention my name to you it makes me feel more timid than I was before, because I don't even know the first principles of book collecting . . . I am looking forward and hoping that after the Depression I then may avail myself of the opportunity to collect something that is really worthwhile."[15]

To catch the gaze of a Quaritch or a Rosenbach and be recognized as a person of means and potential is to be cultivated, educated, enticed, and persuaded that in pursuit of a significant book, money is no object. Estelle will be courted by a number of important dealers in the years that follow, but as biographer Edwin Wolf notes, few can match Rosenbach's "intellectual virtuosity when he set out to ingratiate himself. His manner was effortless; the performance flawless. He had an endless supply of biblio-anecdotes, which made the volumes he handled come alive, and he had the irresistible enthusiasm of a salesman convinced that what he was selling was better than anything else on the market."[16]

Just months after their first exchange, with charm, flattery, and a catalog description likely written with her in mind, he makes his first sale: a 1473 copy of *Imitatio Christi*, a key spiritual handbook and unquestionably worthwhile acquisition, for which she pays $4,650. Though Rosenbach would likely take credit for initiating Estelle into the world of incunabula, this is actually her second. Following her curiosity beyond the *High Spots*, she had purchased a folio of Saint Augustine's *City of God* that had been printed in Mainz in 1473 by Peter Schöffer, Gutenberg's successor, bought from the dealers at Dawson's.

Alerted by Hogan to how much she values her Catholic faith, Rosenbach sends letters stressing the religious significance of the rare books he selects for her, putting each volume in context and tempting her to add another, and another. Slowly, she does. He shares gossip of the book world and feeds her sense of herself as a serious collector with gestures like the pre-auction telegram he sends from a luncheon gathering that includes Frank Hogan:

GATHERED AROUND THE LUNCHEON TABLE AT
ROSENBACHS WE BOOK-COLLECTORS WHILE DISCUSSING
THE GAME ON A GREAT SCALE HAVE COUNTED YOU AS A

PRESENT LEADER AND ARE JOINING IN THIS MESSAGE OF HIGH REGARD.[17]

Early on, Estelle, much like Dyson before her, is pulled in several directions as the urge to collect builds. Edward never regains the vigor he had before the trial and his son's murder, and increasingly, he's an invalid. Some of Estelle's collecting focuses on objects she thinks will raise his spirits. She brings home books bound with small ivory figures in the spines, reminders of similar volumes she'd admired in the library of William Randolph Hearst. She also seeks out books with fore-edge paintings, a delight-inducing (not "important") genre that features images that remain hidden on the closed, gilded front edges of a book until the pages are slightly fanned to reveal the cleverly painted picture.[18] These, along with her more "serious" purchases, have her spending as much as $1,000 a week. Depression or no, money isn't a pressing concern for her. Her working budget starts with the birthday gift Edward always gives her: $1,000 for each year of her life. The total

Estelle Doheny, who became one of the great Woman Bookhunters, chased the Gutenberg Bible for decades. She finally affixed her bookplate to the inside cover of her own copy in October 1950.

in 1931 is $56,000. That's the year when, with books stacking up and dealers' orders to track, she hires Lucille Miller, later adding two more assistants, to help her corral her growing stacks.

"I was put to work in a little dormer-windowed room up under the eaves," Lucille remembers, "but it was several days before I met my employer. Early one morning the door flew open and in came Mrs. Doheny with outstretched hand and friendly smile." She wore a pleated white crepe dress and a flower-laden hat, Lucille recalls, and her welcome was warm. "She looked at the cards I was typing and impressed it upon me that what she wanted was not a complicated, professional sort of catalogue, but a simple card-index enabling her to locate any book in the house. She was in a rush—and soon hurried off, leaving me with an unforgettable impression of her vitality and charm."[19]

The book secretary job, Lucille says, "twirled her into the arms of medieval monks and Romantic poets and authors of classics the world over."[20] The job also pushed her into a thriving, humming network of book aficionados and authorities, all with impressive résumés. Over time, as Estelle's eyesight deteriorates, Lucille becomes Estelle's eyes and ears, transcribing her correspondence and making telephone calls to dealers around the world.

◆ ◆ ◆

COLLECTING IS SOMETHING all Estelle's own. She had walked through fire during Edward's trials, coming out tempered and transformed, with a powerful desire to assert her own taste and a hunger for the respect that Teapot Dome had stripped away. Stepping in to manage affairs that Edward can't, she has taken a seat on the board of Pan American Petroleum, becoming one of the first female directors of a major US company. She has persuaded Edward to fund a lasting memorial to their son—a $1.1 million library at Ned's alma mater, the University of Southern California. Now, she will do something purely for herself: explore the beauty of books and follow that impulse wherever it takes her. Looking back at the high points of her life with Edward, she often sees that moment of asking him for a Gutenberg Bible, whimsical as it seemed, as a measure of what they've lost. They could've had anything all those years ago, even the status and recognition such a book can buy. She wants that more now than she ever did then.

Even as Rosenbach woos from the East Coast, another tutor/mentor/super-salesperson appears much closer to home. In 1933, Estelle is sought out by Alice Millard, a Pasadena bookseller. Millard, who took over her husband's bookselling business when he died, is one of a handful of women in the male-dominated book trade, a "brilliant talker" who can dominate a room with the sweep of her knowledge and her love for rare books. The only significant female figure dealing in rare books when she contacts Estelle, she's audacious, unrelenting, and known, tellingly, as "the Rosenbach of the West."[21]

Alice is sixty, and her angular face and large teeth give her a distinctive appearance that she cultivates carefully, always dressing in shades of blue. She has heard that Estelle is looking for a quality Gutenberg Bible, and she writes from London on August 17 to say she's located a B42 at an unnamed German university, adding some murky details that, she stresses, must be handled with the utmost secrecy, since another wealthy American is also interested:

*This particular copy will only be available because of the Nazi
situation. The old authorities, the "die-hards," have voted against
its sale—but incoming authorities with the spirit of youth have
little reverence for it and voted to do the practical thing. I cannot
tell you more about it now, except that it is one of the great and
well known copies—on vellum, in four volumes[22]—in 15th century
pig skin binding. . . .*

*Roughly, I should say that it will cost about seventy-five
thousand dollars less than the copy which Dr. Vollbehr sold to the
Congressional library, and, of course, perhaps at the opportune
moment one might do very much better than that.[23]*

*I am passing through Germany on my way to Italy in the
beginning of September and shall then carefully examine the book.*

Millard may be stretching the truth in various directions. But like
many others in 1933, she is strapped for cash and very much needs a
sizeable commission. She had enjoyed considerable success in the
1920s and had brokered important sales with collectors William An-
drews Clark and Henry Huntington. But according to Lucille Miller,
the Depression has "nearly finished her," and a transaction like this
would be a lifesaver.

A month later, Mrs. Millard cables Mrs. Doheny to say that she
has "minutely examined the Gutenberg incognito," and more information will be forthcoming. Estelle responds almost immediately, saying that while she appreciates the opportunity, she can't
consider the purchase. The household is still recovering from a
disaster that hit months earlier, and it's not a good time to think
about books.

The magnitude 6.4 Long Beach earthquake struck as Edward

and Estelle were eating dinner in the formal dining room at Chester Place on March 10, bringing books and artworks crashing to the floor and sending the Dohenys and their household staff scrambling for safety in the violent shaking. Fearing aftershocks, or worse, Estelle ordered the staff to load up several cars with the most valuable of her rare books and family possessions and soon had a caravan speeding north toward the Ferndale Ranch in Ventura County.

They emerged unhurt but are still repairing the mansion and its cracked foundation. Estelle is also updating the decor to her taste, replacing the old buffalo head and the petrified wood fireplace with something more elegant. Buying more books is low on her list of priorities, she tells Millard.

Undeterred by the news, the dealer writes again, this time from Rome:

> Of course, the expense of reconstructing your home must have been simply formidable, and impossible of definite estimates in advance, and a realization of such a probability frequently came to my mind—but I should not have really fulfilled my obligation to you had I not carefully investigated this unique opportunity and probably last opportunity of securing "THE GREATEST BOOK IN THE WORLD," especially as I realized that its actual availability may be very much in the future.[24]

Soon, Millard promises, she will return to Los Angeles with suitcases full of rare items, and she warns Mrs. Doheny to "be prepared for a feast!"

Millard makes good on her word, arriving at Chester Place with a substantial cargo: a twelfth-century British concordance and commentary to the four Gospels, with four miniature illustrations on gold grounds; a missal from 1536; the first printed Homer (1488–89); and an Aldine 1502 collection of Sophocles among them. Lucille unpacks the haul and lays it out on the billiard table for Mrs. Doheny to examine later. "I doubt any bookseller in the world could assemble a comparable offering," she recalled. "The prices," reflecting the desperation of pre–World War II Europe, "would make any collector weep."

The power of personal courtship and the presence of the objects exert themselves. With the ancient books and manuscripts arrayed in front of her, so much more alive than even the richest catalog descriptions could make them, Estelle suddenly sees the possibilities Frank Hogan found in Rosenbach's shop. "Mrs. Doheny knew that the books she was looking at were in a different category from her American first editions," Lucille said. "New vistas of book collecting opened to her. She made a decision—she would take everything."

That same day, Estelle writes a check for $34,033 and sends Lucille to deliver it to Mrs. Millard in person in Pasadena, where she lives in a residence designed for her by Frank Lloyd Wright known as La Miniatura. "I can still see Mrs. Millard with that check," Lucille wrote later. "She held it at arm's length in both hands and gave a little cry of triumph."

The relationship between collector and dealer proceeds with the intensity of an infatuation for at least a year or two, with Millard putting herself in the role of Estelle's private tutor and, like Rosenbach, placing her wares in the larger context of history and culture. The books, many of them Bibles, prayer books, and early sacred works, are not only beautiful; they allow Estelle to hold the history of the church in her hands and to absorb the inspiration that once flowed from these pages to monks and priests and popes. Millard makes this connection clear, personal. She is Estelle's version of Sydney Cockerell, close in age, confident of her taste, supremely able to persuade. Millard takes her role as dealer as the "highest form of custodianship, where pride in possession, intimacy with the object, and a feeling of care and responsibility would dominate and be impressed upon her clients," as bibliophile Robert Rosenthal describes it in a 1985 essay.[25] She very much considers herself an arbiter of "highbrow taste."[26]

Millard's lessons take place almost entirely in letters, which Rosenthal describes as a multipronged sales tool, an "educational campaign, amalgams of praise, bibliographical detail, and hard-headed business couched in a lilting, ladylike prose." The notes are often accompanied by books, and of the many that make their way to Chester Place, few are returned. "Mrs. Millard's hallmark as a bookseller was quality. A printed book must be pristine; a binding flawless; a vellum manuscript a superior specimen of the style and period."[27]

As legendary dealers tend to do, Millard takes Estelle to new heights of expense. Her husband had known William Morris, so it was inevitable that the great designer would become part of the Estelle Doheny Collection. In 1933, Millard sends over from London the famous vellum manuscript of Virgil's *Aeneid* (ca. 1874), with calligraphy by William Morris and Graily Hewitt. "It took Mrs. Doheny some time to make up her mind to buy this incomplete but sumptuous volume—probably the most ambitious attempt to re-create medieval arts of calligraphy and illumination," Lucille said. "It was her first ten-thousand-dollar book—a milestone to any collector. Typically, Mrs. Doheny dipped a toe, as it were, in the water—she paid for it in monthly installments!"

That step is a defining one. "Costly as it was, this manuscript helped break the resistance and gave Mrs. Doheny the gratification she required," Robert Rosenthal points out. Estelle now possessed a great work of art, "already acclaimed as the greatest manuscript of the modern age."[28]

Estelle derives great pleasure from her collection as it grows in size and quality. "I love my gorgeous books and manuscripts all the time," she writes Millard, "and the more I love them the more I appreciate all you have done for my library."[29] But even as the dealer tries to "instill direction and even self-confidence" in her client, as Rosenthal puts it, Estelle never seems at ease with her collection "except for the personal gratification she received from the distinctiveness and beauty of its objects." There's a push-pull between the developing collector who wants to like what she likes and lose herself in the aesthetic and spiritual pleasure her books bring and the dealer who sees the objects more coolly and cerebrally as cultural capital.

There are other tensions, too. Millard's audacious, freewheeling ethos and unabashed salesmanship clash with Estelle's straitlaced Catholicism and rigid sense of propriety.[30] Estelle wants respect that Millard doesn't always give. "Intimacy never fully blossomed between the two women," Rosenthal observes, "except in a polite, perfunctory way, forestalled by Mrs. Doheny's inability to commit herself to Alice Millard's ingratiating enthusiasms."[31] They meet socially only once, for a formal luncheon served on the mirror-topped table in the glass-domed Pompeian Room at Chester Place. As Lucille noted, they differ profoundly in "temperament, philosophy, personality. Estelle is a devout Roman Catholic, Millard equally devoted to Christian Science. In almost every other respect as well they are at opposite poles." And eventually, the gaping divide of class, education, temperament, and religion becomes impossible to bridge.

One day, Millard commits the ultimate faux pas, arriving at Estelle's front door with suitcases full of books in her car but with no invitation or warning. Estelle banishes her and her wares from Chester Place. "Mrs. Millard's selling technique was intense and aggressive, and Mrs. Doheny grew impatient with it," Lucille said. "Eventually it was impossible to mention Mrs. Millard's name to her. I was sad for both of them."

But the purchases Estelle made from Rosenbach and Millard have given her entrée to a wide circle of contacts on both coasts: collectors, librarians, dealers, historians, artists, graphic designers, and fine printers. Estelle and Lucille begin to consult Robert Schad, the Huntington Library's rare-books curator, and in him they find an open, non-condescending source of knowledge and enthusiasm. Estelle recognizes something familiar, beyond his expertise, and pulls him quickly into her circle of trust. Schad, like Estelle, isn't an academic, or even formally educated past high school. He began as a low-paid clerk in the New York Public Library and lucked into a job at Henry Huntington's library in New York. Exposure, experience, a receptive personality, and a sharp mind carried him the rest of the way. Estelle and Lucille feel free to ask Robert Schad questions they can't ask anyone else: Which dealers are really trustworthy? What sorts of prices make sense? How do we care for a sixteenth-century book?[32]

Estelle's collecting slows after the rift with Millard, but that might have happened even if the dealer hadn't lost favor. Edward's health rapidly declines after 1933, and over the next two years he becomes increasingly disoriented and bedridden. Estelle juggles the responsibilities that come with overseeing his care and his businesses, and when she can, she turns her attention to cataloging her books, enlisting Schad to organize what will be her splashiest coming-out party as a collector—a one-month exhibition at Ned's library at USC, featuring sixty of her finest works. True to her deepest collecting impulses, she titles the 1935 show *The Book as a Work of Art*, with an introductory essay celebrating the beauty of the objects on display.[33] Highlights, and there are many, include a fifteenth-century illuminated manuscript of Petrarch's sonnets, a 1789 copy of Blake's hallucinatory *Songs of Innocence*, and her William Morris *Aeneid*. Yet she still is ignored as a significant figure in the rare-book arena and scarcely listed among other great collectors with their own private libraries. The elite clubs and bibliophilic societies (New York's Grolier Club, Chicago's Caxton Club, and the Zamorano Club of Los Angeles among them) are open only to men.

Just six months after the exhibit, on September 8, 1935, Estelle urgently summons Edward's doctors. After examining him, they tell her that there is no more that they can do. Estelle calls Ned's widow, Lucy, and the five grandchildren to Edward's bedside, and they are with him when he dies at eight that evening. He is seventy-nine years old.

The funeral takes place two days later as wafts of incense blend with the fragrance of thousands of flowers in the ornate sanctuary of St. Vincent's Church. Eight men carry Edward's bronze casket the short distance from the Doheny mansion to the magnificent Roman Catholic church built with his millions. Accompanied by chanting priests and leaning heavily on the arms of her two oldest grandsons, Estelle walks behind the bier, which is covered in white carnations and lilies of the valley. More than 1,200 guests crowd the church, and another 2,000 stand outside to honor the man who, as the *New York Times* summarizes, had "spent his youth in hardship, his middle years in a phenomenal rise to wealth, power and fame, and much of his old age in grief and humiliation."[34] The bribery scandal that had blazed in headlines for a decade receives scant mention, and Doheny is allowed to depart the mortal world with dignity.[35]

There is one final ritual for Estelle to attend to, an act rooted equally in pragmatism, loyalty, and fear. Returning to Chester Place, she gathers the records of the oil empire her husband had pulled out of the Mexican jungles. With the help of her sister, Daysie May Anderson, she searches Edward's locked file drawers and cabinets, collecting hundreds of personal letters and business documents. Then the women go to the basement, where they open the double doors of the walk-in steel vault that contains his remaining papers, and they add those to the pile. Moments later, they light a roaring fire in the mansion's huge incinerator and throw in every written remnant of Edward Doheny's life, consigning to the flames what has to be an engrossing story. Any last scrap of evidence that could further incriminate the Dohenys and jeopardize Estelle's fortune is reduced to ash before the sisters return to grieving. All hope of further exoneration for her husband and Ned, if that existed, has disappeared as well.

With Edward gone, Estelle takes an even more active part in the management of his business interests, spending her mornings with attorneys and accountants. Legal and financial documents pile up

on her desk, replacing the handsome auction catalogs sent from
Sotheby's, Christie's, Manson &
Woods, or the Anderson Galleries.
Now she builds collections that are
smaller, more personal: antique
glass paperweights, Currier & Ives
prints, porcelain figurines.

But as she considers her books
from a greater remove, a sense of
mission takes hold. During her
many conversations with Robert
Schad, he helps her to define a
goal that is broader than simply

*Estelle Doheny, photographed in the
1940s during the prime years of her book
collecting career.*

seeking beauty or honoring her husband and stepson: saving cultural treasure for posterity. Doing that, he says, carries with it the
obligation to seek only the best. "This logically carries the collector," Schad tells her, "from the superior to the supreme examples."
Adhering to such a standard would set her collection above the
others and steer her into a distinctive process of collecting only the
pieces that were most worthy of preservation. All these years later,
she is hearing Henry Huntington's own ethos from the man who
helped him shape the collection that caught her attention in 1911.
Her vision crystallizes. She wants to preserve the best of the past,
volumes that represent the first appearances in print of great contributions to history and literature.[36]

Once more she thinks of the Gutenberg. Now she feels its importance almost viscerally. This was not only the book that seeded
her own interest, but also the first Bible of her church printed with

the tools that would spread its message faster and more personally than ever before. The Living Word, thanks to Johann Gutenberg, had surged into tens of millions of lives.

In November 1938, Estelle gets her first taste of owning the printer's work, buying eight individual leaves of a Gutenberg Bible from New York book dealer Gabriel Wells. The idea of breaking up the book offends her sensibilities, but parts of the volume are in very poor condition, and it has already been torn apart. Wells sells her Paul's Epistle to the Romans, the book whose text promises spiritual salvation through the gospel of Jesus Christ, for $2,500. With the 10 percent dealer's commission, the final bill of sale totals $2,750.[37] When the leaves arrive at Chester Place, Estelle commissions a special title page by the noted English calligrapher Graily Hewitt and a red morocco binding by the London firm of Rivière & Son to house them.

She renews her contact with A. S. W. Rosenbach in Philadelphia and spends the next decade hunting and buying a world-class array of incunabula and illuminated manuscripts, once more benefiting from the kind of prewar turmoil that sweeps rare books into the marketplace ahead of advancing armies. Her purchases are steady and stellar, filling her shelves with examples of early printing, like the work of Johann Fust and Peter Schöffer, who took over Gutenberg's workshop and quickly refined his art in their own Bibles, Psalters, and intricately illuminated volumes like their 1470 printing of the letters of Saint Jerome. It's possible for even an interested amateur to see the printer's art evolve as the earliest adopters test new possibilities in the Bibles she gathers from the presses of Strassburg and Delft. Estelle can lose herself in earlier works as well, fine manuscripts like a 1410 French Bible with vibrant illuminations imagining the kingdom of heaven before creation, and hell as an animal's open maw; or an extraordinary palm-size book of hours, whose placid scenes of contemplation are framed with gilded branches laden with apple blossoms or ripe pears.

As dealers offer such treasures and broker the transactions that will win them for her, there is scarcely a letter or a phone call that Lucille does not coordinate. The most significant figures in the book trade communicate frequently with "Mrs. Doheny's librarian," and both she and Estelle, drunk on beauty, are caught up in competing for the most noteworthy rare books on the market, which now takes the place of marriage and children for both of them.

When the first major auction of the postwar era arrives in early 1947, the women are captivated by the elegant blue catalog filled with color plates of C. W. Dyson Perrins's books. It comes accompanied by a note from British bookseller Ernest U. Maggs, who directs Estelle's attention to Item 564—the Gutenberg—and notes that Number 45 is "probably the finest copy known, in its contemporary binding."

Estelle becomes fixated on the idea of buying it, but she worries: Can she manage it? She can afford it, she tells herself; why shouldn't she have it? She mulls it over for several days with Lucille. The dream suddenly hovering within reach stirs up a sadness she'd thought was gone, as well as hope, and the corresponding fear of loss. Finally she's clear. Yes, of course she wants it. For Edward and posterity. For God. And, undeniably, for *herself*.

CHAPTER SIX

The Lost Gutenberg

T HE ONLY PERSON Estelle trusts to help her win the Dyson Gutenberg is her old friend Abraham Rosenbach. Anyone who could purchase a copy via wireless radio from the deck of the luxury liner RMS *Olympic*,[1] and land three more copies over the years, is surely her best guide. At age seventy-one, Rosenbach is still a titan of the book world and an unabashed champion of Gutenberg's singular production. "To obtain the very first issue of the Gutenberg Bible," he proclaims, "that is an achievement." He pours it on thick: "There is nothing nobler, nothing finer, nothing more beautiful than the Gutenberg Bible."[2]

On January 30, 1947, Lucille writes the dealer at his office at 15 East Fifty-First Street in New York to officially launch him on the chase:

Dear Dr. Rosenbach:

Mrs. Doheny wishes to know if you would be willing to represent her in bidding for the Gutenberg Bible in the Dyson Perrins Sale in London on March 11. If you can accept her bid, will you please advise her on what procedure she should follow to make sure of obtaining the book. She would like to know how much you think the Bible will sell for and how much her bid should be. Do you think there will be strenuous competition for the Bible?

Needless to say, Mrs. Doheny wants this matter kept absolutely confidential. She will appreciate hearing from you at your earliest convenience.[3]

The Doctor immediately accepts, promises to be discreet, and eases into what will be his most strategic task: preparing his client for what might prove to be a hair-raising price. He would not be surprised, he tells her, if the bids went far higher than the estimate of £15,000 she received from Ernest Maggs. He warns her that the competition among her American peers in addition to the "European regulars" could force bids to new highs. But there's no question that it would be worth it, he promises—he saw this very volume some years earlier, and it is "magnificent."

"The binding is probably the finest on any copy of the Gutenberg Bible being in a superb contemporary Mainz binding," he writes. There are many "ancient Bibles" in the Dyson Perrins sale, Rosenbach adds, but the "Gutenberg Bible is the most thrilling of all."[4]

Though Estelle trusts him completely, the talk of cost gives her pause. She's a businesswoman, not a speculator, and she can't leave herself open to the whims of a wild market. She thinks hard, prays, and sets her limit: $75,000—firm.

As the sale nears, Rosenbach grows increasingly anxious that $75,000 isn't enough. But decades of experience with wealthy and temperamental clients has taught him which strings to pull and how best to pull them. He enlists Lucille to help persuade Mrs. Doheny that she would never regret going higher to get this book: "Volume I of the Gutenberg Bible in the Dyson Perrins Library to be sold on March 11, Lot 564," he writes, "is not only in the finest possible condition but perfect in every respect and is, what is most desirable of all, the FIRST ISSUE OF THE FIRST EDITION OF THE GREATEST BOOK EVER PRINTED. I saw this grand volume and it is everything that could be desired."

In addition to having an exceptional binding, Number 45 is remarkably well preserved. There are no missing pages, which is unusual for a book of its age. Except for a small piece torn from the margin of leaf 231 and a flaw in the original paper of page 147, stains at the lower edges of only a few leaves and a slight foxing (rust-colored stains caused by chemical reactions) of the first three pages, nothing mars its condition. Large initial illuminations, margin ornamentation of foliage and figures, and page headings of Roman capitals alternating in red and blue ink have been carefully done. Red slashes on the first letters of sentences are consistent on every one of the 324 leaves. "The book was a beauty to behold," the Doctor summarizes.

He's not the only one, of course, with these facts in hand, and speculation is rampant that the price for the Bible is increasing by the hour. Rosenbach presses the need to jump on what he stresses might be a never-to-be-repeated opportunity to obtain a copy that is "superior to any other likely to be available for purchase."[5]

As the auction nears, he broaches the possibility of a price much higher than Estelle's bid. His "confidential agent in London," he says in a telegram dispatched on February 27, estimates the final selling price at between £25,000 and £30,000. There's no comfort in his reassurance that "the chances of it bringing over £35,000 are, in my opinion, slim."[6] That £35,000 figure—$140,000—is almost twice the amount she is prepared to pay.

On March 3, eight days before the auction, Estelle writes Rosenbach a thirty-three-line, single-spaced letter saying she wants to withdraw. "The Gutenberg Bible has always been to me the one Book of all books and even to think of securing a whole volume was thrilling," Estelle admits. "But there are many practical considerations which I cannot ignore."

One of her deep concerns is privacy. She still has raw memories of the Teapot Dome agonies, when the papers around the world dissected the Dohenys' every word and gesture, skewered them in editorial cartoons, and dogged them with headlines like "Sinister Shadows Behind the Oil Scandal," "Putting a Hundred Million Dollars in Jail," and "Doheny Weeps on Stand Telling of Loan to Fall." They were besieged by reporters and blinded by swarms of photographers' flashes, and now, she tells Rosenbach, "I dread the publicity. Once the Bible is in my possession, it would become known and I am afraid the Los Angeles papers would be as sensational as possible in writing it up."

And price is no small matter. "When I first learned of the sale I thought the Bible might reasonably be expected to bring about twelve or fifteen thousand pounds, but your estimate of twenty-five to thirty thousand pounds changes the situation completely," she writes.

She thanks Rosenbach for all he has done to build her collection, and she asks him to send an invoice for the time he's spent laying the groundwork for her bid. "I was anxious to make a wise decision and I am confident that I am doing the right thing in deciding not to bid on the Bible," she concludes.[7]

The message only emboldens Rosenbach further. He fancies himself a literary matchmaker, and he believes that some books are fated to meet particular owners. In the second century, Latin grammarian Terentianus Maurus had expressed the same sentiment, famously writing *Habent sua fata libelli* ("books have their destiny").[8] This copy of the Gutenberg Bible belongs in the Estelle Doheny Collection. Rosenbach is sure of it.

Unlike many of his male contemporaries in the book trade, Rosenbach has a fondness for what he calls the "Mighty Women Book Hunters." He had enjoyed working with New York philanthropist Mrs. Edward S. Harkness (who "made a sensation on two continents" when she presented to Yale University the copy of the Melk monastery's Gutenberg Bible he had purchased for her), and he took pleasure in helping shape the collection of arguably his favorite female client, poet and collector Amy Lowell of Brookline, Massachusetts. He takes pride in mentoring female bibliophiles like Estelle Doheny,[9] seeing himself as their champion and protector in the behind-the-scenes machinations of the rare-book trade, which he believes far exceed those in Wall Street's toughest boardrooms. His efforts can seem patronizing, and they're always self-serving—he's got commissions to make, after all—but none of that negates his strong desire to see a Mighty Woman Book Hunter claim her rightful prize.

Rosenbach wires Estelle saying that he has been informed that the prospective bidders from Sweden, Switzerland, and France have not arrived in London. Without the "Continental buyers" in attendance, the Bible could very well sell for less than his previous estimate of $100,000 to $120,000. This news, he feels confident, will change the entire picture for her.[10] He reminds Estelle that he has personally examined the Bible exhaustively, and the auction is a once-in-a-lifetime opportunity. "The feel of the paper always fascinates me, so firm it is, so beautiful in appearance," he writes. "It seems alive, yet there is something definitely final about it. It is as though the paper of the Gutenberg Bible had proudly indicated from its inception that nothing finer, nothing more perfect could be made."[11]

He evokes the power of the object for her with history and poetry: "[Al]though the Gutenberg Bible gives the effect of a fastidiously written manuscript, it is not only the earliest but actually the most beautiful work of printing the world has ever known. It was the first work to come from any press using moveable types . . . the ink now nearly five centuries old, is today as black and glossy as the hair of a Japanese beauty."[12]

Estelle, as intended, is moved to reconsider. Perhaps the Doctor is right about the price. He is the supreme authority on rare books, catalyst and facilitator to the creation of many celebrated libraries. (By the time of Henry Huntington's death in 1927, Rosenbach had brokered more than $4 million in book purchases for that collection alone.) He has a realistic and hard-earned knowledge of the market and its fluctuations, and his estimate for the Dyson Perrins sale couldn't be too far off the mark. Lucille helps to calculate the anticipated exchange rate as Estelle obsesses over the numbers. After a restless night, Estelle telephones Rosenbach at ten a.m. on Friday, March 7, finding him at his office in New York. They talk less than ten minutes, with Lucille taking shorthand notes as she listens on an extension:

> [Mrs. D] told him she was interested in placing a bid on the "parcel" and she had an idea she could get it for less than his estimate. She said, "If I could get it between fifty and seventy-five I would be interested in it." He said he thought there was a chance of its going for seventy-five.
>
> Mrs. D said, "Suppose I send you seventy-five as your limit, taking a chance of getting it for sixty or seventy?" Dr. R. said, "Could you make it seventy-six or seventy-seven?"
>
> Mrs. D said, "I will give you a leeway of one or two thousand up to seventy-seven, with seventy-seven my top limit, but I hope you get it for a great deal less. Be sure you buy on the down side rather than the up." Dr. R. accepted the bid with the definite understanding that seventy-seven was the limit and he said, "I think you have a good chance."[13]

Rosenbach assures Estelle that her name will be kept absolutely secret, and that if she should get the Bible, it can be kept in his New York vault for as long as she wishes.

Lucille's notes also reveal a twist to Estelle's need for secrecy, an odd bit of subterfuge. In early February, as she was engaging Rosenbach, she wrote to dealer Ernest Maggs saying that she had decided not to bid.

Dear Mr. Maggs:

I want to thank you for your letter of January 22nd enclosing a copy of the catalogue of the Dyson Perrins sale. There are many wonderful books in it but, of course, the Gutenberg Bible is the most thrilling of all. Even one volume would be a fabulous possession for any library.

I have read your letter very carefully, and in view of the high prices which rare books are now bringing (the Bay Psalm Book brought $151,000 at auction in New York last week) I would not be surprised if the Bible brought even more than your top estimate of £15,000. I am sorry that I am not in a position to even consider placing a bid, but I'm afraid that the competition among American collectors will result in a record-breaking price.

With cordial greetings to you and Mrs. Maggs, and wishing you a happy, healthy and prosperous New Year, I am,

Sincerely,

Mrs. E. L. Doheny

The motivations for this "white lie" are not entirely clear, but it's possible that Estelle fears that since Maggs came to her, he would not maintain her anonymity during the auction, and not only would she face press attention, but her name and fortune might drive up the price. Better to have Rosenbach, whom she knows better, and trusts, bidding secretly on her behalf. If she wins the book, no one will be the wiser.

The day before the auction, Estelle sends a special-delivery letter to Rosenbach confirming the details of their phone call and committing to a price of up to $77,000, no more than £20,000. "Needless to say, I will expect a telegram from you just as soon as you know the results of the sale," she writes. "Whether I am successful or not, the fact that I actually have a bid on this particular item is the greatest thrill of my career as a book-collector."

Rosenbach travels by train to his Philadelphia office, where he will participate in the bidding via telephone. He wires Estelle one last time, saying that he has spoken with his London agent and believes that she has "a very good chance" of winning the book. "Doing all I can," he writes, "and hope you secure it."[14]

◆ ◆ ◆

ESTELLE WAITS.

Early on the morning of the auction, Lucille watches out the window as she leaves the house through the back door and walks across the manicured grounds, disappearing into the tropical oasis of the Palm House, home to her massive orchid collection. Edward had picked up many specimens during his railcar travels to Mexico and had taken great pleasure in planting them, some of the varieties so rare that they have yet to be named by botanists. This is where Estelle goes to quiet her mind or let it wander. Today the conservatory is a refuge, as it had often been in the past, when she and Edward rested together amid the flowers beneath the fig trees or in a hammock in the shade.

Her other refuge has been the church. Estelle was born a Methodist in a German family, but after she married Edward, frequently finding herself alone as he drilled in Mexico, she welcomed the overtures of Catholic clergy and began studying with her parish

Edward Doheny made a new-money splash in Los Angeles with the fifty-foot-tall glass and steel Palm House and filled it with exotic plants, including ten thousand orchids and rare palms imported from the jungles of Mexico. The swimming pool was large enough to accommodate a gondola and a canoe.

priest, Joseph Glass. Glass became a friend and adviser, grounding her during the pivotal decade and a half when oil riches were radically transforming her life, and it was he, by then a bishop, who performed the ceremony at the "high noon hour" of her life in 1918, when she formally converted at St. Patrick's Cathedral in New York.

The feminine center of Catholicism spoke to her. She was born Carrie Estelle Betzold, and since her marriage to Edward, she has been Estelle, which means "star." She believes deeply that the Virgin Mary is the North Star of the Church and the lambent flame of her own heart. When Catholic leaders offered her the opportunity to give concrete expression to her faith by supporting the building of a new church, she persuaded Edward to foot the entire cost of St. Vincent's, which rose just a block from their Chester Place compound. Estelle insisted that it honor the Virgin with an "ornate golden altar niche with swirling columns, trumpeting angels and ornamental hearts." Rimmed with a halo made of neon, Mary is depicted standing alone in a blue overcloak with rays of light streaming from her upturned palms.[15] The $2 million church, with its oversize tiled rotunda, rose in the darkest days of Teapot Dome, a counterpoint to the scandal narrative or, as one historian describes it, a "religious shield" for a "wealthy communicant in his hour of need."[16] But it was unquestionably an expression of Estelle's devotion as well.

A gift on the order of St. Vincent's earned the Dohenys all the perquisites with which the church rewards faith and significant patronage. The private chapels in their homes, and the regular private Masses said there, with the consecrated host, were one expression of that. Titles were another. In 1925, soon after St. Vincent's opened its doors, they were made Knight and Lady of the Equestrian Order of the Holy Sepulchre—Sir Edward and Lady Estelle. They may have stood outside the bounds of respectability in much of the Los Angeles establishment, but within the church they were nobility. Church officials such as Bishop Francis Clement Kelley and John Joseph Cantwell were there to offer counsel and friendship over private dinners during the scandal, and they provided anchoring solace after Ned's death. In thanks for loyalty they found in few other corners, the Dohenys aimed large gifts at the orders of St. Vincent and their nuns, missionaries, and educators.

After Edward died, Estelle grew close to William J. Ward, the soft-spoken head priest of St. Vincent's, who had served as her private chaplain at Chester Place. He became her confidant and helped her plan and administer her many philanthropic gifts. It was in her talks with him that the most important threads of her life came together and moved her toward the purchase she is attempting to make in London today.

In 1939, Ward had suggested that the ultimate tribute to her husband, her church, and her great book collection would be to build a library in Edward's name that gave access to her books to scholars at the new St. John's Seminary in Camarillo, sixty miles northwest of Los Angeles. It would be her legacy, a gift to Western civilization that preserved its treasures for future generations, just

Edward Laurence Doheny Memorial Library at St. John's Seminary in Camarillo, California, 1940. Estelle Doheny shared both fortune and scandal with her husband, and turned to book collecting in part to help restore respect and honor to the family.

as Robert Schad had suggested. And at a seminary, her many Bibles, books of hours, psalters, and other beautiful works of faith and art would feed the research—and the souls—of those who would most appreciate their importance to Christian life.

Again she hired architect Wallace Neff, who designed the library in his distinctive Spanish Colonial style, creating a two-story building, 110 feet long, with an ornate entrance flanked by roof-high loggias of graceful columns. Its Treasure Room, where Estelle's books would rest, had walls lined with bookcases set behind doors of bronze grillwork. The Western Room contained the Dohenys' collections of Californiana, along with their paintings by Frederic Remington and murals of Native Americans and life in the West by Detlef Sammann and Charles Russell. The centerpiece was a tribute to Estelle that Edward had commissioned in the early days of their marriage, a Steinway grand piano finished in gold lacquer and gold leaf that was decorated with images of Muses and the mythical Greek musician Orpheus, who passed through the gates of hell to be with the woman he loved. A portrait of Estelle as a young woman standing in front of 8 Chester Place had been painted on the underside of the piano's lid.

The Edward Laurence Doheny Memorial Library contained the best of who Estelle was and had been, the best of what she wanted to leave behind. She considered its opening day, October 14, 1940, to be the single most important day of her life.

She hadn't promised the library a Gutenberg Bible, but she had long considered it to be the culmination of her life as a collector, not just for its resounding historical significance but also as the ultimate answer to the men who hadn't seen fit to allow her into

On October 14, 1940, church officials gathered for the dedication of the Edward Laurence Doheny Memorial Library at St. John's Seminary in Camarillo. Estelle Doheny called the library her "little jewel," and loved it more deeply, she said, than any of her other benefactions.

their book clubs and the dealers who had taken her money but talked down to her in dismissive tones, as though she didn't know her own mind.

In 1939, Pope Pius XII had given her the honorary title of papal countess, in recognition of her philanthropy and the gift of the library.[17] Though Estelle is now in the throes of old age and nearly blind, she might have the chance to make her gift complete. The countess might finally have the *book of books*.

◆ ◆ ◆

ACROSS A CONTINENT and an ocean away, an unusually big crowd gathers at Sotheby's large galleries at 35 New Bond Street for the

The Gutenberg Bible at auction in London on March 11, 1947. Estelle Doheny placed a bid in the auction but lost to dealer Ernest Maggs, who paid a record-breaking price for an undisclosed British book collector. At the time, the volume was the last known Gutenberg Bible still in private ownership.

eleven a.m. auction. The most serious contenders sit at a cloth-covered, horseshoe-shaped table stretching in front of the auction-eer, who stands on a podium behind a curved wooden lectern. Behind the raised platform, a series of charcoal male nudes waits for bidders later in the day, creating a curious backdrop as the Gutenberg Bible comes up for display.

An attendant in a long-sleeved cotton coat opens the tall, heavy book with ungloved hands and holds it against his chest, walking slowly in front of the bidders. Necks strain as men in the back jostle to get a better look. Rosenbach's representative is there. So is Ernest Maggs. To his left is one of the two women present in the large crowd, and to his right is London bookseller Charles Dudley Massey, managing director of Pickering and Chatto and the father of Stephen Massey, who will later find fame on the television series *Antiques Roadshow.*

Bidding, led by a balding, bespectacled auctioneer in a dark suit, starts at £5,000 and quickly climbs, as Maggs competes with two main rivals, Rosenbach's London agent and a man identified by the *New York Times* as Mr. W. H. Robinson. The price flashes past Maggs's original estimate of £15,000 and almost immediately hits £20,000. The bidding continues, but having reached Estelle's ceiling, Rosenbach's representative is forced to bow out.

A minute later, the auctioneer smacks down his palm gavel, and the attendant gently closes the book. A round of subdued applause marks the auction's end, and in an instant the Bible is in the hands of a barrel-chested assistant, who pivots and quickly disappears. Ernest Maggs, whose assistance Estelle turned away, has acquired the Dyson Perrins Gutenberg Bible on behalf of an unnamed client for a new record price[18]—£22,000, a US value, at that time, of $89,000.[19]

Maggs is invited to bring the Bible to the studios of the BBC,[20] where it is seen on television for the first time, the fifteenth-century star beaming into the twentieth. The legendary book dealer, aglow, insists that his photograph be taken as he turns the pages of the holy book. The resulting black-and-white image of the bearded book agent and the quarry he's just captured goes into his files. It will soon serve its purpose.

Much as Estelle had mistrusted Maggs's discretion, he is tight-lipped when questioned by reporters about the identity of the buyer. "I have bought the Bible for a private collector but I am unable to divulge his name," Maggs tells them. "It will remain in England, I think," he adds. That is all he will say.[21]

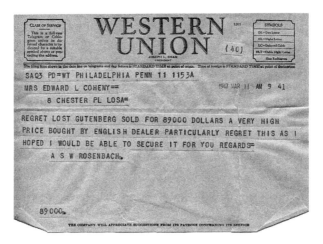

Telegram from American Dealer A. S. W. Rosenbach to Estelle
Doheny informing her that the Gutenberg Bible she coveted had gone
to another book dealer (Maggs), March 1947.

News of the "literary enthusiasts" who "battled it out to reach
this record price" will be plastered on front pages throughout Europe and America the next day, and even regional papers as distant
as the *Decatur Herald* and the *Galveston Daily News* will prominently
feature the sale, with much commentary about the way Number
45 is now valued at forty-four times the £600 pounds Dyson Perrins had paid.

Estelle gets word from Rosenbach nearly six hours after the auction's conclusion but before the news hits the Los Angeles press.
His telegram reaches her at 9:41 a.m. Pacific time:

REGRET LOST GUTENBERG SOLD FOR 89,000 DOLLARS A
VERY HIGH PRICE BOUGHT BY ENGLISH DEALER

PARTICULARLY REGRET THIS AS I HOPED I WOULD BE ABLE
TO SECURE IT FOR YOU REGARDS

ASW ROSENBACH[22]

A "gloomy fog" hangs over Chester Place when Estelle hears
the news.[23] She kicks herself for acting so stupidly and placing the
bid limit too low. A widow with an eight-figure fortune, she had
lost the book over a matter of $14,000.

She refuses to have Lucille read her any of the news accounts
of the sale, but none of them would have answered her most press-
ing question—the identity of the bidder. "We didn't know who
bought it and had no idea who had it or where it went," Lucille
said.[24] Estelle presses Rosenbach to learn whom she'd lost the book
to. Was he a European? Was he a rich American? Was he a great
collector with a worthy library? Despite his extensive contacts,
Rosenbach is unable to find out. All he can do is assure her that he
will never reveal her loss.

"I cannot tell you how much I appreciate your confiding in me
and entrusting me with this bid," he writes. "I have kept it an absolute secret and no one will ever know as far as I am concerned
that you were interested."

He also expresses his deep disappointment over the failure of
their bid. "When the continental buyers did not show up in full
force I thought we would be able to buy it for you but it was probably bought for a private collector in England and it will undoubtedly remain there. Although there are eight copies in public libraries
in England, this is the only one in private hands."[25]

For as close as they'd come, Number 45 was lost.

◆ ◆ ◆

ON MARCH 26, fifteen days after the auction, a letter arrives from London—from Ernest Maggs. Lucille jumps up from her chair to find Estelle. In the note, Maggs politely confirms shipment of a previous order by Mrs. Doheny for a "splendid three-volume set" of fore-edge books. But it is the added handwritten note that catches Lucille's attention. It reads: "P.S. I purchased the Gutenberg Bible Vol. I for £22,000."[26]

Estelle has Lucille read and then reread the words. Does Maggs himself have the Bible? Was purchasing it for an unnamed client just a ruse, perhaps in the hope of holding on to it until he could obtain a higher price? And how much more would he want for it, if that's what he was hinting at? He must be hoping for an offer. Otherwise, why mention it at all?

London book dealer Ernest Maggs gazes at the pages of the Gutenberg Bible following the 1947 auction. The vellum thumb markers used to designate sections of the Bible are visible along the book's fore-edge.

Immediately Estelle feels energized and emboldened. If the Dyson Perrins Gutenberg Bible is now for sale it would be a fantastic turn of events.

"She had me get on the telephone right away," Lucille recalled. "This time there was no quibbling about price. She was absolutely determined to get it."[27]

Estelle now turns her full attention to Maggs. On April 2, she writes to him with a discreet but direct inquiry. She congratulates him on his purchase and chats in a friendly way about having heard about the sale on the radio. Taking care not to sound too eager, she asks whether he had bought the Bible for himself or for a client, and if for himself, what price he might sell it for. She promises to keep anything he tells her in strictest confidence.[28]

Maggs's reply reveals no real clues. All he says is that he had bid on the book for a private party in England, and he regrets he does not have it "in stock" to sell to her. He closes the note by adding that the remainder of the Dyson Perrins library will be sold in June, and there will be other choice volumes available, including highly desired Bibles from the sixteenth and seventeenth centuries.

On May 6, Maggs sends another short note, enclosing two black-and-white photographs taken at the March 11 sale. One shows him with his white goatee and wire-rimmed glasses pretending to turn the pages of the Gutenberg Bible. The other is a single image of the book housed in the auction house glass case. His note to Lucille says that he thought Mrs. Doheny would like to have the pictures. Lucille replies, then pencils a notation on the lower left corner of the back of one of the photographs: Thanked 5/12/47 LM.

The two photographs only darken Estelle's mood. It doesn't

make sense for Maggs to have sent the photos if the unidentified buyer is unwilling to sell. Oddly, he still makes no reference to a possible sale, nor even any suggestion that an offer would be considered. That only adds to her sense of impatience that has been building since the auction. The Gutenberg Bible is the one book that would complete her library, and there have been only five sold since 1930, the year she began to collect books in earnest. She will be seventy-two in a few months, and it is possible that another will not come on the market during her lifetime. With the clock ticking faster than ever, she may have let her last opportunity slip past. Now Maggs, oblique, infuriating Maggs, is toying with her.

◆ ◆ ◆

THE MYSTERIOUS BUYER is in fact fifty-year-old Sir Philip Beaumont Frere, a well-known London solicitor, a tall man with piercing blue eyes and a face marked by a scar from his service in World War I. Distinguished and well-educated, Frere runs in London's tony intellectual circles, but his personal wealth can't compare with that of the Bible's previous owners. He manages Frere, Cholmeley and Nicholson, a family firm founded in 1750[29] that has a long history of representing the legal interests of the great landed estates. Sir Philip has found his niche acting as solicitor to major literary figures of the era, including the Sitwells (Osbert, Edith, and Sacheverell) and Bryher (the pen name of novelist Annie Winifred Ellerman).

Osbert Sitwell, who has become one of Frere's close friends, champions poetry and controversial journalism and takes pride in his aristocratic pedigree and connections to royalty, which span six hundred years.[30] Frere wound up in the thick of literary gossip when Sitwell asked him to address the legal issues involved in Sitwell's breakup with his longtime lover, David Horner. (Horner apparently deserted Sitwell when the latter developed Parkinson's disease.) Homosexuality was a crime in England until 1967, though Sitwell made little effort to hide his relationship. According to Sitwell's biographer, Frere had to hand the case to another partner at the law firm because he "found his friendship with both parties made it too embarrassing for him to act."[31]

For Bryher, Frere is managing personal finances related to an estate valued at approximately £10 million, and in his letters to the writer, Frere describes a wide range of interests in the arts.[32] All this might seem to cast Frere, who had retired from active practice in 1954,[33] as a person who might buy a Gutenberg Bible to enhance his status in the high-profile literary circles he travels. But curiously, he seems never to have told anyone that he wanted the masterpiece, and it's likely that no one but his dealer knew he purchased it. Though he is in no way shy about announcing his accomplishments, he never mentions the purchase in the hundreds of personal letters he writes during this time. It's possible that he buys the book for one of his wealthy clients, but there is nothing in the record to show it. Or he may have purchased it as an investment for the law firm, which in 1947 underwent expansion and reorganization.[34] But there is no indication that it was ever in the possession of the firm or held there for safekeeping.

It is also possible that Frere is keeping the Gutenberg Bible at his Queen Street home in Mayfair, but there is no record of that either. The most likely whereabouts of the book is inside the London vault at Maggs Bros., as Frere perhaps waits for its value to appreciate at an exponential rate. Another theory is that Frere bought the book to tie up funds to keep them out of a creditor's reach.

But Frere isn't telling, nor is Maggs. Number 45 disappears from sight.

CHAPTER SEVEN

The Countess and Her Gutenberg

T︎RY AS SHE MIGHT, Estelle Doheny cannot ignore the Gutenberg Bible after she loses Number 45. In November 1947, the New York Public Library brings out its copy, purchased by James Lenox one hundred years earlier, the first to arrive in America. Lenox had obtained it in a sale hailed as an "unprecedented bibliographical event," paying the "mad price" of $2,600,[1] and the book since then has often been locked away. But the public is mad for the Bible, and a great commotion surrounds its display.

The Pierpont Morgan Library's holiday exhibition, titled *The Bible*, opens a month later, featuring a sampling of the Morgan's outstanding collection of ancient and modern scriptures—and there's another Gutenberg.[2] This one is later escorted by an armed guard with a drawn revolver to the city's premier exhibition hall, Grand Central Palace, where galas, marching bands, displays of aviation and atomic technology, fashion shows, and other works of historical import have converged for the Golden Jubilee Exposition of 1948, celebrating the fiftieth anniversary of the consolidation of New York's five boroughs. Hordes of people line up to see the Bible in its bulletproof glass case, insured by the city for half a million dollars.

The book pops up again, at least symbolically, in January 1949, when President Harry S. Truman is sworn in for a second term on a cold and cloudy day. A photograph of the ceremony that appears in the *Los Angeles Times* shows Truman kissing a Gutenberg Bible (actually a replica created so an original wouldn't suffer clumsy handling). With his left palm raised, Truman had solemnly taken the oath of office on the Gutenberg look-alike, his right hand resting on the text of Exodus 20, the Ten Commandments.[3]

Estelle has a chance to buy a Gutenberg leaf containing that very passage in May 1950. The price for the single page, from a Bible that had been torn apart, is a steep $3,000, but she asks Rosenbach to examine it and to get it for her if it's in fine condition. A description of the leaf indicates that the Commandments are printed on paper bearing the famous watermark of the bull's head and cross.

Rosenbach cables back to say that the leaf has already been sold by the Chiswick Bookshop in New York City, and with that disappointment, Estelle has had enough of seeking the Bible, or even fine pieces of it. Paying a price like $3,000 a leaf for a book with some 650 of them would be an indulgence that she couldn't justify. She could easily pay an astronomical price, but as she senses the end of her life nearing, she has other priorities.

First among them is a foundation she's decided to create to support the advancement of education, medicine, religion, and the health and welfare of children and the needy, the causes that mean most to her. She plans to endow the foundation with the $35 million (the equivalent of more than $350 million in today's dollars) she recently realized from selling her interest in seventy-two producing oil wells on nearly three thousand acres of California land, a gift that will ensure that her philanthropy will continue long after she's gone. It will also, in a sense, let her make herself whole. Estelle had stopped using her given first name when she married because she shared it with Edward's first wife. But this endeavor will reflect her legacy, her best, and she wants to bring every part of her identity to it. She calls it the Carrie Estelle Doheny Foundation, letting the reclaimed Carrie blaze like a neon halo.

Separately, with a grant of $227,000, she creates the Estelle Doheny Eye Foundation and works closely with a group of doctors to establish a pioneering research center on eye disease. Her sight has steadily deteriorated, with glaucoma dimming one eye after a hemorrhage blinded the other, but her foundation's vision will help save that of many others.

She continues to attend to business and put her affairs in order in 1950. Nearly blind, and increasingly housebound, she writes to one of her favorite priests at St. Vincent's Church:

Dear Father Flavin:

I have been thinking of the Masses to be offered for me after my death. We will never know how many have been offered for my

*husband that have not come to our notice, and many have been
offered here which have not been recorded.*

*. . . [I]t will take a very long time to settle my estate. I am
enclosing a check for $2500. Will you please open an account
for Masses to be said for the repose of my soul the day after I
pass away?*

Ma Dee[4]

Though she continues to add books to her collection—which
has grown to nearly seven thousand volumes—the hunt for the
Gutenberg seems as though it's from another time, a world away.

◆ ◆ ◆

AND THEN, SUDDENLY, it's not.

David Randall, head of the Rare Books Department at Scribner
Book Store in New York City, writes to tell Estelle that Scribner's
might soon have for sale "one of the finest Gutenberg Bibles in
existence, absolutely complete and perfect." The price, he says,
"would not be lower than $150,000." He offers to send her more
information but tells her that if she's not interested, she should
"forget all about this letter. I don't want it generally known that a
copy is available."[5]

Randall, one of the many dealers with whom she has an ongo-
ing relationship, had learned of her interest in the Bible months
before, when Estelle mentioned that she had been the underbidder
for the Dyson Perrins Gutenberg. He took note when she added

that she very much regretted losing it and still hoped to find one, though it seemed unlikely that she'd ever have the chance. The conversation set Randall into motion. "Here I was with a customer for THE BOOK and I ought, by golly, to try and do something about it," he wrote later. "I made inquiries of all private owners as to the possibilities of purchasing their copies and received a universal 'no.'" (Gutenberg owner Carl Pforzheimer had harrumphed to him, "After all, I wouldn't have a library without it, would I?") Randall also alerted his colleague John Carter in England that he had a ready buyer if one could be located.

Randall and Carter got their break when they heard that the New York General Theological Seminary had a building project in the works and might consider selling its two-volume Gutenberg Bible to finance it. Randall met with leaders at the seminary, pointing out that the transfer could be completed "without publicity of any kind." How did $150,000 sound? It would be the highest price yet for a Gutenberg Bible, and the purchaser would pay the seminary directly, as well as paying the 10 percent commission to Scribner's. The seminary agreed to proceed. No documents were signed, but according to Randall, none were needed.

That's the news he brings to Estelle. The book is "perfect," he says, and striking in its blue morocco gilt-tooled binding. It had been owned by British collector Sir John Thorold, who bought it for his Syston Park library, and it was sold in 1884, then again in 1898, when Bernard Quaritch purchased it for the seminary for £2,950. And now Randall is poised to steer it to Estelle.

"It is every book dealer's dream to discover a Gutenberg Bible, or failing that to figure in some transaction involving one,"

Randall declares. "There are many dealers in many countries and very few Gutenbergs, so most dreams concerning them must remain just dreams." But this one seems ready to materialize.

All that stands between Estelle and the Bible is the okay of the seminary's board of trustees. Randall is confident that they have the legal right to sell it, and want to. But Lucille is wary. There's "something fishy" about the whole affair—it seems too good to be true. "Why on earth would the seminary give up this precious book?" she asks. As the days pass, she receives more material from Randall about the Bible and its provenance, but the information only deepens her doubt that the seminary will actually sell. Lucille keeps her thoughts to herself, but she grows increasingly anxious as she helps Estelle coordinate the details.

Estelle asks Robert Schad of the Huntington Library to inspect the Bible,[6] sending him to New York to be sure Randall's assessment is sound. Schad is shocked to find that one leaf in volume two is a pen-and-ink facsimile. It is so well done that only the most careful examination could distinguish the replacement from its original, but it is a significant flaw. Schad doesn't think it's a deal breaker—Estelle might not get another chance at a Bible like this— but it does puncture Randall's claim about the book's perfection.

On August 11, 1950, Randall writes to Schad at the Waldorf Astoria, explaining that he had not known about the facsimile leaf and asking if Mrs. Doheny would like to examine the Bible herself. He then offers to lower the price. Although the standing committee of the seminary will decide the final figure, Randall says he'll recommend that it be set at $137,500, which he thinks is fair.[7] The book will be sold WAF (with all faults), to acknowledge Schad's discovery.

Estelle's eyesight will prevent her from inspecting the book, but Schad recommends that she take the opportunity. Randall makes arrangements to have the book shipped to her and sets up a meeting in Los Angeles at which Estelle can discuss the purchase with Lucille, Schad, and other close advisers. Randall flies out to attend, and in his memoir, he recounts the experience this way:

The great day arrived. I was met at my hotel by a chauffeur, driven to Mrs. Doheny's estate in the center of Los Angeles, stopped at the gate by guards, as usual etc., and found myself after lunch, with the "Countess," as some knew her, or "Ma [Dee]," as others did, THE BOOK, and some assorted characters, gathered around a small table in the library.

The confession came first: the gem had a flaw. This disconcerted "Ma [Dee]," not a whit. But her counselors, none of whom, I immediately perceived, wished her to buy the book, saw a quick out. She was reminded on the one hand of the new wing the children's hospital needed, on another that the tax situation was tough (she had just disposed of, according to the Los Angeles papers, some stray oil lands for $40,000,000), and on still another that being imperfect, THE BOOK wasn't worthy of her, etc., ad nauseum.

It was a curious conference. All of her advisers—financial, religious, legal (with the honorable exception of Miss Lucille Miller, her librarian)—agreed that this was not for her. "Back to New York, son, and take your bait with you—go fishing elsewhere," I was advised (not quite in those terms).

The "Countess" listened carefully and then spoke. "I remember [1911] when the Robert Hoe copy of the Gutenberg Bible sold for fifty thousand dollars to Henry Huntington. Ed and I were having

breakfast when I read of it in the paper, and I said 'Will you, some-
day, buy me a Gutenberg Bible, dear?' He said, 'I promise you I will.'
It was an impossible promise for him in those days. Gentlemen, I am
buying this book as a present from him to me."

End of discussion.[8]

Randall flies back to New York in high spirits. Estelle's lawyer, Olin Wellborn III, drafts the four-page contract, and on September 5, a formal offer to buy the Bible for $137,500 is sent air express. The Gutenberg Bible, meanwhile, is shipped back and held in the vault at Scribner.[9]

The seminary's reply to the offer is quick and crushing. A two-sentence letter from the board of trustees unceremoniously informs Estelle that her offer has been presented to the standing committee, which rejected it unanimously.

"It was all terribly embarrassing," Randall said. "I felt that I had let Mrs. Doheny down and the Seminary had let Scribner's down, and a very gracious lady had been needlessly hurt." Randall maintained that no one ever told him why the seminary had a change of heart, but in his memoir, published in 1969, he wrote that he was convinced that his rival Abraham Rosenbach had torpedoed the sale by convincing the board that the price was too low.[10]

Randall also claims that he was blindsided by the facsimile page, though it had been general knowledge among bibliographers and seminary personnel since 1916, when it was discovered. A note on the flyleaf of the volume even calls attention to the substitution.[11]

Whether or not Randall's oversight or Rosenbach's interference has undermined the sale, the unhappy truth remains: Estelle Doheny has now lost the Gutenberg Bible, twice.

◆ ◆ ◆

BUT PERHAPS, AS Rosenbach believed, every book *does* have its destiny. If he or Randall had blocked Estelle's quest for one Bible, they had also, inadvertently, opened the way for the copy she was meant to have—Number 45.

At almost the same moment the seminary deal is unraveling, Sir Philip Frere, Number 45's mysterious new owner, appears in Ernest Maggs's shop. He needs to sell his Gutenberg right away, he says, and in exchange for quick cash, he's willing to take not much more in sterling than he had paid three and a half years before.[12]

The book trade is in a slump brought on, in part, by strained economic conditions in postwar Europe, and an auction is unlikely to bring a higher price than Maggs can get simply by selling to a private individual. And of course, he has the perfect buyer in mind.

He immediately writes to Estelle, and on a page headed with the words *GUTENBERG BIBLE* typed in all-capital red letters, he outlines the turn of events:

"We sold it to an English collector, who has now decided to re-sell it through us and would like to receive £25,000, which at the present rate is equal to approximately $72,000. Thus, in terms of dollars $17,000 less than he paid for it. I am wondering if you would still be interested." The letter is dated September 14, 1950, just days after the seminary debacle.

This time, Estelle doesn't hesitate, quickly moving funds and issuing instructions for the Bible's transfer. As they finalize the details, Estelle asks Maggs to use the code word *commode* instead of *Bible* in their communications to keep the transaction secret, and Lucille silently squirms at all the references to Maggs's commode. Mrs. Doheny thinks the word is simply shorthand for *commodious*, as in a tall chest of drawers, and doesn't realize that it looks as though she has eccentrically decided to refer to her precious Bible as a toilet.

But even the unintentional joke captures her overriding desire to see that *this* opportunity is not flushed away. There's no quibbling over price, and Estelle dispenses with any inspection—she'll buy the book as is and hope it hasn't been altered. Maggs, she trusts, would have mentioned it, if it had.

After all the false starts, this transaction has come at a perfect time to create the discount that Maggs mentions in his note. In 1949, Britain had devalued the pound sterling by 30 percent, dropping the exchange rate for a single pound from $4.03 to $2.80. That means that even as she pays £3,000 more than Frere had at the Dyson auction, she is getting the book for 23 percent less.

When her long-awaited Gutenberg is finally delivered, Estelle is ecstatic. The book, the catalyst for the collecting journey that has transformed her, arrives, quite fortuitously, as she prepares to mark the tenth "birthday" of the seminary library in Camarillo, which will be the ultimate setting for her crown jewel.

She describes the excitement of receiving it in a letter to Maggs dated October 17, 1950:

"It arrived about three o'clock on Saturday afternoon, October the 14th, which happened to be the tenth anniversary of the dedication of the Edward Laurence Doheny Memorial Library. I had planned a small luncheon that day to celebrate the occasion, but I knew from experience that the 'commode' wouldn't arrive in time for the luncheon so I changed it to Sunday.

"Mr. Schad of the Huntington Library came over with Mrs. Schad and their son Jasper, who is rapidly becoming famous as a photographer. Miss Miller was here and my companion Miss Rose Kelly, completed our party. I did not open the package until we were all together and then each one cut the cord with a big shears, so that we all can say, 'I opened the Bible personally.'"

She promises Maggs a souvenir from among the photos of the day, adding, "While I don't think they are going to be especially good because we are all looking down at the book instead of up at

Estelle Doheny and her book secretary, Lucille Miller, examine the Gutenberg Bible at the Doheny mansion in Los Angeles, shortly after it was unwrapped on October 15, 1950. By the time the book was finally in her hands, Estelle was nearly blind.

the camera, nevertheless I will send you one. What we did was for the future and not the present time, because I am just as anxious as the seller to have this kept confidential, and that is the reason I am speaking of it as 'the Mainz Bible.' But later on when it becomes known that I have it, these pictures may be interesting."

Estelle also relays Robert Schad's estimation of her purchase. "When Mr. Schad had examined the book thoroughly, he said it was the most beautiful copy one could ever hope to possess and that it was magnificent in every way—size, binding, illuminations, quality of paper, and provenance."

The elation and pride she feels are clear: "The moment I saw the book in its wonderfully perfect condition I felt as if I wanted to lift it up and kiss it," she tells Maggs. "It will feel perfectly at home

The bill of sale for the Gutenberg Bible, dated October 2, 1950. Estelle Doheny had given up on ever owning the Bible when the copy she had lost suddenly became available. Thanks to an unusually strong dollar, she was able to claim one of civilization's great artifacts at a bargain price.

with the other great Mainz printings in the Estelle Doheny Collection."

♦ ♦ ♦

THERE IS AN unlikely postscript to Estelle's Gutenberg Bible saga. David Randall, who never learned of Estelle's secret transaction with Maggs for her lost Gutenberg, continues to hunt for another copy. And despite the prevailing belief that there would likely be no more, in 1951, he finds one.

A Quaritch associate of John Carter had located the so-called Shuckburgh copy, which had been missing since 1824. Bound in two volumes with crimson-colored morocco covers, it had once belonged to Sir George Shuckburgh, a nineteenth-century British bibliophile, and had been miraculously located in the library of a Shuckburgh descendant. But perhaps *miraculously* is too strong a term, because the finder was Dyson Perrins's old friend Sydney Cockerell, the British book maven who had always had an eye for rarities, and a talent for putting himself in their proximity.

Cockerell had been invited to see a collection of books recently inherited by a Lady Christian Martin, and he noted in his diary that the library included "a slightly imperfect Mazarin Bible" as well as a number of other books of great value. In his inimitable way, he added that "it was a treat to see such an extraordinary collection, of which the owner, a stout ordinary woman, is quite ignorant."[13]

Two men from Quaritch ran into him as he was setting out to view the books, and when David Randall began shaking the trees for Estelle some two years later, they remembered how Cockerell had mentioned that he was off to see a Gutenberg. Cockerell put

them in touch with the owner, and Quaritch secured the book for
Carter and Randall. For his instrumental help, Cockerell received
a dealer's commission as a finder's fee.

With the "new" Gutenberg in hand, Randall writes to Estelle
saying that he feels "morally committed" to give her the right of
first refusal after losing the seminary's Bible. "And as I told Miss
Miller, I was determined not to approach you again unless I had
complete rights to sell you the volume on the spot." Great bookselling involves great theater, and Randall handily delivers:
". . . had it not been for your interest in the Bible," he writes, "it is
extremely unlikely that this would ever have been uncovered. . . .
It was on the wild chance that another copy might be available some-
where, that I set our London agents on the scout, with the results
you know."[14] But the hyperbole isn't really necessary. The facts are
incredible all on their own Randall must've been quite startled when
he read Estelle's terse reply in a telegram dated June 3, 1953:

TELEGRAM RECEIVED. NOT INTERESTED.
—MRS. E. L. DOHENY[15]

There are worse things, though, than being "saddled" with a
Gutenberg Bible whose discovery becomes front-page news in the
New York Times. The find is hailed as the "Forty-Sixth" Gutenberg,
and its unexpected reappearance creates a worldwide sensation,
capturing the imagination of book hunters everywhere. Collectors search their garrets and basements in the hopes of finding a
treasured first edition, hoping they too can make a small fortune.

Scribner decides to pay £40,000 to buy the book for stock, and
then sells it to bookseller H. P. Kraus, who will send the two

volumes to the Gutenberg Museum in 1978. It costs the institution $1.8 million to bring the Bible home to Mainz.[16]

◆ ◆ ◆

ESTELLE MANAGES TO sidestep the publicity that she so feared in acquiring Number 45, but she soon decides that it doesn't make sense to keep her Gutenberg locked up secretly at home. The controlled conditions in the Treasure Room of the Doheny Memorial Library suit the ancient book better, she realizes, and she has the Bible moved there, where it is housed in a handsome, custom-designed antique glass case. Scholars from Europe, the Middle East, and Japan make the trek to view the storied volume and sign the library's guest book, and news crews come to Camarillo to share the Gutenberg with the world. At last Number 45 seems to have found its right resting place, a spot equivalent to the New York Public Library or Henry Huntington's great museum, where it can be studied and admired for generations.

When Carrie Estelle Betzold Doheny dies on October 30, 1958, her estate is valued at $37,500,730, not including her rare-book collection. By anyone's measure she has done right by Edward Doheny, skillfully juggling complex oil and business assets during her husband's decline and after his death. A detailed forensic analysis estimates that she has grown her husband's fortune by roughly 733 percent.[17] More than that, the female book hunter who hadn't been allowed to join the local Zamorano book-collecting club because she wasn't *man* enough, has entered an elite group: the vanishingly small clutch of individuals who could not only gather the most important books in the world, but marshal the resources—personal and financial—to acquire a Gutenberg. She stands with the great collectors of the American West, bibliophiles like Huntington and William Andrews Clark Jr., as well as the ambitious Britons who had previously owned Number 45.

Unlike the book's earlier owners, though, Estelle has taken pains to ensure that her collection won't be scattered after her death, or traded away for the cash to bail a future owner out of trouble. She has willed her precious Gutenberg and the rest of her collection—along with the books' showplace home, the Doheny Memorial Library—to St. John's Seminary, creating an endowment to cover its operating costs in perpetuity and stipulating that nothing be sold for twenty-five years. A quarter century, she reasoned, is enough time to let the library establish itself, and for its Gutenberg to become so identified with the place that no one would consider removing it. The seminary, after all, will have a powerful interest in maintaining the integrity of the library, one of its defining features.

More personally, the church has been Estelle Doheny's spiritual and emotional sanctuary during the most difficult times in her life. Who better to trust to keep her library intact, protected, and well cared for for generations to come?

◆ ◆ ◆

THE GUTENBERG'S STATUS, and price, keep accelerating after Estelle's death. Just twenty years later, the Bibles are taking their place among the most expensive books of all time. That becomes apparent in 1978, when three are put up for sale in what one prominent book dealer describes as "an imponderable coincidence of history."[18]

Most book dealers project a figure in the $2 million range for each of the three (two-volume) paper copies. The price seems unfathomable, but a single leaf has recently sold at Sotheby's, Parke-Bernet, for $4,750. Extrapolating from that figure, a two-volume B42 could bring more than $3 million.

In advance of the sales, experts develop a scoring system that ranks each Gutenberg on offer, resulting in a "total score" based on typographical, artistic, and textual distinctions. The first B42 up for sale, to be sold in March, receives 1,471 points; the second, on the block in April, gets 1,801 points; and the third, to be sold in June, receives 2,318. It's a Miss Universe pageant for B42s. As in such a contest, being judged as having a "conventional appearance" is no compliment, and "Miss March" is, for that reason, deemed to be in "inferior condition." "Miss June" ranks the highest because of its "extravagant and beautiful decoration." And so it goes, with the first substantial pieces of printing, and the heralds of our modern age, being scored on their looks like swimsuit contestants.

Two of these Bibles had surfaced in Estelle Doheny's search. The book offered in March is the one David Randall sold to H. P. Kraus when Estelle rejected it.[19] The copy on the block in April is the same one the General Theological Seminary wouldn't sell her, which goes to the Württembergische Landesbibliothek in Stuttgart for $2.2 million, breaking the price record for a book set the year before by John James Audubon's *The Birds of America*. The June sale moves the copy owned by New York investment banker and collector Carl Howard Pforzheimer Jr. to the University of Texas at Austin, where it is currently on display. Its price, $2.6 million, sets another world-record price for a B42.[20]

The prices draw sustained news coverage and make celebrities

The cover of the Doheny Gutenberg Bible in its original fifteenth-century binding of age-darkened calfskin stretched over heavy wood boards.

of Gutenberg's creations. People from all walks of life now recognize the Gutenberg Bible as not just an expensive book but as the "rarest and most important book in the world," and they crowd in to see it, standing in long lines inside the Great Hall of the Library of Congress, where its unusual three-volume copy, printed on vellum, is on permanent display. The term *Gutenberg Bible* enters the culture's working vocabulary, and the dozen copies in the United States pass all other collectibles in dollar value and desirability.

◆ ◆ ◆

LEFT TO CARE for Estelle's treasure in the lull before Gutenberg becomes a household name in America is Lucille Miller, who in 1960 is chosen to be the first curator of the Estelle Doheny Collection at the Edward Laurence Doheny Memorial Library. Like

Robert Schad, Lucille had no college education or formal training in the humanities, but in the end, few can match her breadth of knowledge about the collection, for which she compiles three catalogs.

Lucille had remained at Chester Place as Mrs. Doheny's primary book secretary until the very end, and she took her death especially hard. "She was absolutely the foundation stone of my life," Lucille said. "We sort of learned the book-collecting game together. She always wanted to know what I thought. She would ask, if there was a choice, which [book] would I prefer?" In her nearly three decades as Estelle's sounding board, go-between, and eyes, Lucille had been courted by the most renowned dealers in Europe and America, who were "eager for her approval," and she learned from the legends of the book trade.[21]

These are the qualifications she brings to the library, where she is not only Number 45's primary steward and champion but also keeper of its story. When important scholars come to the seminary campus to study the Bible, Lucille retrieves the royal folio from its case, carries it to the Treasure Room's polished table, and—if a visitor is smart enough to engage her—offers a sliver of history.

Asked by a journalist if she wishes she could have traded lives with Estelle Doheny, the longtime "book secretary" expresses no regrets about the order of things. "I was perfectly content in my own place," Lucille said. "I thought I was missing a good part of my life by not marrying, but I was happy in my life, building up that collection."[22]

Estelle had not been ungenerous. One birthday gift to Lucille was a 1740 watercolor of a luminous magnolia painted by German artist G. D. Ehret, which shines from the living room wall of the small bungalow Lucille shares with her mother until her mother's death. Money left her by Mrs. Doheny enables her to move from that house and buy a small home on Francis Street in Ventura County. It is a short drive from the Camarillo library, where she works until degenerative eye disease takes her sight, as it had taken Estelle's.

Lucille Valeria Miller, the second exceptional bibliophile and Mighty Woman Book Hunter of the Doheny household, devoted most of her life to Estelle's library. She died on September 27, 1989, and when she was interred five days later at the Ivy Lawn Memorial Park, the graveside ceremony was brief and small. Only three people were present: the Reverend Daniel Fox of Our Lady of the Assumption Church of Ventura, a burial grounds custodian, and the intrepid new curator of the Estelle Doheny Collection, an avid book lover named Rita S. Faulders.

CHAPTER EIGHT

The Nuclear Bibliophiles

T HE EDWARD LAURENCE Doheny Memorial Library isn't as secluded as the European monastery where Number 45 likely
spent its early life, but it's a quiet spot without the pull of the busy
collections in the more prominent locations—the Huntington Library, the Morgan, and the Library of Congress among them—
that house America's other Gutenbergs.

St. John's Seminary is tiny, with around one hundred students,
and the library that Rita Faulders oversees retains the personal feel
it had when Estelle and Lucille were putting it together. Forty
years after its opening, it's still the sort of place where Rita, once
secretary to the library curator who succeeded Lucille, could rise
to oversee the collection. A passion for the books in the Treasure
Room, especially the Gutenberg, is valued as much as formal
training, and the layers of bureaucracy that can surround major
libraries are thinner here.

Which may help explain how Number 45, of all the Gutenbergs in the world, comes to be the first significant subject of pioneering research that draws a physicist, a historian, a librarian, and the great book itself to the proton beam of a cyclotron.

◆ ◆ ◆

Professor Richard N. Schwab of the University of California, Davis, a specialist in the history of early printing, gets to know Rita during research trips to the Camarillo library in the late 1970s and early '80s. He takes advantage of the opportunity to inspect Number 45, and notices how meticulous Rita is when it comes to protecting it, keeping a careful log to ensure that when the book is on display its pages are turned regularly so the binding is never taxed. Like Lucille before her, she knows the volumes in her care well and has an eye for detail, the quality that's so essential in Schwab's work. Rita has another skill that's always useful: the ability to ease

Rita S. Faulders, an avid book lover, served as the curator for the Gutenberg Bible when it was housed at the Edward Laurence Doheny Memorial Library in Camarillo, California. She played a pivotal role in catapulting the ancient book into the realm of advanced particle physics and helping unlock its secrets.

her way forward with a smile, and just enough charm to melt resistance from the seminary's prelates.

None of this is at the front of Schwab's mind as he works the puzzle of his primary research, but a historian is always filing observations for later reference. He turns back to the subject at hand—a decade-long study of one of the most ambitious projects of the Enlightenment, a twenty-eight-volume French encyclopedia edited by Denis Diderot that aimed to capture the world's knowledge in the mid-1700s. Despite its immense length and complexity, the *Encyclopédie* had been massively popular and widely pirated, and some of the fakes are extraordinarily accomplished. There seem to be a full library's worth of tiny variations in the counterfeit copies, some of which are so small he can find them only with a magnifying glass. (One well-known fake uses asterisks with five points, for example, where the original had six.)

Back home in Davis, over dinner with one of his former students, a French literature scholar named Ginny Cahill, and her husband, Tom, the director of the Crocker Nuclear Laboratory, Schwab bemoans the frustrations of weeding out the knockoffs. The three of them are longtime friends and hiking companions, and the Cahills are familiar with the project, but this time, something about Schwab's frustrations with studying those black blotches on paper hits Tom in a new way. Cahill has been studying smog at the nuclear lab, and his work, too, could be described as studying black spots on paper—with the caveat that it also involves using a three-hundred-ton particle accelerator, a machine also known as a cyclotron or atom smasher. His equipment, several orders of magnitude more sophisticated than a magnifying glass, is a rebuilt version of the cyclotron invented by Nobel Laureate Ernest O. Lawrence and used as part of the Manhattan Project to isolate plutonium for the first time, helping create the first atomic bomb.

The machine was designed to accelerate atomic particles to extremely high speeds—one-third the speed of light at the Crocker lab—and aim them at target particles to blow them apart, releasing yet-unknown subatomic particles, or to get them to absorb particles and change form, potentially creating new elements. But Cahill had figured out how to convert the device from an atom smasher to something more akin to an atom pusher, by accelerating protons to lower speeds and creating a less powerful proton beam. Swedish researchers had discovered that when they aimed a lower-intensity proton stream at target material, instead of blasting and scattering the target's electrons out of their orbits, it just nudged them out of their path, and other electrons rushed in to replace them. The energy created in that process is released in the form of X-rays.[1]

Every substance put under the beam releases X-rays of different energy, its own "signature," which can be read and analyzed by a computer. The nudge/X-ray/ID process is called proton-induced X-ray emission, or PIXE (pronounced *pixie*). Cahill had been collecting smog on air filters and using PIXE to identify the pollutants in the gathered particles.

At that dinner in 1978, he tells Schwab how his group is looking for new applications for PIXE, and Schwab, who has been lamenting the impossibility of detecting the fake *Encyclopédie* pages among the real ones, has an inspired thought as their flaming dessert arrives. So does Cahill. "Your books and my air filters aren't that different," the physicist tells his friend. "They are both made of paper, and my garbage is called smog and your garbage is called ink." The next step, Schwab recalled, comes "like a revelation during the flambé." They'll see what PIXE has to say about Schwab's books.

Cahill thinks that the spray of X-rays emitted after the protons collide with the atoms in a book's ink and paper might be distinctive enough to distinguish a real *Encyclopédie* from a counterfeit. But finding out won't be easy. They are talking about focusing the cyclotron's beam on fragile artifacts that are hundreds of years old, and there's no room for error. After all, as Cahill points out, the cyclotron's proton beam, at higher settings, has the power to drill a hole through a thick steel plate,[2] break down the material it interacts with, or make it radioactive. Before aiming his beam at a book, he'd need to be certain that the interaction would be utterly noninvasive, the book unchanged in any way.

There they have a great advantage. Smog, the focus of Cahill's work, turns out to be a delicate material that is easily degraded, and Cahill has worked out how to calibrate the proton beam so it won't break down or alter any component elements. But that will be of small comfort to rare-book owners, who will want to see convincing evidence that what's good for smog isn't somehow lethal for centuries-old paper and ink. Cahill and Schwab will need to demonstrate that PIXE testing will be risk-free. They start by putting the campus newspaper under the proton beam, but its cheap newsprint is so uncomplicated that "the project almost died," Cahill recalls, because "the newspaper was as uninteresting chemically as it was editorially." Fortunately, he adds, "we had a few pieces of very old paper." Small scraps are just right for the job, because Cahill will be exposing them to the proton beam inside a vacuum chamber, on a glass slide frame that can't accommodate anything bigger than two square inches.

These samples prove to be chemically complex. "When we analyzed them we found out that, lo and behold, elements like manganese, chlorine, and sulfur jumped out all over the place. This was the key that something interesting was going on," Cahill remembers.

Schwab races home and retrieves an eighteenth-century book from his library—he'll sacrifice it for the good of science. Small samples from the edges of thirty-two sequential pages go into the cyclotron next, and the X-ray patterns PIXE produces reveal something unexpected: the paper appears to change in composition every eight pages. Cahill doesn't know what to make of the finding, but it's instantly clear to Schwab. In traditional book production, one large sheet of paper, a quire, was folded several times to make a set of eight sequential pages. To create a finished book, many of these folded quires were stacked together and bound. PIXE is picking up the slight changes in the composition of different quires.[3] The analysis shows that "each batch of paper, nay each sheet of paper" has a unique chemical identity, says Cahill.

"Neither of us had imagined the analysis would be so subtle that it could distinguish between different sheets, apparently even from the same batch of paper out of the same papermaker's vat," Schwab explains. That makes it possible to determine where quires begin and end, to pick out pages that were added later, and to collect the chemical "profiles" of paper from a known time or region to make it easier to compare books and better pinpoint their origins. As hoped, PIXE's data offers path-breaking insights. And to the researchers' great relief, the proton beam passes the safety test: The paper samples emerge unchanged by their time in the cyclotron.[4] "It turned out," Cahill mused, "that old books are much more stable than recent-vintage California smog."

That leaves them with the question of how, exactly, to test a book like the *Encyclopédie*. It won't be possible to cram an entire leaf into the cyclotron's two-inch slide window, and the notion of cutting even the smallest sample from a three-hundred-year-old book is unthinkable. The solution, Cahill realizes, is to modify his machine. "Since we could not bring the books to the vacuum-sealed cyclotron beam, we would bring the beam to the books," he explains. In the open air, book pages could be tested whole.

Figuring out how to bring the proton beam safely out of the cyclotron and to focus it precisely on a delicate book takes time and money. Starting with a university grant of only $2,200, Cahill and his team set to work. Proton beams are operated in a vacuum in the first place because when they collide with air molecules, they can travel only four inches or so before they lose energy and fall apart. So the team begins designing a device that will make the most of the beam's four-inch range. Four inches, as it happens, is plenty of space in which to arrange a leaf of a book in front of the proton beam, let the beam pass through it to an X-ray detector on the other side, and capture the protons as they exit.

Ultimately, Cahill comes up with a milliprobe that can be aimed with a laser and focus the proton beam on a spot the tenth the size of a period. There's no danger to book or people from the "unboxed" protons. The energy they release is "roughly equivalent to that provided by a 100-watt light bulb at 50 cm," about twenty inches, Schwab writes later, "much less than sunlight."[5]

Cahill runs repeated tests to be sure the beam causes no unintended or latent damage. He aims it at sheets from other ancient books, including medieval manuscripts, and even runs a test on one of his own possessions—a leaf of a manuscript from the year 1080. The page from the Book of Kings handwritten in Latin is not just historically important. Given to him by his father, it also has deep personal significance. If he's going to ask other people to risk their irreplaceable books, he'll do it, too. He's not at all surprised, but relieved nonetheless, when the page emerges unharmed.

As the work progresses, the experimenters realize that their method is delivering layers of details not only about paper, but also heretofore unknown scientific data about ancient ink. "We found these [inks] to vary almost as much as fingerprints," Schwab said, "from era to era, region to region, and even scribe to scribe and printer to printer, in ways that help in determining date, provenance, and authenticity." The initial experiments are so promising that Cahill and Schwab begin in earnest to lay the foundations for a new branch of bibliography focused on the chemical profiles of writing and printing materials. They are convinced that even the most fragile artifacts can be subjected to the particle beam without damage. And increasingly people are willing to believe them. They even manage to borrow and test a number of single leaves from several dismantled Gutenberg Bibles owned by the University of California at Riverside and Santa Barbara.

The tests uncover revelatory information about the ink the printers had used, a unique, oil-based mixture with high concentrations of copper and lead—more similar to the oil paints used by artists of the time than to later inks. "We found within a few seconds of our first analysis of the ink that it is unusually rich in compounds of lead and copper," Cahill said. Every other ink of the period had "browned up" as the carbon in it had oxidized, but Gutenberg's ink is still lustrous and deep black after five hundred years. "Everybody said the ink was carbon-based. It was taken for granted," Cahill explains. "Everyone was wrong."[6]

The findings galvanize the book world.

"At this point," as Cahill recalls, "the right person walked into our lives." One of America's leading fine printers, San Francisco–based Adrian Wilson, reads about the tests with the cyclotron in a local newspaper and immediately calls Cahill and Schwab. Wilson is not only a book designer and a scholar, but also a visionary whose word carries weight among print connoisseurs.[7] What they need now, he insists, is a complete volume of the Gutenberg Bible so that PIXE can analyze it, page by page. An atomic examination, he tells them, could reveal secrets of the problems Gutenberg faced, help unlock more of the mysteries of the Bible's eternally fresh ink, and offer deeper insights into the origins of printing. They hadn't considered such an ambitious project, but Wilson is persuasive. (His encouragement and knowledge eventually lead to a "genius grant" from the MacArthur Foundation, which will help fund their work.) There's a significant stumbling block, though. Borrowing leaves of a Bible that's already been torn apart is one thing. But who would be willing to loan a priceless, undamaged B42 for testing with a piece of equipment known primarily as a catalyst of mass destruction?[8]

◆　◆　◆

THEIR FIRST STOP is the Huntington Library, which holds one of the only two bound Gutenberg Bibles in California. The answer is a quick and emphatic no.

But Schwab has always been warmly received at the Doheny Library. "So at that point," he says, "Tom and I drove down to Camarillo and tried to sweet-talk the librarian and the rector—Rita Faulders and Monsignor Eugene Frilot."

The rector is skeptical, but Rita is intrigued by what secrets the cyclotron might unlock. "I think that she was persuaded that it would be a fine thing to do for the history of scholarship," Schwab recalls, "and a credit to the Doheny Library. It was not so much about her ego, but an intelligent decision that this was something worthwhile."

Perhaps her curiosity and openness have something to do with living with an engineer. Rita's husband, Dr. Charles R. Faulders, is an aerodynamics specialist for North American Rockwell, with advanced degrees in mechanical engineering from UC Berkeley and MIT. Both she and the monsignor have many questions remaining at the end of the meeting, but no one slams the door on the possibility of loaning the Bible. They keep the conversation going even after getting a nervous no from church officials the first time they broach the subject.

So Schwab and Cahill mount a campaign of what Schwab describes as delicate "research diplomacy." They write detailed memos explaining their methods and techniques, underlining their track record with earlier testing, and highlighting the findings of their work to date. PIXE is totally noninvasive, they promise, and they will safeguard the Gutenberg Bible the entire time it is undergoing testing, a process that won't take longer than forty-eight hours. The project will be wrapped in secrecy, and not even the operators of the control room will know the true identity of the book under the beam.

It's impossible to know what would've happened had they approached the library even a couple of years earlier, before Rita became the collection's curator, but luck is with them: Rita is both a true believer in the experiment and in a position to persuade. After lengthy discussions with the board of trustees, on July 26, 1982, the church gives Cahill and Schwab a verbal go-ahead—and Schwab gives Rita significant credit for making it happen. "She was probably the only person in the United States, possibly in the world, who could do it." The scientists will have the Bible for four days and three nights during the first week of October.

The seminary secures a multimillion-dollar insurance policy for Number 45, and a nerve-racked Rita prepares the book for travel. "If anything happened to the Gutenberg Bible, my goose would be cooked," she recalls. While she worries over how to pack it, her biggest concern is security. The detailed plans she orchestrates for keeping the book undercover and safe during its travels are something out of a John le Carré novel, to spy-novel fan Tom Cahill's delight. Rita and the research team exchange voluminous letters and memos detailing procedures for what the researchers dub "The Great Gutenberg Fishing Expedition." In all their communications, Number 45 is referred to by its code name, "the WHALE," chosen, as Schwab explains it, because for the researchers, that Bible was "the biggest catch of all."

As "G-Day" nears, the research team works with Chuck Faulders to design a lectern covered in soft foam rubber and white felt to hold the Bible in front of the proton beam. In consultation with rare-book specialists, they engineer the custom cradle to place no more pressure on the book than it would experience on display in the library.

Finally, on Wednesday, October 6, it's time. Rita's itinerary for the day begins with "6:00–6:30 am: Pick up fishing tackle," and she, Chuck, and Jim Hawkins, the seminary business manager, arrive at the library to carry Number 45 out of its vault and bundle it for travel. The book gets a wrapping of fireproof paper, then disappears into the padded case Estelle Doheny had custom built three decades earlier. They slide that into a fireproof box marked Liquor, pour in Styrofoam pellets to fill the empty spaces, and tie up the sealed parcel with a heavy white cord.

The box goes into the back bay of the Faulders' twelve-year-old Mercury station wagon, where it's visible through the rear window. Chuck will drive the library's contingent—Rita, Monsignor Frilot, and Hawkins. A second vehicle, driven by a plainclothes policeman from UC Davis, will provide security. Officer Shad Canington has a gun strapped to his ankle and a revolver on the passenger seat of his unmarked car.

Davis is some four hundred miles north of Camarillo, a trip that takes upward of six hours. The two cars make radio contact at predetermined intervals, and stop for gas and lunch, parking in front of a large plateglass window at a Denny's restaurant, where everyone hurriedly eats cheeseburgers, never taking their eyes off the Faulders' family Mercury. At UC Davis, they take the WHALE straight to the campus police department—chosen not for its security, though that's a plus, but because its evidence room is the only spot they can store the book on campus that doesn't have an automatic sprinkler system. Number 45 spends the night in a locked cage next to a pile of handguns, bags of marijuana, and other contraband confiscated by university police.

ABOVE LEFT: *Historian Richard N. Schwab and Bruce Kusko position the Gutenberg Bible so the ink and paper of its pages can be tested by the proton beam of a cyclotron.*

ABOVE RIGHT: *A team of scientist/engineers and a book scholar used the same machine that first isolated plutonium for the atomic bomb to solve the five-hundred-year-old mysteries surrounding the Gutenberg Bible and the origins of modern printing. Left to right: Richard N. Schwab, Rita S. Faulders, Charles R. Faulders, Thomas A. Cahill, and Bruce Kusko.*

◆ ◆ ◆

TOM CAHILL IS uncharacteristically nervous as he fires up the cyclotron the next day. He's been running tests on ever-more-valuable samples for four years, and he's confident that nothing will happen to the irreplaceable book now in his hands. But confronted with the five-hundred-year-old Bible that he'll put under his proton beam for some forty-one hours, he can't brush aside what's at stake. If anything goes wrong, the costs will be steep.

As the muted hum of the machine intensifies, so does his anxiety. "We'd never done anything like this before," he says. Neither had anyone else. "The ancient book was now face-to-face with a modern nuclear accelerator, the pointy end of modern science."

He checks and rechecks settings, all too conscious that "if somehow I made a mistake in my physics, I could put a hole permanently in one of the pages of the Doheny Gutenberg Bible."

Dick Schwab is equally nervous, having awakened to the fleeting memory of a "Gutenberg dream."

They take some comfort in knowing that Cahill has had a red panic button installed in the room, nicknamed "the North Cave," that houses the cyclotron. It's a safeguard against a strong-arm theft if there happens to be a heist in the works. "I could put my finger on it," Cahill says, "and a SWAT car would be there within two minutes. We were very aware of the value of what we had." But there's no backup to call in if the protons go rogue and decimate the book. The tension is thick, yet the team remains outwardly calm.

The crew preparing the computers in the aboveground control room, whose array of screens and equipment makes it look like a scaled-down version of NASA's Space Center Houston, has been spared the Gutenberg jitters. They've been told that they're analyzing a seventeenth-century Bible once owned and annotated by Martin Luther, composer Johann Sebastian Bach, and theology professor Abraham Calovius, a book known to experts as the Calov Bible. The control room crew have no idea they are testing one of civilization's great masterpieces.

Rita and Chuck Faulders help Schwab and Cahill stabilize Number 45 in its cradle. Photos from the day show the heavy book resting securely there, with felt arms holding it firmly in place. The whole apparatus[9] is made to be tilted so that a single leaf can hang

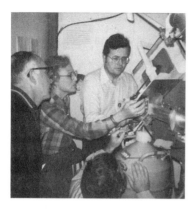

*Richard N. Schwab and Rita
S. Faulders join physicist Thomas
A. Cahill during the testing of the
Gutenberg Bible at UC Davis in
October 1982.*

free, and rest on an analysis plate in front of the beam. The protons
will come through the leaf from behind, and the plan is to first test
all the verso sides of the leaves—the surfaces that would face the
back of the closed book—and then turn the book upside down and
analyze as many of the recto sides as possible in the allotted time.
The beam will be carefully aimed each time at a spot where there's
only ink on one side of the leaf. (In the data, they'll use the bookman's convention of giving the same page number to each two-
sided leaf, so the first leaf will be referred to as "1, recto and verso,"
instead of as "pages 1 and 2.")

When the first leaf is in place, Cahill signals for the testing to
begin. Every leaf takes a few minutes, and when one is complete,
the gentle hug of the felt pad arms is loosened to present a new
page. Cahill carefully moves each one that's completed out of the
way and positions the next one on his equipment, always mindful
of the clock. He also keeps a vigilant eye on the dosimeters that
measure radiation. The process will be safe as long as the settings
are correct, but if they are not, the beam is "utterly mortal if you
get hit by it," he says.

After four hours, the crew hands off to a new shift of technicians. It's not economical to start and stop the machine, so three shifts will work around the clock in four-hour blocks until the work is done or time runs out. Rita watches with fascination as the process settles into a gentle routine, and the researchers begin to talk to the Bible. "Let me turn you over," they murmur under their breaths, telling each other, "be careful now." The positioning isn't always easy. Number 45, Rita observes, is like a cat that "seeks the most comfortable position and resists change or being moved." The team decides that this Bible is a "she" and begin to refer to it as "HER."[10]

The upstairs computers instantly and continuously plot out the chemical analysis PIXE is producing in real time. High concentrations of any element appear as tall peaks on the graph paper spewing out of the printer. By comparing an area of the page with ink on it to an area without, the researchers can determine what is in the ink on a particular page.[11]

Rounds and rounds of four-hour shifts return reams of data, and when the testing finally has to stop, Ginny Cahill holds a party for the weary team. Rita takes home a gift from the team, a sweatshirt reading, *I survived the Great Gutenberg Run.* Having done its duty, the book is soon back in the Treasure Room. But for Cahill and Schwab, the work has just begun.

◆   ◆   ◆

To GET AN overview of the PIXE data, Cahill spreads printouts across the lab's concrete floor, page-by-page chemical analyses that his old track-line printer spits out like eight- or twelve-foot-long paper snakes. He and Schwab are looking for the stories the ink can tell, many of them captured in simple graphs that show the relative amounts of copper and lead—those signature ingredients of Gutenberg's formula—on each page. A change in copper/lead ratio indicates a change in the formulation of the ink, something that would likely come with stirring up a new batch. From their earlier study of Gutenberg leaves, they expected that there would be variations, but they're surprised at how many they find. Cahill begins to suspect that Gutenberg must have mixed up a new batch nearly every day. "He seems to have made his ink like a grand-mother makes apple pie," Cahill said, meaning that Gutenberg's measurements seemed more personal than precise.

By studying these ratios, the team can spot which pages have chemically matching ink, and surmise that they were printed at the same time. That gives them an unexpectedly detailed sense of the Bible's production process.

Of special interest are four pages where the copper/lead ratios are notably higher than those immediately surrounding them. They dub these "Pole Star" pages, all printed from a single, distinctive

Cahill and Faulders study the findings from the cyclotron tests. The analysis allowed researchers Cahill and Schwab to determine the components of the distinctive ink Gutenberg used for the Bible. Their pioneering discoveries represent a leap forward in Gutenberg scholarship and have generated a new field of forensic investigation into the history of the book.

batch of ink on the same day and used nowhere else. The Pole Stars aren't sequential—they fall on widely separated pages (verso pages 74, 114, 201, and 273). Schwab's guess is that each specially inked page marked the beginning of a different section of the Bible being run at the same time as the others. "These unique pages alone," he writes later, "would suggest that in Gutenberg's printing shop at least four sequences of volume 1 of the Bible were being printed concurrently."[12]

The evidence of that deepens when they spot another cluster of pages with an unusually high copper/lead ratio in the ink. They call these the "Tower" pages, and look to see where they fall in comparison with the Pole Stars. The distance between the Pole Stars and their nearest Towers is consistent—either sixty or sixty-one pages—and within each of those sixty-page units, the same sequence of copper/lead ratios largely repeats, leaf by leaf.[13]

Schwab is eager to see how their findings mesh with the work of Gutenberg scholar Paul Schwenke, who closely studied variations in the printing and paper of the Bibles and in 1923 published one of the most authoritative descriptions of how, when, and in what order sections were probably printed.[14] There, they've got a match. Pole Star/Tower data from PIXE almost perfectly lines up with what Schwenke detailed, and the new data allows them to correct and elaborate on his theories as well. (Schwenke believed, for example, that the three quires containing the Psalms were printed one after another, but the ink formulations show that two of them were printed concurrently.)[15]

These are breakthrough findings. As Schwab and company continue to mine the PIXE data, the ink evidence proves to be an astoundingly accurate means of tracking the order of printing. It allows them to see when accidents or delays probably occurred and how they were rectified (with replaced or reprinted pages, for example). They can also detect changes that likely resulted from a new organization or distribution of the work in the shop. The PIXE team is even able to infer when Gutenberg's workers on one press unit fell behind in their output and subsequently caught up with the others.[16]

The great American scholar of incunabula, Paul Needham, viewing the new page-by-page, day-by-day ink evidence, combined with Schwenke's work and his own in-depth studies of the watermarks, typography, and compositional evidence in Gutenberg's Bibles, is moved to write: "One can almost hear, across the centuries, the faintly echoing creak of the press as inked types were pushed into paper."[17]

Gutenberg's workshop seems to have been far more sophisticated than many had imagined. Since the compositors were working on widely separated pages, they would have to know where each page started, even though hundreds of pages in between had not been printed. That intricate organization was echoed in how the compositors working on the project were assigned. Schwab will be able to piece together the complete process when the PIXE team later studies two complete B42s and analyzes the pages of the entire Bible, adding their profiles, and New Testament readings, to the Old Testament data from the Doheny Gutenberg Bible.

"We are able to confirm beyond any doubt that the Bible was ultimately produced in six compositional units being composed and printed concurrently," Schwab writes in one journal.[18] The books of

Numbers, 2 Chronicles, Isaiah, Judges, Esther, and Matthew—five from the Old Testament and one from the New—show the same sequence of copper/lead ratios, for example, suggesting that they comprised one of the "compositional units" that then had to be pieced together in proper page order in order to create a Bible, first page to last.

Schwab adamantly insists, however, that this did not mean there were six presses. Two or three presses could have handled the actual printing.

After much analysis, he is able to devise a flow chart showing how Gutenberg manufactured his Bibles. "Our ink data demonstrated in minute detail Gutenberg's genius for organization," he says. "In his way, Gutenberg was a sort of fifteenth-century Henry Ford, organizing an early form of mass production using interchangeable parts. This, of course, prefigured the characteristic manufacturing patterns of the Industrial Revolution, which was itself made possible by the invention of printing."

Thanks to PIXE, and the in-depth work that began with Number

Rare-book scholar Richard N. Schwab poses with Rita S. Faulders as she delicately cradles the Gutenberg Bible during the historic encounter with the cyclotron.

45, he says, "We've pretty much cracked the code of the day-to-day or page-by-page organization of the Bible."

◆ ◆ ◆

PHYSICIST TOM CAHILL comes away from testing impressed, perhaps more than anything, by Gutenberg's ink. Though his work has identified at least some of the primary elements that go into making the Bible's letters so glossy and enduringly black, it can't deliver a recipe for reproducing them. A chemist in Cahill's group works out a possible formula by guessing at the compounds Gutenberg used, and Adrian Wilson, the book designer, reproduces it successfully on his San Francisco press. But the ink remains a mystery. "My theory is that Gutenberg's greatest discovery was not the movable type. The type had been known already," Cahill tells reporters years later. "It was the ink. It would stick to metal type. I think when he left the project, he took the ink secret with him."[19]

◆ ◆ ◆

NUMBER 45'S ENCOUNTER with the cyclotron yields one more discovery. A previously undetected leaf of Estelle's Bible, 134, had been cut out and replaced, likely in the print shop.

Schwab zeros in on leaf 134 because the PIXE data shows that its ink has a copper/lead ratio that appears on no other page of Number 45. It should have been similar to that of leaf 133 because the two leaves fall on the innermost sheet of a quire. They are conjugate, meaning that they are—or should have been—two halves of a folded sheet of paper, divided by the fold. But the PIXE readings show that not only is the ink unusual, but also the paper of leaf 134 doesn't match the chemical composition of leaf 133, or any of the four common paper stocks used for the Bible.

Schwab travels to Camarillo and sits with Rita at the Treasure Room table to look closely at Number 45's replacement page. On close examination, they can see that, indeed, leaves 133 and 134 aren't directly connected to each other. They are, instead, separately attached to opposite sides of a hinge of paper known as a "conjugate pair of stubs."[20]

The substitute leaf differs in numerous ways from its immediate neighbors. Its ink has practically no lead, and Schwab and Rita can see immediately that it is much duller than that on the other pages, giving its type none of the glossiness of that printed with Gutenberg's signature recipe. No one had known precisely what gives the text its sheen, but now it seems likely that lead is a key factor. The pinholes at the edges of the page, used for alignment

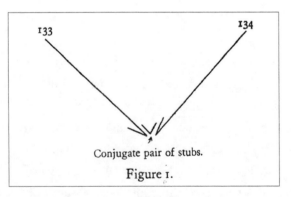

Conjugate pair of stubs.

Figure 1.

A "conjugate pair of stubs," essentially a paper hinge, allowed the Bible's printers to tip a substitute page 134, printed later with different ink, into the book.

on the press, are different from those on surrounding pages, too—there are six instead of ten, and the holes are larger, cruder, and closer together than elsewhere in the book.

When Schwab has a chance later to compare the text on leaf 134 with that on the same leaf in other Bibles, he gets a rare look at how much leeway the compositors had on spelling, spacing, type combinations, abbreviations, and the arrangement of words, as long as the type fit. The shop had set the type once for the first print run, and reset it, with slight variations, when it needed more copies midway as demand increased, then had to do it all over again on the fly for the replacement page. As he studies the replacement and compares it to other versions of the page, he notes thirty-eight places where its type differs from the first setting, sixty-nine instances where it differs from the second, and seventy-three spots where the spelling, spacing, or arrangement of words doesn't match either one. The typesetter of the replacement page sometimes spells the name Benjamin with an *I*—*Beniamin*—as the compositor of the second setting did, and sometimes spells it with a *Y*—*Benyamin*—as did the compositor of the first setting.[21] Both spellings were apparently acceptable in the workshop's makeshift solution.

The typesetter "was not at all slavishly tied down to the first printing . . . but followed his own inclination and habits of operation when he wished to," Schwab writes.[22] In Gutenberg's print shop, making up a page of type was as much an art as a science.

◆ ◆ ◆

RICHARD SCHWAB CONSIDERS his work with the cyclotron data to be the highlight of his career as a historian, opening the way for paradigm-shifting examinations of Gutenberg's work and the history of printing using technology far more discerning than the human eye. He and the PIXE team still marvel at the serendipitous chain of factors that propelled their pivotal project—Schwab's unlikely link to Thomas Cahill through Ginny Cahill, his access to the Gutenberg volume through Rita, and the willingness of all the parties to abandon their habitual trajectories and take the risk of putting a hallmark of the humanities on a collision course with atomic physics.

"It was a great deal of fun being an historian and encouraged to use a cyclotron by a nuclear physicist who was interested in history and had an amazing instrument at his disposal," Schwab said.

Cahill is especially struck by the way "everyone put their lives and their careers on the line" to discover new revelations about Gutenberg's ink and production schema.

Both men gain worldwide fame for their techniques, and the PIXE findings that flow from Number 45's encounter with the cyclotron open a new era of science-based research in the understanding of antiquities. Cahill's refurbished atom smasher goes on to scrutinize an ancient Greek manuscript, a sixteenth-century samurai sword, a priceless oil painting by Renoir, and a meteorite from deep space.[23] Perhaps the most well-known item of the ancient world to divulge its secrets to the proton beam is a group of seven fragments from the Dead Sea Scrolls.[24] The *New York Times* notes: "Few instruments of science have continued to make dazzling discoveries over so a long period as the cyclotron used to decipher Johann Gutenberg's printing techniques."[25]

From the moment Number 45 left the lab, Schwab hoped to bring it back to finish testing the recto sides they'd had to skip when time ran out. He began angling for a second round almost right away, writing Rita in November of 1983 to say:

"I am looking forward to a kind of model of bibliographic description of the Gutenberg bible that the two of us will produce, which will include a unique feature, the complete chemical bibliographic description of every page of it. How does that strike you? It would involve the challenge, fun, and collaboration of another 'Fishing Expedition,' because it is now evident that the key to several of the important specific questions of the day-to-day production in Gutenberg's shop lies in having analysis of *all* the rectos. The sections where we have the Copper/Lead ratios for both the rectos and the verso show that vital information is found on *both* sides of each leaf. . . ."

But the return trip is not to be.

It's not that the project lacks money or support. Printer Adrian Wilson sets aside $15,000 from his MacArthur grant to fund additional cyclotron sessions. Rita is enthusiastic, and the Reverend Monsignor Eugene Frilot, who witnessed PIXE in the lab, has become a passionate advocate. "We came here for the sake of knowledge and truth," he says at the time. "You wouldn't have science, you wouldn't have had a man on the moon without the invention by Gutenberg. This is a study to determine some historical questions about the invention of printing. It opens up a whole world of knowledge."[26]

But neither he nor the rest of the participants in the Great Gutenberg Run can stop the sequence of events that will ultimately eclipse the study and leave hidden the worlds it hopes to decode. Number 45 is about to meet a force as powerful and disruptive, in its way, as anything in Tom Cahill's cyclotron bunker: the mercurial politics of the Catholic Church.

PART III

THE ASIAN CENTURY

CHAPTER NINE

The Unexpected Betrayal

THE FLOOD OF GLOBAL interest in Number 45 and the PIXE project arrives at a vulnerable moment for Estelle's Bible and the
Doheny Library at St. John's Seminary. The autumn of 1983 is not
just the season the book meets the proton beam. October 30 also
is the silver anniversary of Estelle's death—a date that triggers a
shift in the terms of her bequest. Until now, her legacy has been
protected by a provision that no parts of her gift be sold, but time
is about to snip the legal strings that bind the library's holdings
together—and at the Archdiocese of Los Angeles, an intricate
strategy is quietly set in motion to pull the collection apart.

As Rita Faulders looks back,[1] it's clear that as early as 1981
groundwork is being laid for a sale that would dissolve the Doheny
holdings and send Number 45 to its next owner. The first hint is
the appearance of an unidentified man, who comes to the library
to photograph the two huge Charles Russell murals hanging in

the museum's Western Room. He visits again in 1981 and 1982, testing film and exposures to try to get prints that perfectly match the colors in the paintings that Edward Doheny commissioned to tell the story of the American West. Guiding him is Monsignor Frilot, who is supervising the project under the direction of a cleric in the chancery office of the Archdiocese of Los Angeles.

At last the photos are approved, and a pair of finished prints, each twenty feet long and three feet high, are mounted on five eight-foot sheets of Styrofoam and delivered to the library. The cost for printing, mounting, and laminating alone is close to $15,000—but no one specifies what the replicas will be used for. The pricey posters disappear into a closet.

Two years later, in 1984, a London broker representing the J. Paul Getty Museum library becomes a frequent guest of Monsignor Frilot. The Getty had recently established a new department of illuminated manuscripts with an en bloc purchase of 144 medieval and Renaissance books and leaves, and in preparation for the opening, the department's head had come to Camarillo to study Estelle's books. Now, the Getty's dealer brings Frilot a wish list of twenty-five items from the library—"the choicest of the choice,"[2] as Rita emphasizes to the monsignor—and makes a cash offer. A crew of four from the museum spends a day photographing those items, plus a host of others, and the monsignor laughingly tells Rita that the Getty's broker had told him to keep the "charming dragon lady" out of the way.

No sales are finalized, but the monsignor's bosses are clearly testing the waters to figure out how much the books might bring in. Next comes a prominent New York dealer who arrives after hours with the director of a local museum and the two men's wives. With the monsignor's blessing to look at "anything they wanted to see," they "poked into every corner," Rita notes.[3] Her alarm is rising. She tells the prelate that such visits are "unprofessional and detrimental to the Seminary's best interests. . . . One does not let prospective buyers go through the entire house to pick and choose what they want to buy," she says, especially not without a master plan for what will stay and what will go. She urges him to articulate his long-range vision for the collection instead of letting potential bidders roam at will and selling items piecemeal, but Frilot is not inclined to listen.

As these shopping expeditions mount, there are no consultations with the library's trustees, the people representing Estelle's interests and intent. But in the world of institutions, dealers, and collectors, Rita recalls, "the news was out, and it spread like wildfire."

In early 1985, someone claiming to represent what he called the Cowboy Hall of Fame in Oklahoma City comes prospecting. A tall man in cowboy boots and hat, he breaks the ice for the church, brokering the first sale from the Doheny Library. Seminary officials secretly agree to part with artworks by Charles Russell and Frederic Remington in exchange for $6 million.[4] The deal can only be so secret, though. It's impossible for students to miss the departure of *History of the West I* and *II*, the two panoramic Charles Russell paintings whose photo replicas have long been standing ready for this moment. A large truck draws up to the library, and workers pack the Russell originals for removal. But when the panels prove to be too long to carry down the library's curved stairwell, workmen have to build a scaffold outside a window on the second-floor hall and ease them out through a narrow grillwork, then lower them to the ground with heavy ropes.

Students ask Faulders what's going on, but she has been told not to answer questions. The Russells, she has learned, aren't going to the Cowboy Hall of Fame at all—and the broker is not what he had seemed. Other dealers had alerted Rita that the man was no longer connected with the museum, and a *National Geographic* editor had called her to be sure the seminary had heard that the charming man in the cowboy hat was planning to buy the paintings, then resell to a private client. But none of this had been enough to persuade the monsignor to reconsider. The murals head to the private collection of an Oklahoma natural gas executive, and Rita rushes to have the copies hung. They glare too much, though, and never quite line up, so they're taken away, too, and workers bring in two lesser artworks to fill the space. Wherever the $6 million goes, it's not to the seminary.[5]

The trustees of the library get no warning of the covert dealings. Board members receive a short note informing them only after one of them hears of the transaction and calls Monsignor Frilot to complain. (Rita overhears the monsignor's end of the conversation, part of which goes, "Didn't we tell you?")[6] The board responds to the news with shock and anger. The sale may have been legal, but it clearly violated the spirit of Estelle's bequest. She had commissioned and donated a Wallace Neff building to honor her husband with a showcase for his art collection and her books. It doesn't seem likely that she intended for the recipients to sell off the contents.

Further evidence is the endowment Estelle Doheny had provided to keep up the library in perpetuity, with funds to cover care, preservation, maintenance, repair, security, administration, taxes, and insurance for the books and building, as well as the salary of the book collection's curator. Payments have been made routinely for decades, but when the insurance on the book collection comes due soon after *History of the West* is trucked away, the affronted trustees refuse to pay the $6,000 bill. "It belongs to you now," trust secretary Arthur E. Thunell tells the seminary.

The response reflects an effect of the sale that is vastly more far-reaching than the disappearance of art from the library walls. Estelle had tried to ensure that her collection would be kept together by stipulating that the trust fund for the library would terminate if anything were sold before she had been dead twenty-five years. But the Western art sale is completed in April, six months shy of the twenty-five-year mark, irrevocably breaking the trust and ending its support.[7] Whether by accident or wily calculation, the church is buttressing its case for selling Estelle's collections: now it can argue that they are just too expensive for the seminary to maintain.

As 1985 progresses, the church's push to trade the library's books and artwork for cash intensifies. After Roger Mahony, a Los Angeles bishop, is elevated to archbishop, he initiates a reorganization of the seminary's leadership to address the dilemma that's building across the church: producing enough priests to replenish the thinning ranks. The man he puts in charge of the changes at St. John's is Rector Charles Miller, a stocky man in his late fifties whose principal job has been teaching aspiring priests how to perform church ceremonies. Miller favors an ascetic approach to worship and Catholic education, and finds the seminary's chapel complex overweening, its religious murals and hand-painted decorations unseemly. He pushes to have the grand spaces painted a simple white that will cover the art, an ultimately unsuccessful effort that Rita Faulders says "would have been a desecration, like painting over the Mona Lisa."

Rector Miller can't see the point of housing a collection of rare books and art at the seminary. Such things have no place in the education of priests, he tells Rita. Beyond that, he says, there's no need for the church to be involved in preserving the kind of history and art in Estelle's books—secular institutions, he argues, can do it better.

Archbishop Mahony's predecessor, the Most Reverend J. Francis McIntyre, had assessed the library in spiritual terms, telling a meeting of the Zamorano Club held in the Treasure Room that the worth of the books "is far greater than their rarity." What they represent in terms of character and history, he said, lifts the reader "so far above the material concepts of life that easily do we soar into the heights where values depart from the language of compensation and enter into the strata of the non-compensatable."[8]

But under Mahony and Miller, "compensation" is the new lingua franca. Miller, who is running St. John's by the end of 1985, installs a like-minded board of directors and a library committee that quietly endorses cashing out Estelle's gift. Leading the group is Gerald Lynch, a retired Ford Motor Company and aerospace executive, who argues for selling the library's "inert assets"—or, put another way, its raison d'être—at auction. The idea that a collection might have its own integrity, or a value to the larger community that transcends money, doesn't seem to enter the discussion.

Rita braces for a full-on questioning of the need for the library and prepares a report for Miller that quantifies visits by scholars and requests for information, tours, special exhibits, and projects like PIXE. She also tries to make a "bread and roses" case, including an article from a Catholic lay publication that quotes San Francisco Archbishop John Quinn saying, "Art represents the striving of human beings for the divine. . . . The church uses art to lift our gaze toward God, to exalt what is most noble in human beings."[9]

Miller doesn't respond, but Rita persists, asking him for permission to solicit endorsements of the collection from distinguished scholars familiar with its holdings. Miller says he will allow it, as long as she simply asks for endorsements and doesn't mention plans for a sale. But she doesn't need to. Richard Schwab tells Faulders that he is horrified by what her request implies. "All I can think of is the sadness of the real loss to the best of things that still remain on earth," he says.[10] Others write warm letters about what the collection has meant to them, and how it has advanced their research. To Faulders's knowledge, the only St. John's faculty member to protest the idea of a sale is Father Douglas Slauson, who sends a letter directly to Mahony decrying the great loss to scholarship.

None of this slows the steady march toward an auction. Lynch, the ex–Ford man heading the library board, comes by Rita's office twice on the same mid-June day in 1986, first with two executives from Christie's, then with two from Sotheby's. He lays out the rules of engagement: Each company will have its own week in the library during a school holiday to assess, catalog, photograph, and appraise the collection—8,500 books, 3,500 manuscripts, and several hundred art objects. Then each will submit a proposal outlining its plans for producing an auction that will maximize revenue to the church.

Rita dutifully assists the teams that sweep in, paying attention to the comings and goings in the room, and making notes in her diary. "One day when John Plummer, Prof. Emeritus from Princeton and head of rare books at the Morgan Library, was in the Library working as a consultant for Christie's, Mr. Lynch came by to see how things were going," she writes. "Mr. Plummer was sitting at the big table examining one of the early printed books. Mr. Lynch looked down and asked, 'Who would want to buy an old book like that.' The room became very quiet. . . . Plummer hesitated, not knowing if it was a serious question or a joke.

"He judged correctly," she comments, "and carefully explained that many people and institutions would love to possess that very book, that he had coveted a copy for the Morgan Library but that none was ever available because of its rarity."[11]

The board meets in early September, after the church has selected Christie's, to decide formally whether to hold the auction, and Rita is asked to speak in favor of keeping the collection. But she knows the invitation is just pro forma. At the end of the month, someone takes down the wooden sign that directs people to the library. Finally, two days before Christmas, she receives a memo telling her the Doheny Collection will be closing on February 15, 1987.

By the time news of the sale leaks to the press at the end of February, the library offices have been emptied.

◆ ◆ ◆

ARCHBISHOP ROGER MAHONY steps in front of the cameras at a widely attended morning news conference on March 3 to announce that the rare-book collection and artworks will be sold at a series of auctions over the next two years. Christie's has estimated that Number 45 and its shelf mates will bring in more than $20 million, which Mahony says will be used as an endowment for recruiting and training new priests. The need is dire, he says. Each of the past twelve years, only about ten priests were ordained in the archdiocese, and the previous year the number had fallen to six.[12]

The case for the sale is spelled out in a slick twelve-page brochure with a tissue overlay that's printed with a replica of Estelle's bookplate. "Will you do all in your power to help realize the many new directions which our Archdiocese must take in being true to the spirit of the Gospel in our day?" reads the cover. The copy and photos inside are careful to describe the library without ever evoking the astonishing richness inside Estelle's books. An unidentified photo showing a corner of a Gutenberg page stands in for the collection—because even a small sampling of the saints and angels on the Treasure Room shelves would create a hunger for them.[13]

Though Mahony describes the collection as predominantly secular, it contains some of the finest examples of the Bible anywhere, not just Number 45 but also a rare Complutensian Polyglot Bible, the first complete Bible in multiple languages to appear in print, as well as fine examples of the Aldine Greek, the Coverdale, and the King James editions, among hundreds of others.[14] Kevin Starr, the great California historian, had described the collection as one of the finest in Roman Catholic Church bibliographical treasures ever assembled in the region, brimming with "riches of a thousand years of European monasticism . . . culled from the libraries of cardinals and bishops."[15]

But the brochure ignores such assessments and makes the case Rita has been hearing for months: "The rare books and works of art . . . are contributing very little to priestly formation," and they're expensive to keep. "In order to maintain the Collection properly, we have determined, based on expenses for comparable institutions, that the cost would be close to $300,000 per year, which translates to . . . $822 per day." (However, records indicate that the endowment would have covered that, and more.) A chart compares that sum to the income that might be generated from $20 million in auction proceeds: up to $38,461.54 per week at a 10 percent rate of return.

Mrs. Doheny never intended for the collection to be a "permanent tribute to herself," the brochure argues—she would have wanted whatever the church thought best. And the church thinks it's time to sell.

As press coverage ramps up, the church hears myriad arguments for keeping the collection from stunned scholars, historians, and bibliophiles. Some have already tried to dissuade church officials from proceeding, to no avail. Martin Ridge, chief of research at the Huntington Library, insists that the library is a Southern California treasure that should not be broken up: "You cannot place a monetary value on the collection," he tells the *Los Angeles Times*. "The whole is enormously more valuable than the parts. . . . In Southern California we're so new that anything we have is so precious and important to us."[16]

One local book collector tells the *Times* that he thinks people in the community would have been willing to donate enough money to create Mahony's $20 million fund without selling the books. "I personally would have contributed," he says.[17] Another writes the paper to denounce the decision to "loot" the collection as appalling and unforgivable. "Why must ignorance always prevail?" he asks. "Shall we look back at this hypocrisy and be amazed at the stupidity and lack of foresight on the part of the current archdiocese and its supporters? Or shall we stop it? . . . . Who passed this torch of destruction and anti-gnosis on to the archbishop and his fellow executioners?"[18]

Mahony acknowledges the difficult trade-off between "culture and need" but says that the cost of training priests has risen from less than $10,000 per year to almost six figures. The whole affair, as he puts it in the brochure, requires a "redeployment" of church assets.[19]

A skeptical Nicolas Barker, keeper of rare books at the British Museum, calls the sale "another sad example of the church's—any church's—all too frequent failure to understand or respect what books have done or can do for Christianity." He quips that Mahony's brochure "resembled a dubious company flotation" and asks one of the most pertinent questions of the day: "Will cash buy priests?"[20]

One aspect of the brochure alarms Rita and the collection's defenders. It's the way the archdiocese interprets the "twenty-five years" clause of Estelle's bequest as defining her intent to make her library an "unrestricted gift" once those years had passed. That language, which was modeled on wording in J. P. Morgan's bequest, was intended to keep the collection "as she established it, truly reflective of her interests" for twenty-five years, before changes were made, Rita says.

Lucille Miller reported in her oral history that Estelle liked J. P. Morgan's template and believed that changes after a quarter century would simply reflect a curator's need to update reference books or replace books in the collection with better copies if they became available. If that was good enough for J. P. Morgan, Estelle reasoned, it was good enough for her "small library." But the language was her undoing, Rita says, and "the very phrase that she thought would ensure permanence and growth was used to provide a legal loophole for selling her rare books. It was a twisting of truth and a complete abnegation of her gifts."

Estelle's intention was never in doubt, Rita believes, and a visitors' brochure long handed out at the library recounts an official history that suggests she's right: "In 1939 when Archbishop Cantwell asked if Mrs. Doheny would like to build a library for the newly founded Seminary," it reads, "she welcomed the opportunity to honor her beloved husband, as well as to establish a place for her burgeoning collection of books and art objects, and to carry on the tradition of her church as the preserver of Western civilization by making the Seminary the repository for so many fine manuscripts and printing treasures."[21]

◆ ◆ ◆

IN HINDSIGHT, PERHAPS Estelle Doheny's greatest mistake was her decision not to donate the collection to a university. Great East Coast schools like Harvard and Yale had a jump-start of nearly two centuries over public and private universities in the West, and their success was fueled by world-class libraries. It would have made sense to give her collection maximum visibility, security, and importance at a prominent local institution—and in fact, that was likely her plan. It had long seemed almost inevitable that Estelle's books would go to the University of Southern California, where the Doheny family had already built the Edward L. Doheny Jr. Memorial Library in 1932. But the bumbling of an administrator, USC president Rufus B. von KleinSmid, soured the plan.

One of Estelle's gifts to USC had been the book collection of California historian J. Gregg Layne, which she had stipulated should be housed at the Doheny Memorial Library. But Von Klein-Smid, oblivious or unconcerned, had the Layne collection removed from the library and integrated into the university's main collection, using the cleared space to expand his own office suite. Estelle was so furious when she learned of the move that "USC ceased to be the primary object of her largess," Kevin Starr wrote. "Rarely has a blundering president, ambitious for better office space, cost an institution more in probable future dollars than Von KleinSmid cost USC by his high-handed treatment of the Doheny bequest."

The current USC librarian, Charles R. Ritcheson, tells the *Los Angeles Times* after the sale is announced that he hopes at least some substantial portion of Estelle's collection might be kept intact and remain in Southern California, perhaps going to a major research library. "Dispersal of this collection is a very sad affair in terms of scholarship," he says.[22]

Mahony and company discuss the auction with the press in ways that sometimes display a casual, and hazy, familiarity with what they're getting rid of. Rita hears the archbishop tell an interviewer that an autographed copy of a Mark Twain book "will possibly bring $10." (She notes that the least expensive Clemens item is a postcard with an estimated price of $300.) Asked if the printer of the Gutenberg Bible was a Catholic, Mahony says, perhaps jokingly, "No, he was Lutheran."[23] The appalled curator, not one to make light of history, corrects the facts in her diary: "The date for

Gutenberg's Bible is pegged at 1456. Martin Luther was born in 1483. I think it is safe to say that Gutenberg's Bible was Catholic."

Seminary Rector Miller, who agitated for the sale, sums up the diocese's prevailing mind-set, telling seminarians that their recently revised New American Bibles are "intrinsically more valuable" than the Gutenberg.[24]

There's no going back. The library receives its final public visitors on Friday, March 13, 1987. William Doheny Jr., Ned's grandson,

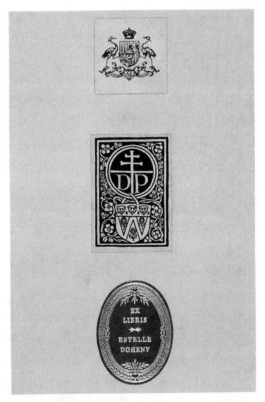

The three bookplates of the known modern owners of the Gutenberg Bible grace the rare book's inside cover.

comes with his wife and their two young sons to say good-bye—
but the rarest of the rare books, including Number 45, have already
been packed.[25]

♦ ♦ ♦

THERE WILL BE six auctions to dispose of the Estelle Doheny Collection. The first, which will feature Number 45 and Estelle's
fifteenth-century books, is set for October 22, 1987, and Stephen S.
Lash, Christie's effusive executive vice president, tells the Associ-
ated Press that the Doheny Collection will be "the largest single
assemblage of books in terms of value and volume ever to have
come on the market."

The moment seems opportune. Bolstered by a robust economy
in the 1980s, aggressive collectors have flooded the field. The demand is so strong that scholars are calling it a new golden age in
book collecting, with sales records demolished in auction after auction. But "in a way," says Lash, "we feel that all of these other sales
have been dress rehearsals, if you will, for the sale of the Doheny
Collection."[26]

Old-timers liken the sale to the colossal 1911 dispersal of the Robert Hoe collection, where railroad tycoon Henry Huntington purchased many of his most notable volumes, including the Gutenberg
that set Estelle on a quest for her own. John Fleming,[27] a well-known
New York dealer who had appraised Estelle's collection in the 1970s
with his mentor, A. S. W. Rosenbach, declares that the auction will
be "the greatest book and manuscript sale of the last half century."[28] Number 45 alone, he says, should bring at least $2 million.

It takes a small army of specialized professionals to catalog and prepare the books for auction. Most of the collection will be making a cross-country trip from Camarillo to New York City or London, the sites of all but one of the sales. The Christie's crew, which includes Stephen Massey, then head of the book department, and his colleague Hillary Holland, starts work on Monday, March 9. They set up folding tables in the two book rooms, and Rita watches as the library quickly comes apart "by implosion."[29] The company's strategy, she notes, is "to begin the auctions with a 'big bang'" in the fall and winter—first the incunabula, then a London sale of Estelle's gemlike collection of illuminated manuscripts in December—and those are the packers' priority.

Workers roll the custom cabinet holding Number 45 out of the vault and into the Treasure Room, where Rita unlocks the case with her small key. Massey removes the heavy book and slides it into its maroon-colored padded leather sleeve. It's checked off the accession list, tagged, numbered, and labeled with its auction date. The Bible is followed by a stream of books from the vault and shelves that continues for four days. Guillaume Durand's *Rationale divinorum officiorum* from 1459, Saint Jerome's *Epistolare* from 1470, and a 1470 copy of Saint Thomas's *Summa Theologica* are lined up on the table, then first editions of Mark Twain's *Adventures of Huckleberry Finn* and Walt Whitman's *Leaves of Grass*. Each precious volume is processed, swaddled in tissue and Bubble Wrap, and wrapped in white paper closed with masking tape, then put into a cardboard box. A mountain of boxes grows under the library balcony.

On the twelfth of March, forty-two cartons of books valued at $11.8 million—the titles to be sold first—are double-checked and set aside, and twelve days later, shipping crews arrive to build twenty-one wooden crates and pack the boxes inside. Massey uses a black marker to label the box containing the Gutenberg Bible. It's now A-31/1, BOX 21. Monsignor Francis J. Weber, the author and archivist of the archdiocese, grabs the marker to write Johannes good-bye, and hands it to Rita. She hesitates, then draws a broken heart and adds her initials.

She stands beneath the rococo arch of the library, watching in disbelief as the rest of the boxes are labeled and hauled to the front brick sidewalk of the Wallace Neff building, where packers crate them up and load them onto the semitrailer truck. She and Weber stand forlornly at the curb as the truck pulls away at 1:19. At a special loading dock at the Los Angeles International Airport, the crates go onto a TWA jet in a single, wheeled fiberglass fire- and waterproof container. They fly through the night and arrive in New York at six a.m. By midday, Massey calls the archdiocese to inform Monsignor Weber that all the books, including Number 45, are safe and sound.

A few days later, though, it appears that one book has gone missing. Rita Faulders runs to the vault to see if it's been left behind, and indeed, *Le Morte d'Arthur*, illustrated by William Morris, is sitting alone in its regular spot on the shelf.[30] The parties breathe a sigh of relief, and the sumptuous Morris volume is packed and shipped to New York.

Interest in the items on offer is so high that executives at Christie's decide to send the auction's stars on a first-class excursion. The auction preview is like a concert tour, playing to throngs in Tokyo, Munich, and London before a final display in New York. Beyond Number 45, there's a stunning array of marquee items: a broadside folio once owned by fifteenth-century Pope Alexander VI,[31] a unique printing of the Bull of Demarcation, which separated the New World into Spanish and Portuguese territories, Giovanni Boccaccio's *The Fall of Princes* from 1494,[32] and a copy of the works of Aristotle in Greek printed by Aldus Manutius. Along for the tour are some of Estelle's exceedingly rare Fust and Schöffer Bibles, works of Geoffrey Chaucer printed by William Morris's Kelmscott Press, and William Blake's *Songs of Innocence.*

A signed manuscript essay by Mark Twain on Gutenberg and the art of printing is a particularly apt companion for Estelle's Bible. Written in 1900 to museum officials to commemorate the opening of the Gutenberg Museum in Mainz, it reads, in part:

> *Gutenberg's achievement created a new and wonderful earth, but at the same time also a new hell. During the past 500 years Gutenberg's invention has supplied both earth and hell with new occurrences, new wonders and new phases.*
>
> *It found truth astir on earth and gave it wings; but untruth also was abroad, and it was supplied with a double pair of wings.*
>
> *What the world is to-day, good and bad, it owes to Gutenberg. Everything can be traced to this source, but we are bound to bring him homage, for what he said in dreams to the angered angel has been literally fulfilled, for the bad that his colossal invention has brought about is overshadowed a thousand times by the good with which mankind has been favored.*[33]

Christie's creates an eight-volume catalog for the auctions that will feature these items and all the rest. It's a full-color opus bound in red leather and weighing more than twenty pounds. Volume 1, which encompasses the initial "big bang" sale, is the most opulent, with twenty-three pages devoted to Number 45, its provenance, and its place among the world's remaining Gutenbergs. A foldout leaf and six additional color reproductions show the Bible's distinctive type and the spidery touches of one of the book's illuminators, and one page shows the grayed ink of the replacement leaf Richard Schwab discovered. Through the catalog's next three hundred pages, it's possible to see church history, and the history of printing and illustration, unfolding as if in a highlight reel.

Included in the lot are almost a dozen examples from the earliest Mainz presses, Bibles and religious texts, with six printed on vellum. There are copies of Cicero's *De officiis*, dated 1466; and Guillaume Durand's *Rationale*, from 1459; and the 1470 Saint Jerome *Epistolare*, with its brilliant illumination, considered one of Peter Schöffer's most ambitious publications. The showstopper, in terms of visual impact, is Lot 73, the *Biblia pauperum* blockbook, a slim, forty-leaf Dutch work from the late 1400s whose distinctive panels, as they sprawl over both sides of a foldout leaf and spill onto an additional page (plus the frontispiece), look like nothing so much as a fifteenth-century graphic novel of the Bible. Eve confronts a snake stretched to her height in the opening panel, and the story rolls on from there, filled with colorful scenes in distinctive oranges, yellows, and greens. The book was a later addition to Estelle's collection, bought in 1951 for $30,000. Its price is estimated to be between $400,000 and half a million dollars.

The descriptive text through all the volumes of the catalog is direct and scholarly, as though the auction house knows well that these works can speak for themselves, without the customary hyperbole. Following the provenance notes page by page, it's possible to see exactly how Estelle Doheny achieved her goal of amassing books and objects of the highest quality—careful purchase by careful purchase, over decades.

◆ ◆ ◆

THEN, THERE'S AN unplanned, world-shaking drumroll. Just three days before the first auction, on October 19, 1987, the Dow Jones Industrial Average tumbles 22.6 percent, and billions of dollars are lost in a global financial panic. Nerves are on edge so soon after Black Monday, still "the sharpest market downturn in the U.S. since the Great Depression,"[34] but when the double doors of the Christie's auction room open at 6:30 p.m. on October 22, more than six hundred people, including Rita Faulders, Monsignor Weber, and many of the premier dealers and collectors in the world, crowd inside.

At seven p.m., Christie's president, Christopher Burge, steps to the lectern to say, "I am pleased to offer Lot 1, the Gutenberg Bible," opening the bidding at $700,000. The crowd collectively leans forward to take in the action as the price rises in seconds to $1 million, then to $1.3 million from an overseas bidder. Millions blur by as an intense duel develops between Japanese publishing conglomerate Maruzen Co. Ltd. and London rare-book dealer Thomas E. Schuster. Eiichi Kobayashi, director of the book and journal division of Maruzen, bids for company officials by phone as Schuster paces nervously near the podium.

The bidding breaks $4 million, and Schuster's face turns stony as he takes the amount to $4.8 million. Kobayashi, acting for Maruzen, whispers another bid over the telephone and pushes the price 10 percent higher. The only sound is silence as Burge calls for a counterbid, one that Schuster can't make, and after a pause the gavel

The auction paddle used by bidders at the historic sale of the Doheny Gutenberg in New York City on October 22, 1987. Intense bidding for the book realized a final price of $5.4 million, making the Gutenberg Bible the most expensive book in the world at the time.

comes down. Maruzen Co. Ltd. of Tokyo is the new owner of Estelle Doheny's Gutenberg Bible. The final price, including Christie's commission, is $5.4 million,[35] making Number 45 the single most expensive book in the world. It is now worth seventy-five times what Estelle had paid for it in 1950.[36]

♦ ♦ ♦

LATER, A DISAPPOINTED Schuster answers reporters' questions. "You don't know if you will ever find another one," he says in a flat voice. He seems stunned that someone could pay a price that topped $5 million, musing, "Perhaps the people on the phone had unlimited money."[37]

In Tokyo, Maruzen's press representative says that the firm had long been looking for the right opportunity to buy a historic book. Shuji Tomita emphasizes that Japanese interest in the Gutenberg Bible centers on its "historic significance rather than its religious nature." The Gutenberg, that great signifier of cultural importance—at least to those who seek it—gives Maruzen a kind of currency that cannot be purchased with advertising.

There are, of course, other books yet to sell. Estelle's vellum copy of Saint Jerome's *Epistolare* goes for $950,000 to London book dealer Quaritch. Estelle had paid just $16,500 for it during a period of depressed prices in 1949. And the block-printed fifteenth-century *Biblia pauperum* with the "Bible comic book" feel is a standout. Quaritch takes it for $2.2 million, more than four times the estimate. In total, the first auction of only the incunabula earns the archdiocese more than $12 million.

The second auction, of medieval and illuminated manuscripts, includes some of Estelle's earliest major purchases, many from Alice Millard and A. S. W. Rosenbach. A tiny sixteenth-century French book of hours that she bought from Millard in 1931 is Lot 160. Lot 174 is a remarkable 1528 book of hours, whose illuminated pages, by an artist now known as the Doheny Master, are shown in five color pages of the catalog. The book sells for £880,000, almost $1.6 million. Elsewhere in the sale are books of hours that once sat in the Dyson Perrins library or were held by the sister of Napoleon. The exquisite collection yields $22 million for the Archdiocese of Los Angeles, far exceeding expectations and recommending rare books and manuscripts as a refuge for capital after the unknowns of Black Monday.

Auction four, of Western Americana, literature, fine printing, and bindings, brings Christie's back to Camarillo in February 1988 and features Estelle's extensive collection of autographed documents and letters, which includes the signatures of all forty US presidents, each of the signers of the Declaration of Independence, and such distinct and disparate figures as California's Father Junipero Serra and French emperor Napoleon Bonaparte. One of the rarest items is a manuscript signed by Georgia representative Button Gwinnett, who died in a duel less than a year after signing the Declaration of Independence. Estelle and A. S. W. Rosenbach had chased the Gwinnett signature for years. Also on the block is Mark Twain's personal copy of *The Adventures of Huckleberry Finn*, dedicated to his wife with the inscription "To Livy L. Clemens with the matured and perfect love of the author." A clutch of letters from Walt Whitman includes a poetic note to his friend naturalist John Burroughs that reads, in part:

"No news particular—I sell a book now & then—No I have not been to any watering place—they are no company for me—the cities magnificent for their complex play & oceans of eager human faces— But the country or sea for me in some sparse place, old barn & farm house—or bleak ice shore nobody around—Meanwhile I get along very well here—Walt." As such pieces scatter—and with them the voices, images, and history of America, and its art and literature— it's easy to wonder if the archdiocese understood what it had.

The final auction, on May 19, 1989, is perhaps the most anticipated among younger collectors. It focuses on what the auctioneers title "William Morris and his Circle," many of the pieces purchased by Mrs. Doheny with the help of Alice Millard. The items—calligraphy, original autographed manuscripts, special bindings, and Kelmscott Press books—are a choice assembly of the artist's work. The hottest item on the auction list is *Das Kapital* by Karl Marx in a fine binding by Thomas James Cobden-Sanderson. Also under the hammer are the works of Geoffrey Chaucer, brilliantly printed by Morris's Kelmscott Press. Experts unrelated to the auction call the Kelmscott Chaucer on vellum the "summit of the private press movement."

An Estelle Doheny collecting milestone—her first $10,000 book—comes on the block in this round. It is Morris's calligraphic masterpiece on vellum, Virgil's *Aeneid*, which Alice Millard had cajoled her into purchasing during the cash-scarce post-Depression period. The work, particularly noteworthy for containing the contributions of a handful of renowned artists, including Graily Hewitt, Louise Powell, Charles Fairfax Murray, and Edward Burne-Jones, fetches $1.23 million.

The "Morris and His Circle" category yields sales of $2.2 million, bringing the grand total to a record-breaking $37.8 million, almost twice what the archdiocese had anticipated. The staggering figure exceeds the final dollar value of Edward Doheny's far-flung Mexican and US oil empire (even when adjusted for inflation). As a collector and investor, Estelle proved to be more than equal to the famed oil tycoon she married.

Estelle's library had never had more visibility than when it was put up for sale, and the great tragedy is that only then—when it was too late to speak up for her vision and mount a powerful defense for preserving it—was it widely apparent how significant her collection had been. Flip through the small encyclopedia of catalogs from the Christie's sale, with masterpiece following masterpiece, and it's undeniable that Estelle Doheny stands with the foremost American book collectors of the century.[38]

◆ ◆ ◆

FOR PEOPLE LIKE Rita Faulders and Richard Schwab, who understood what Estelle had wanted for her books, the sense of sadness and betrayal that remains after the auction is strong. Estelle had trusted the Catholic Church to provide a lasting sanctuary for her collection, and Rita is certain that she'd be heartbroken to see how easily that trust had been broken. Yet, as the journey of Number 45 through the lives of Gosford, Amherst, and Perrins has shown, the integrity of any great library is at the mercy of history. As historian Albert L. Hurtado wrote, "War, pestilence, and famine blow books around the planet like so many hostages to uncertain fortune. Thieves steal, vandals deface, pious clergy burn, and worms eat books. Whether threatened by worms or war, there is nothing permanent about books and libraries."[39]

But some books do manage to slide from the grip of what seems to be their certain destiny. Two truckloads from the Edward L. Doheny Memorial Library, volumes related to the history of the West, escape sale and wind up close to home—together, as Estelle intended. While Christie's was cataloging and packing at the library, Rita watched as Monsignor Weber, the book-loving archivist, quietly wandered through, "pulling out the books he wanted" and enlisting a clerk to help him as he collected more and more.[40] In all, 887 titles were sent to the archdiocese's archival center, where Weber christened them "The Estelle Doheny Collection of Californiana."

Rita is grateful for that, but she is still saddened that there was no one like Weber to protect the most significant books in the library. Decades later, it's striking to see the archival center clearly articulating the value of collections like Estelle's, using words that no one in the archdiocese could muster at the time of the sale: "The Archival Center," its website says today, "long ago embraced the notion expressed by Lawrence Clark Powell that: 'the collecting of books is . . . the *summum bonum* [highest good] of the acquisitive desire, for the reason that books brought together by plan and purposely kept together are a social force to be reckoned with, as long as people have clear eyes and free minds.'"[41]

Apparently, the trick is finding a way to somehow manage enough clarity and freedom, as decades drift into centuries, to remember that.

◆ ◆ ◆

WITH TIME, RITA Faulders has grown philosophical about the sale. "For the seminary to have that [collection] was a gift beyond understanding—and they *didn't* understand it." Selling it was the wrong thing to do, she says, but "giving is always a risk, is it not? It is a gamble on any level, whether in affairs of the heart or monetary substance."[42]

Despite the most careful planning, it's impossible to know what will become of one's legacy or what forces a bequest will set in motion. Estelle's gamble hadn't created the lasting library she envisioned, yet again changed the path of history, spinning Number 45 toward new scientific revelations and thrusting it on a world tour, giving Gutenberg's work a visibility that only such late-twentieth-century celebrity could ignite. Now, as Estelle's Bible travels to Japan, it whirls onto a path that will give it its widest exposure in history, on the fledgling browsers of the World Wide Web.

CHAPTER TEN

The Virtual Gutenberg

NUMBER 45 MAKES the 6,750-mile trip over the polar ice cap to Tokyo lofted by the iridescent economic bubble that has carried Japan to the heights of the global economy. For the first time, Japan's assets have surpassed those of the United States[1] (at least on paper), and inflated real estate prices have ushered in an extravagant age that has the *nyuu ritchi* drinking $500 cups of coffee dusted with gold leaf[2] and scooping up art treasures at record-breaking prices. "The flashy yen that struts,"[3] as one reporter describes it, is gathering Picassos and Kandinskys, Henry Moores and Ming vases for corporate galleries and private viewing. With Yasuda Fire and Marine Insurance Company in Tokyo having recently plucked up one of Van Gogh's sunflower paintings at Christie's for $39.9 million[4] to celebrate its centenary, it hardly seems out of the ordinary for the publishing conglomerate Maruzen to lay down $5.4 million for a Gutenberg Bible as a 120th anniversary present to itself.

Maruzen is no cultural interloper, though. Established in 1869, the year after the Meiji Restoration began opening Japan to Western knowledge and technology after three centuries of isolation, the company that now owns the first Gutenberg in Asia was built on importing, translating, and publishing important works from the West. Schools and the scholarly market comprise much of its clientele—and each of its forty-seven retail stores features an exhibit space for rare books and artifacts. Asked by American reporters why Maruzen wanted a Gutenberg Bible, company officials reply, "If it were not for Gutenberg, there would be no Maruzen."[5]

The company kicks off its yearlong anniversary celebration in February of 1988 with a highly publicized exhibit of Number 45 at its flagship store, a short walk from the Imperial Palace in the historic Nihombashi section of Tokyo. Thousands line up for a quick look at Gutenberg's work, but one visitor takes his time. Naruhito, the twenty-eight-year-old crown prince of Japan and heir apparent to the Chrysanthemum Throne, dons a pair of white gloves and sits turning pages and asking questions for half an hour, joining the company of others who have lingered over this book: monks, an earl, a lord, a sauce tycoon, a papal countess, and a nuclear physicist.

The *Asahi Shimbun*, a leading national newspaper, cheers Japan's acquisition of "history's oldest moveable type book," but without a nod to the ambitious history of printing in Asia long before Gutenberg. In 770, Japan's Empress Shōtoku had famously sought to mark the end of a civil war by having a million small Buddhist prayer scrolls block printed and distributed. (According to one account, this edition required 157 men working six years to finish.[6]) Movable type was an eleventh-century Chinese invention, refined in Korea in 1230, before finally meeting the conditions that would allow it to flourish—in Europe, during Gutenberg's time. It's taken nearly a millennium for the most celebrated product of that process to find its way to the region of its inception. But this is Asia's ascendant moment, and the presence of Number 45, which has crossed seas and continents with historic shifts in global power, reflects that.

Maruzen, which has so long braided Eastern and Western scholarship, seems perfectly cast as Number 45's new, and perhaps permanent, owner. But its role in the life of Estelle's Bible is brief. The exuberance of the anniversary year passes, and Japan's economic bubble pops soon after, triggering a decline that will trudge on for decades. It's not clear precisely what prompts Maruzen to transfer the book in 1996, but that year, it is on the move.

Had Number 45's Japanese owner been an insurance company or a real estate mogul, the Bible might easily have cycled back into the international auction market to be churned into cash. But fortunate connections carry it instead to a new home within Japan, Keio University, one of the top-ranked private institutions in Asia.

◆ ◆ ◆

ACCOUNTS DIFFER OVER whether the Bible goes to the university by sale or as a gift. Either is plausible, as Maruzen and Keio University have a long-standing relationship rooted in the nineteenth-century friendship of Maruzen's founder, Yuteki Hayashi, and Keio founder, Yukichi Fukuzawa, an educational innovator who was also behind the first private elementary and secondary school systems in Japan. Maruzen's business, built on sales to the institutions Fukuzawa pioneered, is indebted to his vision and was designed, in part, to serve it. Notably, Fukuzawa, considered to be a founder of modern Japan, is believed to be the first Japanese person ever to see a Gutenberg—on a visit to the Imperial Library in Saint Petersburg in 1862. In his diary, he remarked on seeing a "book said to have been published in 1440, Germany," and in 1996, the Saint Petersburg library, which holds a copy of the Gutenberg, confirms that Fukuzawa had, indeed, signed its guest book.

The man pushing the Japan-Gutenberg connection into the twenty-first century and the digital frontier is Toshiyuki Takamiya, a Keio professor and leading authority on medieval manuscripts. As part of a government-backed initiative to digitize rare books and documents, Takamiya is spearheading a project called HUMI, for Humanities Media Interface, that will focus on digitizing parts of Keio's holdings—which include eight thousand Western manuscripts and rare books—to create a pioneering digital research hub. This, he believes, is the role of the modern research library, not simply to collect important cultural artifacts but to share them online "for the benefit of today's scholars and for the greater goal of preserving these treasures for posterity without further decay."

With a strong suggestion from Takamiya, the HUMI project selects Number 45 as its inaugural subject, the first Gutenberg Bible that will sail—in its entirety—onto the internet.

Takamiya, a slender man with regal posture and close-cropped, jet-black hair, began collecting ancient Western manuscripts from a Tokyo antiquarian bookshop in his twenties, continuing while he was a graduate student at Cambridge University, studying Sir Thomas Malory's *Le Morte d'Arthur.* "Many young Japanese who are pessimistic about the future appreciate the romantic world of the medieval past," he says. The overlap between samurai instincts and the code of chivalry, with concepts of honor, dishonor, and shame, caught his attention,[7] and held it for a lifetime of scholarship.

He often illustrates his Keio seminars for postgraduate English literature students with medieval manuscripts and early printed books from his library. A former student remembers the way he "always emphasized the importance of examining original materials, and taught us the excitement of discovering individual stories embedded in specific copies."[8] With projects like HUMI, Takamiya and his teammates believe, such materials, once available only to a few, might be studied globally by many. The professor has long supported the use of facsimiles to help scholars examine rare books and compare them with others, and he's excited by the possibility that a digital copy of a Gutenberg Bible, a book almost no one can currently read or touch, might be explored and analyzed even by young students, without damage, and with tremendous potential for discovery.

The HUMI group is interdisciplinary, pulling in not only Takamiya and colleagues with expertise on physical books and means of analyzing them, but also members of the university's physics and technology labs, who are testing the books, and the environmental information department, which is developing virtual reality applications that might make it possible for readers and researchers to have a more visceral sense of volumes like Number 45. Once more, the pages of this Bible will serve as a testing ground for path-breaking technology.

◆ ◆ ◆

FOR TWO WEEKS in early March 1997, Takamiya and research engineer Masaaki Kashimura direct students and technicians as they photograph the entire Doheny Gutenberg Bible, page by page. Like the cyclotron team before them, they have had to design a special cradle to hold the book, maneuvering each stiff leaf into a position that will allow them to capture it clearly and without distortion, while not damaging it in the handling. Their camera, a prototype developed by Nippon Telegraph and Telephone and Olympus, takes five seconds to create a high-resolution image, and the technicians experiment to determine how much artificial light will create an optimal result, and how far the lens should be from the surface of each page. They struggle to calculate how to position the camera, and make digital adjustments that will render curved and wavy pages flat and without shadows, since they can't press down the fragile paper.

There's a Kabuki-like feel to the shooting process, which is set in a room cloaked in black curtains, with the carefully lighted Bible, in its black-sheathed cradle, manipulated by technicians dressed all in black except for their white gloves and face masks, to help minimize reflections.

The painstaking work produces a digital revelation. Number 45 goes live on the internet in January 1998, and for the first time, viewers can see the pages of a Gutenberg Bible on their desktops.

Until now, most people who've viewed Gutenberg's work have done so in an extremely restricted way, limited to seeing perhaps just the pair of pages on view when a book is put on display. But HUMI's digital version allows readers to examine whatever they'd like, for as long as they care to, turning the book's pages and zooming in on details.

Digitally lifting the dark, embossed cover, viewers can experience the book with the same rush of discovery that greeted generations of its caretakers. There on the upper left corner of the front pastedown page are the distinctive signatures of Number 45's owners, the last one written in ballpoint pen. Opposite the signatures are the words *Before 15 August, 1456*, identifying this book as one of Johannes Gutenberg's. The illuminator's gleaming turquoise peacocks and brilliant yellow flowers shine from the screen on later

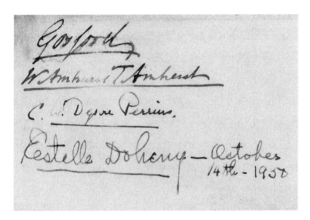

Signatures of the Bible's modern owners—Archibald Acheson, Third Earl of Gosford, Lord William Amherst of Hackney, C. W. Dyson Perrins, and Estelle Doheny—inscribed inside the Gutenberg Bible's front cover. Ownership of the artifact was considered the ultimate trophy in rare-book collecting.

pages, and a scholar anywhere in the world with internet access can enlarge them for study, or focus on individual letters to examine their shape and consistency, compare one impression with another, or measure spaces and lines precisely.

This simple capacity, to see and study an entire volume of a rare manuscript online, is commonplace today, but in the late 1990s, it is revolutionary. While the internet has only a fraction of the reach and speed it will gain in the twenty-first century, government agencies, forward-looking corporations, educational institutions, and libraries increasingly have access to high-speed connections that make it possible for motivated scholars to view the HUMI images as intended. And even people relying on slow dial-up connections and using early web browsers, such as America Online or Netscape, can peruse the entirety of Number 45 for free, if they are willing to wait minutes, not seconds, for the images to load.

The project makes the "otherwise unavailable text available, and in ways that before were unimaginable," says Mark Dimunation, chief of the Rare Book and Special Collections Division at the Library of Congress.[9] At the same time, it ushers in a new era in the field of library science as the book morphs into "digital material." HUMI's work helps generate a new field of study known as "digital bibliography," spurring the production of other powerful new cameras, lenses, and groundbreaking software for comparing and analyzing texts.

At the heart of it all, below the pixel counts and algorithms, there is something deeply Japanese about the HUMI project, notes Serbian philology scholar Divna Tričković. HUMI is pronounced *fumi*, which sounds like the Japanese characters for book or manuscript, and the project, says Tričković, "gives a modern embodiment to the deeply established and almost metaphysically profound Japanese love of tradition and the drawing on from the past in order to create a future."[10] It's as though, in the hands of Toshiyuki Takamiya, the Japanese Arthurian and bibliophile, the story of the future of the book could only begin with Gutenberg. Takamiya expansively views HUMI as "an opportunity for transcending the confines of the traditional format, with its bound pages. Once digitized, every component can be unbound and rebound in an infinite number of ways," he says, becoming a "new entity . . . perhaps more vivid than ever possible in the real world, where rare books are often inaccessible."[11]

The team refines its processes and tests new versions of equipment, taking a mobile version of its setup on the road to collaborate with research libraries and museums holding other copies of Gutenberg's Bible. It spends four days in Cambridge in November of 1998, creating the next complete digital copy of the Bible, and goes on to shoot nine more, including those owned by the British Library, the Gutenberg Museum in Mainz, and the three copies owned by the Morgan Library and Museum. Now various Bibles can be compared side by side. Sophisticated navigational tools allow detailed close-up views of the text and the decorative illumination, and when the team finds that it's unwieldy and time-consuming to make minute comparisons, they develop software that allows them to instantly perform such functions as overlaying individual letters from different locations to compare them, revealing tantalizing clues about the printer's methods and practices.[12]

There's a voracious hunger for these images. When the British Library posts HUMI versions of its two copies of the Gutenberg Bible, it generates one million hits during its first month,[13] underlining the power of HUMI's vision of a grand digital library that can open the study of the liberal arts to anyone with a computer.

At a series of international symposia, the HUMI team not only shares the knowledge and technical expertise of its own work but also gathers input from other institutions and interested scholars, refining its approach and presenting exhibits around the world. Now, says Professor Takamiya, "digitized rare books, including the Gutenberg Bible, will never become forgotten relics of past wisdom. They will come alive every time someone has access to them. This, then, is the raison-d'être of the HUMI Project."[14]

◆ ◆ ◆

AS HIGH-RESOLUTION GUTENBERG images enter the digital realm, fast-evolving technology opens the way for increasingly sophisticated analysis of the text, creating deeper ways of seeing. In January 2001, Gutenberg expert Paul Needham and Blaise Agüera y Arcas, a young computational mathematician, announce a disruptive new theory about how Gutenberg created his type. A prevailing narrative had it that the printer had used an assembly-line process involving a "punch matrix" system. Individual letters would have been carefully carved on the ends of steel rods and punched into sheets of copper to create sturdy molds (each called a matrix) that could be filled with a lead alloy to create a piece of type. One punch could be used to create multiple molds, from which could come an endless stream of identical letters.

The process had long been celebrated as the core of Gutenberg's invention, but it had not gone unquestioned. In the late 1980s, Needham, now the librarian of Princeton's Scheide Library, had worked with a colleague to study the individual letters in an early Gutenberg document, trying to determine how many punches were used. They expected to find large groups of near-identical letters, each group reflecting the use of a single punch, and a relatively low number of punches overall. It would've taken a day for a skilled craftsman to carve a letter in steel, so the process would be most economical if a small library of punches was used repeatedly. Instead, though, as the scholars looked at the letters and counted variations by hand, they noted so many differences that they theorized there were 204 different punches by the time they stopped counting. It didn't make sense. And that's where they left things—with many questions about the old assumptions, but no answers.

Needham circled back to the investigation a decade and a half later when a Princeton colleague introduced him to Agüera y Arcas, a student from his graduate seminar on the history of the book. The twenty-five-year-old computing wunderkind became interested in the problem (enough so to make it the basis of his applied mathematics dissertation) and built a sophisticated model to compare the letters on computer-enhanced copies of several early Gutenberg documents from the Scheide Library.

Now, the algorithm allows them to overlay all the instances of a single letter and to cluster the ones that are similar, making it possible to easily spot individual pieces of type as they recur on the pages. They find *hundreds* of versions of each letter. The clamor of variations leads them to theorize that the early foundry created its type not with a metal punch matrix system but individually, by hand. (Agüera y Arcas wonders later how it happened that so many people, for so long, looked at pages of type they called a triumph of uniformity without noticing how different the letters were[15]—something Needham had quickly discerned without the help of advanced mathematics.)

Gutenberg, they posit, was trying to re-create the complexities of a scribe's shorthand, which used an extensive array of letter combinations and abbreviations to compress as many words as possible onto each expensive vellum leaf of a book. He did this, they theorize, by shaping his type in individual, one- or two-use molds pressed into a soft material like sand, possibly combining shapes modeled on pen strokes. Needham notes that this sort of complex system, called *cuneiform typography,* was known to be used by early fifteenth-century European craftsmen, including goldsmiths. He contends that the metal molds attributed to Gutenberg were probably invented by someone else, perhaps two decades after Gutenberg first began printing the Bibles.[16]

The scholars present their findings at a standing-room-only lecture in New York City at the Grolier Club, the noted society of bibliophiles, and find themselves in headlines around the world. "The announcement is causing the kind of excitement among rare-book collectors and scholars that the Super Bowl is generating among sports fans," writes Dinitia Smith in the *New York Times.*

One leading scholar labels the fruits of this latest intersection of Gutenberg and advanced technology "a landmark in the study of early typography," and Anthony Grafton, the Princeton book historian who brought Needham and Agüera y Arcas together, tells the *New York Times,* "They have figured out that the whole history of early printing is wrong."

National Public Radio's report wonders if history has been too generous to the printer from Mainz, and whether Gutenberg's invention will be diminished by the findings. But Agüera y Arcas, who will later head the pioneering machine intelligence group at Google, says simply that the findings show that the development of printing moved forward in many smaller steps, instead of one great leap. Acknowledging Gutenberg as a "great, great engineer," he emphasizes to the *Financial Times* in 2014 that technology evolves with the contributions of many. "The idea that a technology emerges fully formed at the beginning is nuts. Anyone who does technology knows that's not how it works."[17]

◆ ◆ ◆

PERHAPS THE IMAGE of Johannes Gutenberg as a lone genius who transformed human culture endures because the sweep of what followed is so vast that it feels almost mythic and needs an origin story to match. The sheer ambition of heralding new printing technology with a 1,200-page book is breathtaking, a fitting overture to the avalanche of change it would so quickly bring. By the end of the fifteenth century, more than 130 other editions of the Holy Bible had been printed and distributed throughout the world.[18] Some 240 European cities had set up printing shops, which are estimated to have printed at least 28,000 different editions of innumerable works, producing an astonishing total of ten million books.[19] The mechanically printed word created the world's memory, as some scholars have put it, helping ignite the Renaissance, the Protestant Reformation, and centuries' worth of revolutions in science, politics, and industry. And Gutenberg and his Bibles stand as embodiments of the first moments when so much human possibility could be tapped, multiplied, and unleashed.

With the spread and development of Gutenberg's techniques,

historian John Man writes in his book *The Gutenberg Revolution*, "Hardly an aspect of life remained untouched. Scholars could compare findings, stand on each other's shoulders and make better and faster sense of the universe. Gutenberg's invention made the soil from which sprang modern history, science, popular literature, the emergence of the nation-state, so much of everything by which we define modernity."[20]

Life magazine concurs, naming Johann Gutenberg, maverick printer who reshaped human advancement, its "Man of the Millennium" in the fall of 2000 and putting the printing of his Bibles atop its list of the most important events of the past one thousand years. *Life* portrays Gutenberg as a mysterious underdog hero-genius: "What Gutenberg devised was the first Western moveable type system that worked—so well that it remained largely unchanged for the next 350 years," the tribute says. "Gutenberg, however, got none of the glory. His brainchild bankrupted him, the year his Bible was published, a creditor took over his business. Little more is known of the inventor—in part because he never put his name in print."[21]

As the long millennium shaped by printing gives way to an era being rewritten in computer code, there's a widespread desire to honor the value of Gutenberg's legacy and see in its disruptions a harbinger of the emerging age. The city of Mainz celebrates the printer as a tech revolutionary when it stages the Gutenberg Year 2000, a year-long affair that marks the six hundredth anniversary of his birth with a series of museum exhibitions, multimedia presentations, festivals, and a 227-page catalog, *Gutenberg Man of the Millennium: From a Secret Enterprise to the First Media Revolution*, a veritable Gutenberg encyclopedia.

The Bibles themselves gracefully stride through time, continuing to offer insights. In no small part because of the unusual will-ingness of Number 45's caretakers to collaborate with scientists, more people than ever before will have a chance to study the texts online. It's not inconceivable that the next breakthrough percep-tions will be crowd-sourced.

One unanticipated consequence of the HUMI project is Keio University's decision to protect Number 45 by cutting off access, not only by the public but also by scholars and researchers, no mat-ter how qualified. Once the book had been digitized and made available to all, the reasoning seemed to go there was no longer a need for physical contact with the object itself. But for a time, when the earliest digitized images were deemed too low-resolution to be of value as the technology advanced, Number 45 disappeared com-pletely from the internet, only resurfacing in a significantly higher-quality version in the spring of 2017.

Professor Richard Schwab is overcome with emotion when he recounts how Keio officials refused his request to visit Tokyo to examine Number 45 and complete his cyclotron research project. He realized then that his time with the book had forever ended,[22] and that it would be impossible for him to analyze the paper and ink of every page of that volume, or gain the insights into Guten-berg's processes that the additional data could bring.

As of this writing, Number 45 remains locked away, inaccessi-ble in a Keio University vault.

✦ ✦ ✦

As FOR AN individual owning a Gutenberg Bible again, the chances are vanishingly small. There have been no copies put up for sale

Estelle Doheny, the only American woman to own a Guten-
berg Bible as a private collector. She succeeded in her forty-
year quest to own the "greatest book in the world."

since the auction of the Estelle Doheny Collection in 1987, and it seems unlikely that another will ever be sold again (though that has been said many times in the life of Number 45). Fragments of the great book, however, have entered the marketplace, some selling for staggering sums.

The so-called Rendsburg Fragment was discovered in 1997 in the Evangelical parish of St. Marien, in Rendsburg, Germany, when a church librarian went looking for a missing book and tracked the fragment to a restoration workshop where it had been languishing for years on a dusty shelf. Leaves had been ripped from between the oak-board covers, illuminated initials torn out. It had been badly vandalized. But what remained were 129 leaves from volume 1 of Gutenberg's Bible. The church fathers decided to sell the fragment to raise funds to refurbish a community church built in 1287, turning down a reported offer of $2.5 million from a prospective American buyer after pressure to keep it in Germany. It was sold to another German church for 3.5 million deutsche marks (just over $2 million) and is now on permanent loan to the Schloss Gottorf, a museum in Schleswig, Germany. Debate swirls among book lovers and bibliophiles, but some experts go as far as calling the unusual Rendsburg Fragment the forty-ninth Gutenberg.[23] (The full history of the copy designated by some experts as Number 48 is cloaked in mystery. Confiscated by the Soviet Army during World War II, it is currently at the Lomonosov University Library in Moscow.)

On June 19, 2015, the building hunger for Gutenbergs became apparent when a much smaller fragment of a Bible sold at Sotheby's for $970,000, exceeding the auction house's expectations by almost half a million dollars. The fragment, eight consecutive leaves from the Book of Esther with handsome red, blue, and gold rubrication, came from a Bible purchased by dealer Gabriel Wells in 1920—the same copy from which he sold Estelle's St. Paul's Epistle to the Romans. Wells made numerous sales from that copy at $150 a leaf, calling the pieces "Noble Fragments," a strategy that was wryly tweaked by the *New York Times* as "spreading the Gospel among the rich."[24]

Based on the most recent auction price, each leaf of the Gutenberg Bible could be valued now at an extraordinary $121,250. Extrapolating from that, it's conceivable that a two-volume Gutenberg Bible consisting of 643 leaves (1,286 single pages) might be priced at almost $80 million. One museum official goes even higher, estimating that if such a book suddenly became available on the world market today, its price would be in the $100 million range.[25]

And it's certain that there would be an individual bidder for the volume, even at the most extravagant price. In 2017, $100 million might buy a 20,500-square-foot home in Beverly Hills,[26] a personal 757 jet,[27] or most of a Jean-Michel Basquiat skull painting—the sorts of purchases that put the gleam on modern wealth and are easily within the reach of the billionaire class. Though Gutenberg's Bibles have long been part of such catalogs of signifiers, they have always stood apart, occupying a realm all their own. A volume like Number 45, after all, "symbolizes one of the small handful of the greatest accomplishments of all time," as James Thorpe, former director of the Huntington Library, once wrote. To own

The signatures and bookplates of the owners still visible on the inside cover of the Gutenberg Bible.

one is to possess the remarkable first fruit of a single invention that profoundly changed everything.

Not all of Number 45's individual owners thought deeply about that history, or even counted the Bible among the most valued items in their collections. Gosford, a Don Juan of book collecting whose every acquisition seems only to have energized him for another, carried the Gutenberg home to his never-finished castle because it was cheap. Dyson Perrins added it to his carefully curated shelves, probably on a dealer's recommendation, but gave it little of the love he lavished on the illuminated manuscripts he shared with his ailing wife. Estelle Doheny pursued it for decades in large part because it reminded her of a time in her life she wanted badly to reclaim. Philip Frere, the short-term owner who apparently left the book in the dealer's vault, seemed not to value it at all. Only Lord Amherst, tutored by Bernard Quaritch to appreciate the book's value, and determined to connect its story with the threads of history that spun out through the rest of his library, seemed to appreciate it as a scholar should.

If titan book dealer A. S. W. Rosenbach is correct that every book has its own destiny, then perhaps each owner had a particular role to play in the larger narrative—or even particular "mission"—of Number 45 as it crossed the globe, triggering serendipitous contacts between the worlds of art and science, weaving direct connections between Gutenberg and the technologies shaping the future.

Looked at one way, the story of Number 45 is strewn with revolution, betrayal, and loss. But seen from something more akin to the book's own point of view, it's a study in the way a single significant object provoked responses that carried it into the orbits of unlikely risk takers and innovators through time—people as different, and often invisible, as Estelle Doheny and Rita Faulders and Toshiyuki Takamiya. In the same way that Gutenberg's technology no doubt grew from accidents and chance intersections of ideas, Number 45 has continued to yield new insights through unexpected and serendipitous meetings triggered by the people in its owners' sphere.

Book dealers and scholars, the people at the core of the rare-book world, often regard amateur collectors in slightly dismissive terms, seeing them as temporary travelers in a world they're unlikely ever to appreciate fully. But each owner and his or her circle left a mark on Gutenberg Bible Number 45, and it's possible that someday, a yet-unimagined technology will allow the pages of the book to be read for the genetic DNA stories left by their touch.

We change the book, and it changes us.

In an era when newness is prized, Gutenberg's Bibles ground us in the richness of age, showing us how time deepens beauty, as layers of meaning accrue to physical objects in ways that can't be replicated in a digital world. The gravity that builds in the process pulls us in. Even Takamiya, whom his HUMI teammates regarded as a digital ambassador, told an interviewer, "I would like to make my last mission to encourage people to get more interested in real books."

What gathers in ancient books as we add them to our transitory collections may be as ephemeral as the prayers said over them, or as explosive as the human dramas that have propelled Number 45 through its singular life, and may yet send Gutenberg's creation into the care of another obsessed individual for another unpredictable spin. The only certainty, if the past is any indicator, is that the next exchange will deepen our understanding of what the book has made us. The first mass-produced printed books, after all, are unlike any other thing in the world. Little else that we have produced is so rich with story, with lifelines that flow through one object—and bind us together in the pages of human existence.

EPILOGUE

Final Bows

T HE PEOPLE, PLACES, and institutions that touched Number 45 form a modern parable about the volatility of fate and fortune.

❧ After the Acheson family was financially ruined by the gambling debts of the young 4th Earl of Gosford, it was forced to abandon Gosford Castle, leaving the walls crumbling in decay. The site was commandeered by the British government during World War II for use as a prisoner-of-war camp, and then again by film crews shooting *Game of Thrones* in 2012. The castle changed hands several times until 2008, when it was divided into twenty-three units in a multimillion-dollar redevelopment project—with not a trace of a library.

❧ The home of the Bible's second owner, Lord William Amherst's Didlington Hall, was passed to Mary, the eldest of his seven daughters, after Amherst died, seemingly of a broken heart, after being forced to sell his collection. Mary was "styled under special proclamation" Baroness of Amherst so that she could inherit her father's seven-thousand-acre estate under the British rules of entail. But after only a year, she was forced to sell the house and its remaining contents. At the height of World War II, the mansion and grounds were requisitioned and served as headquarters for the commander of the British Army during the D-Day landings. Didlington Hall, once a sprawling cabinet of curiosities filled with some of the finest artifacts to be gathered from the corners of the British Empire, was torn down in the 1950s.

❧ C. W. Dyson Perrins, the Bible's third owner, died in January 1958, having helped ensure that the Royal Worcester Porcelain factory and its artisans would endure into the twenty-first century. The Royal Worcester name still appears on china, but the company's last fifteen porcelain painters, along with the other remaining workers, left the Severn Street factory for good on September 29, 2006. Dyson Perrins is remembered today through the Worcester Porcelain Museum, established by his widow, Frida, at the factory site. The Perrins' Davenham house, once a hive of bibliophiles, is now a home for the ill and elderly.

❧ Little is known about the final years of Sir Philip Frere, the only individual owner who chose not to add his signature to the Bible. Frere slipped from London's society pages in 1950. According to his death certificate, the hard-charging solicitor died in a coma on December 6, 1981, in the city of Westminster at age eighty-four.

❧ Estelle Betzold Doheny, the owner who undoubtedly felt the deepest emotional connection with Number 45, is remembered today primarily for the charitable works she endowed so amply before she died. A list of the 237 grants her foundation awarded in 2017 shows widespread support for the poor and homeless, for the education of children, and for the works of the Catholic Church through its ministries, programs, and schools. Her foundation is a major funder of the Doheny Eye Institute, one of the top eye centers in the nation dedicated to groundbreaking research at the forefront of "vision science."

And what became of the proceeds from the sale of the Estelle Doheny Collection, the funds the Catholic Church insisted it so urgently needed for the training of priests? In 1996, a front-page article in the *Los Angeles Lay Catholic Mission* raised the question, noting that the Los Angeles archdiocese had "dipped into the seminary endowment" several times to cover operating shortfalls, including a $4 to $5 million deficit in 1991. Quoting named and unnamed sources, the paper estimated that the endowment was short $23 million to $25 million—more than half the sale amount—with the money having gone to cover such things as a $1 million makeover of the archbishop's quarters. Seminarians, meanwhile, noted that St. John's facilities had been modernized—in a cheap and sterile way. "They took down all the ecclesiastical art," said one, "and made the place look like a Denny's."[1]

❧ Keio University continues to prohibit physical access to Number 45, but in April 2017, a new, high-resolution copy appeared online. The majestic leaves, including the signatures of the book's owners, can be viewed in splendid clarity at http://dcollections.lib .keio.ac.jp/en/gutenberg.

Number 45 was the first Gutenberg Bible to enter the digital frontier. No longer a three-dimensional book of ink printed on paper, the virtual Gutenberg is a twenty-first-century creation of the digital age. Today, Number 45 resides in a library vault at Keio University in Tokyo, Japan.

ACKNOWLEDGMENTS

The story of Estelle Doheny and the Gutenberg Bible might have vanished if not for Rita S. Faulders, the library curator who became the unlikely protector of the Bible's history, saving centuries' worth of its ephemeral traces. Her quick hand preserved not only the record of one woman's quest for the most important of all printed books, but also the remarkable saga of the single Gutenberg Bible that Estelle Doheny finally won—designated as Number 45.

This book was six years in the making. I am truly indebted to Rita S. Faulders, who has worked closely with me since May 2012, for her help researching and writing this story. I am also indebted to Dr. Theodore Faulders, adjunct professor at St. John's Seminary in Camarillo, California, for his careful read of the manuscript. I also extend my heartfelt thanks to Nicholas A. Curry for his critical eye and input regarding the Doheny family's business interests.

I greatly appreciate the talents of Dr. Olwen Purdue, Queens University, Belfast; Lorraine Bourke, records management, Public Record Office of Northern Ireland; and Belfast-based researcher Louise Canavan. Enormous thanks are owed Professor Merrill Distad, former associate director of research and special collections at the Thomas Fisher Rare Book Library at the University of Toronto. Many thanks to researcher Eric Mitchell for his extensive review of the papers of Lord William Amherst at the Hackney Archives, Dalston CLR James Library, London. Very special thanks to Derek Chin, who assisted in the translation with scholars at Keio University, Tokyo. At the Archdiocese of Los Angeles, I extend my great appreciation to prolific author and historian Monsignor Francis J. Weber and library archivist Kevin Feeney.

My profound appreciation is extended to physicist Dr. Thomas A. Cahill, former director of the Crocker Nuclear Laboratory, and rare book scholar Dr. Richard N. Schwab for graciously granting me repeated interviews to better understand the Gutenberg Bible's complex and history-making encounter with the cyclotron.

I am deeply indebted to Donna Frazier Glynn, Walter Bode, Jack Miles, and Victoria Steele. I gratefully acknowledge Dr. Lawrence D. Dorr and Marilyn Dorr, John Waiblinger, Kathryn Donatelli, Brandon Schmook, Michael Caldwell, Rachel Winfree, Mark Spohn, David Bice, Alex and Kim Gallego, Eugene You, Linda Howard, Carol Easton, Kelly Kinnon, Jeffrey Forer, Nancy Reimann, Don Russ, Susan Levinson, Joe and Justine Medeiros, Eileen C. White, Noel Riley Fitch, Albert Sonnenfeld, Eric Evavold, and intuitives Julie Hunter and Shelby Ingram. I extend my utmost gratitude to my new husband, Roger Vincent.

Hail to the amazing ladies of my Los Angeles book club, the Women's Literary Society, for their continuous support: Dr. Deborah Lynn, Abigail Walsh, Kim Nemoy, Jeanne MacDonald, and Meena Nainan. I would like to posthumously honor my mentors Kevin Starr, Jim Bellows, and T. Sumner Robinson. In loving memoriam: James H. Davis, Frank D. Vincent, Jack Dunlap, Tom X, and Taylor Negron. I am very grateful to Patrick A. Doheny, who gave me his enthusiastic blessing to pursue this project shortly before his death in 2014. Very special thanks to Leslie Siewierski.

My remarkable editor, Megan Newman, publisher at Tarcher-Perigee, inspired my best work and made this book possible. My heartfelt thanks are owed to my gifted editor, Nina Shield. I would also like to thank Marian Lizzi, editor in chief at TarcherPerigee. Very special thanks to Hannah Steigmeyer, editorial assistant; Erica Rose, senior production editor; and consummate copyeditor, Kathleen Go. Many thanks are owed to Tiffany Estreicher, director of design, for this book's beautiful interior design in addition to cover artist Jess Morphew.

Finally, I extend my deepest gratitude to my literary agent, Betsy Amster, who brilliantly guided *The Lost Gutenberg* from idea to publication.

Long live the book.

In memory of Catherine Chabot Davis

NOTES

Chapter 1: Million-Dollar Bookshelf

1. **"carelessly wrapped":** Rita Faulders, audio interview with Lucille Miller, August 15, 1984.
2. **"any old way":** Ibid.
3. **The copy now in Estelle Doheny's possession:** One indirect gift we have from Estelle Doheny is the ability to examine Number 45 as she and its other owners will throughout this book. If you'd like to open the cover or look closely at any detail on any page, you can do so at the website of Keio University in Japan, whose groundbreaking digital work with Estelle's Bible is described in chapter 10. Follow along in Number 45 at http://dcollections.lib.keio.ac.jp/en/gutenberg.
4. **most scholars believe:** The census used here of vellum versus parchment copies is from the Gutenberg Museum in Mainz, Germany. See http://gutenberg-museum.de/41.0.html?&L=1.

   For a census of known Gutenberg Bibles in 1950, see Lazare, Edward, "The Gutenberg Bible: A Census," *Antiquarian Bookman*, November, 18, 1950.
5. **forty-five known to exist in 1950:** Lazare, Edward, "The Gutenberg Bible: A Census," *Antiquarian Bookman*, November, 18, 1950.
6. **"collection of collections":** "Bible Exhibit One of Finest, Huntington Library Curator Descibes Collection," *Los Angeles Times*, October 26, 1930.
7. **"boiling hot":** Rita Faulders, audio interview with Lucille Miller, August 15, 1984.
8. **$70,093:** In today's dollars, adjusted for inflation, the price is roughly $694,067.
9. **first and only woman:** Only two other women have a direct connection to the Gutenberg Bible. Lady Christian Martin of Great Britain inherited a Gutenberg

Bible, widely known as the Shuckburgh copy, which was acquired by Arthur A. Houghton Jr. in 1953.

The so-called Melk copy of the Gutenberg Bible was purchased by Mrs. Edward Harkness through book dealer A. S. W. Rosenbach for the purpose of donating it to Yale University.

Estelle Doheny is the only woman to purchase a Gutenberg Bible as a private collector for her personal library.

10. **"pulp novel":** Hamilton, Denise, "Curator Rekindles Early Chapter of Doheny Archives," *Los Angeles Times*, February 4, 1988.

11. **"lookie-loos":** Rita Faulders, audio interview with Lucille Miller, August 15, 1984.

12. **"up to me":** Ibid.

13. **"positively terrified":** Ibid.

14. **booklice:** Richardson, John, "Bookworms: The Most Common Insect Pests of Paper in Archives, Libraries and Museums," December 15, 2010, http://jvrichardsonjr.net/insects/pests.htm.

15. **rag paper:** Carter, John and Nicolas Barker, *ABC for Book Collectors*, New Castle: Oak Knoll Press, 2004, p. 232.

16. **"new baby":** Rita Faulders, audio interview with Lucille Miller, August 15, 1984.

17. **watermarks:** Schwenke, Paul, *Johannes Gutenbergszweiundvierzigzeilige Bibel: Erganzungsbandzur Faksimile-Ausgabe*. Leipzig:Insel-Verlag: 1923, pp. 25–28.

18. **northwest Italy:** "The Gutenberg Bible, Treasures in Focus," The British Library, 2006, p. 40. Also see Ing, Janet, *Johann Gutenberg and His Bible: A Historical Study*, New York: Typophiles, 1988.

19. **hideous little knots:** Rita Faulders, audio Interview with Lucille Miller, August 15, 1984.

20. **Füssell:** Füssell, Stephan. *Gutenberg and the Impact of Printing*, Burlington, VT.: Ashgate, 2005, pp. 20–21. Author John Man has suggested a number in the range of 46,000; see Man, John. Gutenberg: *How One Man Remade the World with Words*, New York: John Wiley & Sons, 2002, p. 166.

Chapter 2: Treasure Neglected

1. **Norman Revival castle**: The castle had 197 rooms and 45 basement rooms. See http://www.chrono.qub.ac.uk/local/armagh/Gosford/.

2. **humanist scholar:** *Aldus Manutius and Renaissance Culture: Essays in Memory of Franklin D. Murphy*, Acts of an International Conference (Venice and Florence, 14–17 June 1994), ed. David S. Zeidberg with Fiorella Gioffredi, Superbi, Florence, Leo S. Olschki, 1998. p. 1.

3. **concept of personal reading:** Statement made by G. Scott Clemens, former president of Grolier Club, quoted in "A Tribute to the Printer Aldus Manutius, and the Roots of the Paperback," *New York Times*, February 26, 2015.

4. **"pure Renaissance":** Ibid. Also see *Printing and the Mind of Man*, edited by John Carter, New York: Holt, Rinehart and Winston, 1967, p. 21.

5. **symbols:** Hunt, Arnold, "Private Libraries in the Age of Bibliomania," in The History of Libraries in Britain and Ireland, 2: 1640–1850, ed. Giles Madelbrote and K. A. Manley, Cambridge: Cambridge University Press, 2006, p. 444.

6. **"fondling his treasures alone":** Weiner, Norman D., "On Bibliomania," *Psychoanalytic Quarterly* 35: 217–232.

7. **"scant" attention:** White, Eric Marshall, "The Gutenberg Bible at the Harry Ransom Center Description and Analysis," CD-ROM, Austin: The University of Texas at Austin, 2004.

8. **consigned to oblivion:** Scholar Eric Marshall White writes: "'The revolutionary year of 1789 is a very early date in the history of Gutenberg research. Following nearly three centuries of oblivion, the B42 had been recognized as Europe's 'first printed book' by several mid-eighteenth-century scholars." White, Eric Marshall, "Gutenberg Bibles on the Move in England, 1789–1834," *Transactions of the Cambridge Bibliographical Society* 15, no. 1 (2012): p. 81.

9. **"We do not hesitate":** de Bure, Guillaume-Francois, Bibliographie Instructive, vol I. (Theologue), 1764, p. 32–40. Also see Arnold Hunt, p.447. The Cardinal's library is also known as the Bibliothèque Mazarin, of the Collège des Quatre Nations. The term *Mazarin Bible* was attached to the Gutenberg Bible following the publicity stemming from de Bure's discovery.

10. **Thomas Payne II:** White, Eric Marshall, "Gutenberg Bibles on the Move in England, 1789–1834," *Transactions of the Cambridge Bibliographical Society* 15, no. 1 (2012): p. 84. White discovered the Spencer receipt for the Mazarin Bible (Gutenberg Bible) in the British Library's Althorp papers.

11. **Four years later:** Folter, Roland. "The Gutenberg Bible in the Antiquarian Book Trade," *Incunabula: Studies in Fifteenth-Century Printed Books Presented to Lotte Hellinga*, ed. Martin Davies. London: The British Library, 1999, p. 11.

12. **Spencer and his cousin:** Spencer lost the book but eventually came out the winner, buying it for less than half the price seven years later when his over-extended cousin had to sell his library. See John Rylands Library Special Collections Blog, https://rylandscollections.wordpress.com/tag/george-john-2nd-earl-spencer/

13. **"Not a living creature":** Dibdin, Thomas Frognall, *The Bibliographical Decameron*, vol. 3, London, 1817, p. 65. Also see Granniss, Ruth S., "What Bibliography Owes to Private Book Clubs," *The Papers of the Bibliographical Society of America* 24, no. 1/2 (1930): 14–33.

14. **"point maniac":** Carter, John and Nicolas Barker, *ABC for Book Collectors*, New Castle: Oak Knoll Press, 2004, p. 171.

15. **"make the lot worth":** Gilbert, Rosa Mulholland, *Life of Sir John T. Gilbert*, London: Longmans, Green, and Co., 1905, p. 133.

16. **carved plaster:** Larmour, Paul, "Gosford Castle, Co. Armagh: A Neo-Norman Novelty," *Ulster Architect* (March 1985): 4–5. Also see http://landedfamilies .blogspot.com/search?q=Gosford.
17. **"byzantine":** Proudfoot, Lindsay, "Placing the Imaginary: Gosford Castle and the Gosford Estate, ca. 1820–1900," in A. J. Hughes and W. Nolan (eds), Armagh: History and Society, Geography Publications, Dublin," p. 907.
18. **"book that gave us Shakespeare":** See Folger Shakespeare Library at: folger .edu/first-folio-tour.
19. **157 guineas:** A price of £13,760, or $21,123 in today's valuation.
20. **considerable historic value:** The Athenaeum, No. 4144, March 30, 1907 p. 384. Gosford's attachment to the Folio is based purely on its perfection. (Years after Gosford's death, it is discovered that the book is not perfect, as he had believed: two of its leaves have been repaired, possibly even replaced—a fact that would've drained the joy of ownership from the point maniac of Markethill.)
21. **4th Earl of Gosford:** *Freeman's Journal* (June 21, 1864): p. 2.
22. **fetching a price:** Percy Hetherington Fitzgerald, *The Book Fancier*, London: Ballantine, Hanson and Co., 1886, p. 24.

Chapter 3: The Bibliophile

1. **"deny himself":** Distad, Merrill. "William Amhurst Tyssen-Amherst, First Baron of Hackney, Country Gentleman, Collector, and Connoisseur, 1835–1909." Unpublished, Courtesy of Merrill Distad, p. 11.
2. **unyielding, and irascible:** *Dictionary of Literary Biography, Vol. 184: Nineteenth Century British Book-Collectors and Bibliographers*, Detroit: Gale Research, 1997. p. 370.
3. **flurry of letters:** Letter from Quaritch to Amherst, March 12, 1858 and March 15, 1858, Thomas Fisher Rare Book Library, Toronto, Box 1.
4. **link in the chain:** Distad, Merrill. "William Amhurst Tyssen-Amherst, First Baron of Hackney, Country Gentleman, Collector, and Connoisseur, 1835–1909." Unpublished, Courtesy of Merrill Distad, p. 13.
5. **hidden door:** Duggan, Brian Patrick, *Saluki: The Desert Hound and the English Travelers Who Brought It to the West*, Jefferson: McFarland & Co., 2009, p. 15.
6. **"afraid of the price":** Letter from Quaritch to Amherst, February 19, 1870, Thomas Fisher Rare Book Library, Toronto, Box 1.
7. **"scarcer and dearer":** Letters from Quaritch to Amherst, October 12, 1871, and December 22, 1886, Thomas Fisher Rare Book Library, Toronto, Box 1.
8. **"booksellers are the horses":** Letter from Quaritch to Amherst, May 1, 1873, Thomas Fisher Rare Book Library, Toronto, Box 1.
9. **cut his usual fee:** Letter from Quaritch to Amherst, March 1, 1873 (written on the back of a notice of the Perkins sale), Thomas Fisher Rare Book Library, Toronto, Box 1.

10. **vellum copy:** Folter, Roland, "The Gutenberg Bible in the Antiquarian Book Trade," *Incunabula*, ed. Martin Davis, The British Library, 1999, pp. 27 and 43. Quaritch sold the two-volume paper Gutenberg Bible in 1874 to the great British collector Henry Huth. In 1911 the Huth copy was sold to J. P. Morgan.

11. **"sardonic humor":** Weedon, Alexis, "Bernard Quaritch," *Dictionary of Literary Biography, Vol. 184: Nineteenth Century British Book-Collectors and Bibliographers*, Detroit: Gale Research, 1997, p. 370.

12. **"last day of my life":** Distad, Merrill. "William Amhurst Tyssen-Amherst, First Baron of Hackney, Country Gentleman, Collector, and Connoisseur, 1835–1909." Unpublished, Courtesy of Merrill Distad, p. 16.

13. **translation by Saint Jerome:** Dr. Theodore Faulders, adjunct professor at St. John's Seminary in Camarillo, CA, adds: "St. Jerome (347–420) wrote numerous letters and more than one hundred of his letters are preserved today in various libraries. According to Thomas Lawler, St. Jerome's correspondence 'is a significant source of information on the world of Jerome and . . . the general social and ecclesiastical life of his time.'" E-mail to the author, June 18, 2018. See Thomas C. Lawler, *The Letters of St. Jerome*, New York: Paulist Press, 1963, p. 3.

14. **needle or an awl:** Kapr, Albert, *Johann Gutenberg: The Man and His Invention*, Aldersgot: Scholar Press; Brookfield, VT: Ashgate Publishing, 1966, p. 136.

15. **pinholes:** Ing, Janet, *Johann Gutenberg and His Bible: A Historical Study*, New York: The Typophiles, 1988, p. 98.

16. **forty-two lines:** Ibid., p. 59.

17. **mix of line settings:** The fact that there were different settings had been identified in 1881 by Cambridge University Librarian Henry Bradshaw, who made a table of the resetting based on the evidence he found in four other copies. See Ing, Janet, *Johann Gutenberg and His Bible*, p. 60. Also see British Library, Treasures in Full: Gutenberg Bible, "The difference in line lengths per page," http://www .bl.uk/treasures/gutenberg/flash4.html.

18. **Before 15 August 1456:** The date derives from an illuminator's inscription in a two-volume forty-two-line Bible now at the Bibliothéque nationale de France in Paris, where he writes at the end of each volume: Vol. 1: "Here endeth the First Part of the Old Testament of the Holy Bible, which was illuminated, rubricated and bound by Henry Albech, or Cremer on Saint Bartholomew's Day [August 24] in the year of our Lord 1456. Thanks be to God, Hallelujah." Vol. 2: "This book was illuminated, bound and perfected by Henry Cremer, vicar of the Collegiate Church of Saint Stephen in Mainz, on the feast of the Assumption of the Blessed Virgin [August 15] in the year of our Lord 1456. Thanks be to God." See Malkin, Sol. M., "Johann Gutenberg: 1400–1468," *Antiquarian Bookman*, November 18, 1950, p. 6.

    Unfortunately, the illuminator did not record the date on which he first received the Gutenberg Bible.

The phrase *Before August 1456* is written in pencil and still visible in the inside cover of Number 45.

19. **"Thanks be to God":** Ibid, p. 6.

20. **minuscule red dots:** Digital Gallery of Rare Books & Special Collections, 036 The 42-Line Bible [Mainz]; Digital Gallery of Keio University, http://www.mita.lib .keio.ac.jp/collection/b42.html.

21. **celebrated Cambridge Bible:** Sotheby, Wilkinson & Hodge, *Catalogue of the Magnificent Library of Choice and Valuable Books & Manuscripts, the Property of the Rt. Hon. Lord Amherst of Hackney,* Item 117, London: Dryden Press, 1908, p. 25.

22. **"prolongs your life":** Letter from Quaritch to Amherst, October 11, 1889, Thomas Fisher Rare Book Library, Toronto, Box 1.

23. **about 1474:** See https://warburg.sas.ac.uk/pdf/neh1740b2329729B.pdf.

24. **"now so rich":** Ibid.

25. **"Titan of the auction room":** In Quaritch's obituary, *the Times* (London) declares: "It would scarcely be rash to say that Quaritch was the greatest bookseller who ever lived. His ideals were so high, his eye so keen, his transactions so colossal, his courage so dauntless, that he stands out among men who have dealt in old literature as a Napoleon or a Wellington stands out among generals."

26. **1st Baron Amherst of Hackney:** The subject of Lord Amherst's ancestry and title is complicated. Dr. Merrill Distad of the Thomas Fisher Rare Book Library, Toronto, succinctly summarizes it as follows: "Amherst was born 25 April 1835 at Narford, Norfolk, the eldest son and heir of William George Tyssen Daniel-Tyssen (1801–55) by his wife Mary (d. 1854), eldest daughter of Andrew Fountaine of Narford Hall. Descended from the MacDaniels or MacDonnells of County Mayo in Ireland, his grandfather assumed the additional Tyssen surname in 1814 when he inherited the estate of Francis John Tyssen of Hackney, which included the manors of Hackney, Middlesex, and Foulden, Norfolk. In 1852 Amherst and his father both assumed, by royal license, the name Tyssen-Amhurst, in lieu of Daniel-Tyssen, as part of the inheritance or the property of still another maternally related family, the Amhersts or Amhursts. In 1877, by a further royal license, Amherst altered the spelling of his name from Tyssen-Amhurst to Tyssen-Amherst. When he was elevated to the peerage in 1892, he chose as his title 'Baron Amherst of Hackney.'"

Interestingly, Lord Amherst signed both surnames when he added his signature to the Gutenberg Bible, writing *W. Amhurst T. Amherst.*

In this book, we use the later family name, Amherst.

Also see: Cockayne, G. E., revised by Vicary Gibbs, Dictionary of National Biography, 1901–12, *The Complete Peerage of England, Scotland, Ireland, Great Britain and the United Kingdom,* vol. 1, London: The Saint Catherine Press, p. 125–126. Also see *Debrett's Peerage and Baronetage 1976,* Kingston Upon Thames: Kelly's Directories, 1976; *Burke's Genealogical and Heraldic History of the Peerage, Baronetage and Knightage,* London: Burke's Peerage Ltd., 1970.

27. **one of the great bibliophiles:** Distad, Merrill, "William Amhurst Tyssen
-Amherst, First Baron of Hackney, Country Gentleman, Collector, and Connois-
seur, 1835–1909," p. 14.
28. **defrauded Amherst:** "Wills—Mr Charles Cheston," *London Times*, July 13, 1906;
"Heavy Losses by Fraud," *London Times*, December 9, 1908; "Lord's Losses
Through a Fraud," *Luton Times and Advertiser*, August 3, 1906; "Earl of Amherst
Ruined in Old Age," *Washington Times*, August 12, 1906; "Lost in Speculation:
London Solicitor Robs Clients of Immense Funds," *Bemidji Daily Pioneer*, July 12,
1906; "English Peer Sells Library to Pay off Debt of Honor," *Deseret Evening News*,
December 26, 1908; "Is To Be Feared . . . Lord Amherst of Hackney," *Richmond
Times-Dispatch*, December 9, 1908.
29. **"coward's way out":** Duggan, Brian Patrick, *Saluki: The Desert Hound and the
English Travelers Who Brought It to the West*, Jefferson: McFarland & Co., 2009,
p. 68.
30. **"cruel and heavy":** "Sad Reverse of Fortune, Lord Amherst's Pathetic Speech,"
Tamworth Herald, August 4, 1906, p. 3.
31. **negotiates a bank loan:** Letter from Alan Missen to Amherst, April 22, 1907,
Thomas Fisher Rare Book Library, Toronto, Box 11.
32. **"brown paper parcels":** Duggan, Brian Patrick, *Saluki: The Desert Hound and the
English Travelers Who Brought It to the West*, Jefferson: McFarland & Co., 2009,
p. 68.
33. **"still possible":** "Lord Amherst of Hackney," *London Times*, September 6, 1906.
34. **sells to J. P. Morgan:** "Caxton Books Morgon Got: Description of Rare Volumes
from Lord Amherst's Library Sale," *New York Times*, December 6, 1908; "$5,000
Bible Mr. Morgan's: He Was Purchaser of the King Charles I Copy at Amherst
Sale, *New York Times*, Dec. 6, 1908.
35. **"reason for living ceased":** "Lord Amherst is Dead: Spent Lifetime Gathering
Great Library Which He Was Lately Forced to Sell," *New York Times*, Jan. 18, 1909.
Also see "Lord Amherst of Hackney," *London Times*, Jan. 18, 1909.
36. *Victoria Concordia Crescit:* Loosely translated into English, Lord Amherst's motto
was "Victory Grows by Harmony."

Chapter 4: The Patriot

1. **His entire library:** Julian Brown, The fate of Mr. Dyson Perrins's mss., Portfolio
& Art News Annual, No. 5, 1962, p. 57.
2. **Plan B:** Handley, John L., *The Quiet Hero: The Story of C. W. Perrins 1864–1958*, Malvern: Aspect Design, 2010, p. 18.
3. **herbs and spices the store stocked:** Keogh, Brian, *The Secret Sauce, A History of
Lea & Perrins*, Worcester: Leaper Books, 1997, p. 3.
4. **marketing trick:** Ibid., p. 28.

5. **getting their product onto ocean liners:** Shurtleff, William and Akiko Aoyagi, *History of Worcestershire Sauce (1837–2012)*, SoyInfo Center, 2012, p. 182.

6. **secret:** Only a few people knew the recipe for more than 170 years. But in 2009, a copy of the formula was found in a trash bin after some clean-up at the factory. It turned out that the sauce is a blend of water, cloves, sugar, soy sauce, fish, vinegar, lemon zest, peppers, pickles, and tamarind.

7. **seven hundred:** Sandon, Henry, *Royal Worcester Porcelain from 1862 to the Present Day*, London: Barrie & Jenkins, 1973, p. 30.

8. **product that equaled its inspiration:** Lund and Dr. Wall: Savage, George, *The Story of Royal Worcester*, London: Pitkin Pictorials, 1979, p. 3.

9. **early pieces:** See http://collectorsweekly.com/china-and-dinnerware/royal -worcester

10. **"early experimental work":** Perrins, C. W. Dyson, "Mr. Dyson Perrins' Collection of Early Worcester China," *The Connoisseur* 4, no. 13 (September 1902), p. 101.

11. **On the factory floor:** A Guide Through The Royal Porcelain Works, Worcester, 1895, p. 12, https://archive.org/details/guidethrouhroyaooroyarich.

12. **fingerprints:** Ibid., p. 30.

13. **cricket:** Sandon, Henry, *Royal Worcester Porcelain from 1862 to the Present Day*, London: Barrie & Jenkins, 1973, p. 46.

14. **five-figure profits:** Ibid., p. 24.

15. **Whatever the catalyst:** Panayotova, Stella, *I Turned It into a Palace: Sydney Cockerell and the Fitzwilliam Museum*, Fitzwilliam Museum, 2008, p. 34.

16. **Sydney Cockerell:** De Hamel, Christopher, "Cockerell as Entrepreneur," *The Book Collector*, spring 2006, p. 65.

17. **"welcome guest":** Ibid., p. 68.

18. **"a single glance":** Brown, T. J., G. M. Meredith-Owens, and D. H. Turner, "Manuscripts from the Dyson Perrins Collection," *The British Museum Quarterly* 23, no. 2 (1961) p. 28; Also see "C. W. Dyson Perrins," *London Times*, July 2, 1958.

19. **many doors Cockerell opens:** De Hamel, Christopher, "Cockerell as Entrepreneur," *The Book Collector*, spring 2006, p. 65.

20. **"rewarded for the journey":** Four letters from Charles William Dyson Perrins to Charles Fairfax Murray. Harry Ransom Center, The University of Texas at Austin, Digital Collections, http://hrc.contentdm.oclc.org/cdm/ref/collection /p15878coll57/id/2484#nav_top.

21. **Cockerell advises him:** De Hamel, Christopher, "Cockerell as Entrepreneur," *The Book Collector*, spring 2006, p. 65.

22. **"showy":** Ibid., p. 66.

23. **auction catalog:** Sotheby, Wilkinson & Hodge, *Catalogue of the Valuable Library of Ancient Manuscripts and Valuable & Rare Printed Books, the Property of L. W. Hodson, Esq.*, London: Dryden Press, May 1906.

24. **Epistole et Evangelii:** See *Epistole et Evangelii* at https://loc.gov/item/48035464/.

25. **"opportunity"**: Dyson, C. W. Perrins, preface, *Italian Book-Illustrations and Early Printing: A Catalogue of Early Italian Books in the Library of C. W. Dyson Perrins*, Oxford: University Press, 1914.
26. **"Far too many cripples"**: "The Dyson Perrins Sale," unsigned, *Times Literary Supplement*, July 5, 1947.
27. **"gummed together"**: Ashby, Thomas, British Archaeological Association, Royal Archaeological Institute of Great Britain and Ireland, "An Unknown Sixteenth Century Topography of Rome," *The Archaeological Journal* 65 (March 1908), p. 245.
28. **"bibelots"**: *The Dyson Perrins Collection, Part 1*, with an introduction by Francis Wormald, London: Sotheby and Co., December 1958, p. 7.
29. **owned by the Duke of Warwick:** The manuscript is now housed at the Morgan Library in New York. See the Annunciation image, and the others in the book, at http://ica.themorgan.org/manuscript/page/1/159610.
30. **value of the collected works:** De Hamel, Christopher, "Cockerell as Entrepreneur," *The Book Collector*, spring 2006, p. 70.
31. **"frontispiece page"**: Konig, Eberhard, "Illuminated Incunabula in the Doheny Library," Notes on the Gutenberg Bible, Christie, Manson & Woods International Inc., Estelle Doheny Collection from the Edward Laurence Doheny Memorial Library, St. John's Seminary, Camarillo, California, New York: Christie, Manson & Woods International, 1987–89, Christies Catalog, Part 1, p. 285.
32. **"not only in America"**: "Collectors to Bid on a Gutenberg Bible; One of the Seven Known Vellum Copies to be Sold at the Hoe Sale on April 24," *New York Times*, April 12, 1911.
33. **"jealousy"**: "Books Westward Ho; England's Plaint that America Takes her Bibliographic Treasures," *New York Times*, August 2, 1902.
34. **"Brailes-ish"**: Pollard, Graham, "Obituary Notices, C. W. Dyson Perrins," undated, Papers of Rita Faulders.
35. **Worcestershire Regiment:** For statistics regarding the the Worcestershire Regiment, see Forces War Records, https://www.forces-war-records.co.uk/.
36. **one hundred illuminated manuscripts:** The British Library holds fifty-two manuscripts from the Yates Thompson collection. See pages from them at: https://bl.uk/catalogues/illuminatedmanuscripts/results.asp.
37. **earthenware and female nude figurines:** Sandon, Henry, *Royal Worcester Porcelain from 1862 to the Present Day*, London: Barrie & Jenkins, 1973, p. 48.
38. **more than repaid:** Pelik, Rowena, C. W., *Dyson Perrins: A Brief Account of His Life, His Achievements, His Collections and Benefactions*, Worcester: Dyson Perrins Museum Trust, 1983, p. 20.
39. **"to be a collector"**: de Ricci, Seymour, *English Collectors of Books and Manuscripts (1530–1930) and Their Marks of Ownership*, New York: Cambridge University Press, 2010, p. 193.

Chapter 5: The Mighty Woman Book Hunter

1. **Rosenwald:** See Library of Congress at http://loc.gov/exhibits/heavenlycraft/heavenly-exhibit.html.

2. **$75 million:** Davis, Margaret Leslie, *Dark Side of Fortune*, Berkeley: University of California Press, 1998, p. 80.

3. **411-acre:** See Library of Congress regarding Frank Lloyd Wright at https://www.loc.gov/exhibits/flw/flw04.html.

4. **"May Break Records":** "Hoe Library Sale May Break Records; Gutenberg Bible, Which Last Sold for $20,000, to be Offered on First Day, *New York Times*, March 31, 1911.

5. **bidding had advanced:** Ibid.

6. **"Man Who Paid $50,000":** "The Man Who Paid $50,000 for the Gutenberg Bible; Henry E. Huntington Leaps Into Fame as a Book Collector by Buying the Church Library for $1,300,000, as Well as the chief Treasure of the Hoe Collection," *New York Times*, April 29, 1911. Also see "Gutenberg Bible Sold for $50,000; Buyer for Henry E. Huntington Gets It as the Highest Price Ever Paid for a Book," *New York Times*, April 24, 1911.

7. **"all that practically unlimited means can procure":** Bonino, MaryAnn, The Doheny Mansion, p. 75.

8. **calm and convincing:** "Doheny Declares Robison said Japan had Mobilized; Defends His Loan to Fall . . . Wife and Son on Stand, Mrs. Doheny Tells of the Torn Note and Younger," *New York Times*, December 9, 1926.

9. **five years of torture:** Edward Doheny was formally indicted on federal charges of bribery and conspiracy on June 5, 1925. He was acquitted of all criminal charges in March 1930. However, numerous civil trials related to the scandal continued over the next decade.

10. **"distract or sway":** "Rich Men Scared," *Time* magazine, March 11, 1935.

11. **"broken and changed man":** Davis, Margaret Leslie, *Dark Side of Fortune*, Berkeley: University of California Press, 1998, p. 246. Also see Diaries of Henry W. O'Melveny, Papers of Henry W. O'Melveny, Huntington Library, San Marino, CA.

12. **George Bernard Shaw:** Wolf, Edwin with John Fleming, *Rosenbach: A Biography*, Cleveland: The World Publishing Co., 1960, p. 359.

13. **steady exodus:** "Fifty Years an Ardent Book Collector; Rosenbach, Now Sixty, Started His Career as a Boy of Ten," *New York Times*, July 18, 1936.

14. **"fun to pay through the nose":** "Gutenberg Bible Sells for $106,000; Dr. A.S.W. Rosenbach Pays High Price for Rare Work of First Printer," *The New York Times*, Feb. 16, 1926.

15. **"such a novice":** Wolf, Edwin with John Fleming, *Rosenbach: A Biography*, Cleveland: The World Publishing Co., 1960, pp. 360–61.

16. **"intellectual virtuosity":** "It Was Fun to Pay Though the Nose," Book Review, *New York Times*, Nov. 20, 1960.

17. **"MESSAGE OF HIGH REGARD":** Wolf, Edwin with John Fleming, *Rosenbach: A Biography*, Cleveland: The World Publishing Co., 1960, p. 406.

18. **fore-edge paintings:** See examples at http://twistedsifter.com/2013/09/hidden -artworks-on-the-edges-of-books/.

19. **"I was put to work":** Miller, Lucille V., "Edward and Estelle Doheny," *Ventura County Historical Society Quarterly* 6 (November 1960): pp. 3–20.

20. **"twirled":** Hamilton, Denise, "Curator Rekindles Early Chapter of Doheny Archives," *Los Angeles Times*, February 4, 1988.

21. **"Rosenbach of the West":** Rosenthal, Robert, "Los Angeles & Chicago: Two Cities, Two Bibliophiles," *A Bibliophile's Los Angeles, Essays for the International Association of Bibliophiles on the Occasion of Its XIVth Congress*, Los Angeles, 1985, p. 12.

22. **"in four volumes":** Exceedingly rare, a four-volume Gutenberg Bible is currently owned by the Universitaetsbibliothek Leipzig in Germany. The only other known four-volume copy is in Paris at the Bibliothèque nationale.

23. **"the copy which Dr. Vollbehr sold":** Dr. Otto F. H. Vollbehr of Berlin, German, purchased a three-volume Gutenberg Bible from the Benedictine Abbey of St. Paul in Carinthia, Austria, for $305,000 in 1926.

24. **"fulfilled my obligation":** Letter from Alice Millard to Estelle Doheny, Rita Faulders Collection. (This is one of two extant Gutenberg Bibles bound in four volumes. The other copy is in the Bibliothèque nationale de France in Paris; the "German university" where Mrs. Millard saw the four-volume Gutenberg was most likely in Leipzig. In 1933, there were reportedly three complete Gutenberg Bibles in that city, a copy at the Buch- und Schriftmuseum and two copies at the Library of Leipzig, which became the Karl-Marx Universitatsbibliothek after World War II. After the reunification of Germany in 1991, the university's name was restored to Leipzig University.

    See Norman, Don Cleveland, *The 500th Anniversary Pictorial Census of the Gutenberg Bible*, Chicago: The Cloverdale Press, 1961, p. 70.)

25. **"highest form of custodianship":** Rosenthal, Robert, "Los Angeles & Chicago, Two Cities, Two Bibliophiles," *A Bibliophile's Los Angeles, Essays for the International Association of Bibliophiles on the Occasion of its XIVth Congress*, Los Angeles, 1985, p. 12.

26. **"highbrow taste":** Danky, James P., and Wayne A. Wiegand, *Women in Print: Essays on the Print Culture of American Women from the Nineteenth and Twentieth Centuries*, Madison: University of Wisconsin Press, 2006, p. 160.

27. **"Mrs. Millard's hallmark":** Rosenthal, Robert. "Los Angeles & Chicago, Two Cities, Two Bibliophiles."

28. **"Costly as it was":** Ibid., p. 24.

29. **"my gorgeous books":** Ibid., p. 25.

30. **self-confidence:** Ibid., p. 24.

31. **"ingratiating enthusiasms":** Ibid., p. 23.

32. **source of knowledge:** Dickinson, Donald C., "Robert O. Schad: A Treasure of a Bookman," *Southern California Quarterly* 81, no. 2 (Summer 1999), p. 236.

33. ***The Book as a Work of Art:*** *The Book as a Work of Art: An Exhibition of Books and Manuscripts from the Library of Mrs. Edward Laurence Doheny*, Los Angeles: Printed by Ward Ritchie, 1935. https://babel.hathitrust.org/cgi/pt?id=mdp.39015033647671.

34. **"youth in hardship":** Davis, Margaret Leslie, *Dark Side of Fortune*, Berkeley: University of California Press, 1998, p. 1.

35. **mortal world:** Ibid., p. 3.

36. **"logically carries":** Schad, Robert O., "The Estelle Doheny Collection," *New Colophon III*, New York: Duschnes Crawford, Inc., 1950, p. 13. She may have turned to book collecting as a form of "grief therapy and memorialization."

37. **buying eight individual leaves:** From the George C. Smith sale. See letter from Gabriel Wells to Estelle Doheny, November 4, 1938, and attached bill of sale.

Chapter 6: The Lost Gutenberg

1. **via wireless:** "Buys Ancient Bible at Sea by Wireless; Dr. A.S.W. Rosenbach Uses Olympic's Radio to Acquire Gutenberg Volume Here," *New York Times*, April 25, 1923.

2. **"nothing nobler":** Rosenbach, A. S. W., *Books and Bidders: The Adventures of a Bibliophile*, Boston: Little, Brown and Company, 1927, p. 215.

3. **"absolutely confidential":** Letter from Lucille Miller to A. S. W. Rosenbach, January 30, 1947.

4. **"most thrilling of all":** Ibid.

5. **a never-to-be-repeated opportunity:** Letter from A. S. W. Rosenbach to Lucille Miller, February 27, 1947. Also see *Catalogue of the Magnificent Library Principally of Early Printed Books and Early Illustrated Books Formed by C. W. Dyson Perrins, Esq.*, London: Sotheby & Co., 1947, pp. 24–25.

6. **"confidential agent in London":** Letter from A. S. W. Rosenbach to Lucille Miller, February 27, 1947.

7. **"I was anxious":** Letter from Estelle Doheny to A. S. W. Rosenbach, March 3, 1947.

8. ***Habent sua fata libelli:*** The Latin expression *Pro captu lectoris habent sua fata libelli* loosely translated is: "According to the capabilities of the reader, books have their destiny."

9. **"Mighty Women Book Hunters":** Basbanes, Nicholas A., *A Gentle Madness: Bibliophiles, Bibliomanes, and the Eternal Passion for Books*, New York: Holt, 1999, p. 31. Also see Rosenbach, A. S. W., *A Book Hunter's Holiday*, Boston: Houghton Mifflin Co., p. 129.

10. **"Continental buyers":** Telegram from A. S. W. Rosenbach to Lucille Miller, care of Mrs. Edward L. Doheny, March 4, 1947.
11. **"nothing more perfect":** Rosenbach, A. S. W., *Books and Bidders: The Adventures of a Bibliophile*, Boston: Little, Brown and Company, 1927, pp. 213–14.
12. **"Japanese beauty":** Ibid. p. 213.
13. **"leeway":** Lucille Miller, memorandum, March 7, 1947. Also see Wolf, Edwin with John Fleming, *Rosenbach: A Biography*, Cleveland: The World Publishing Co., 1960, p. 146.
14. **"Doing all I can":** Telegram from A. S. W. Rosenbach to Mrs. Edward L. Doheny, March 10, 1947.
15. **"ornate golden altar":** Wright, Wendy M., *The Lady of the Angels and Her City*, Collegeville: Liturgical Press, 2013, p. 86.
    Edward's condition for the gift was that the design be based on Santa Prisca, a 1748 Spanish Renaissance church in Taxco, Mexico.
16. **"religious shield":** Author Dan La Botz quoted in Davis, Margaret Leslie, *Dark Side of Fortune*, Berkeley: University of California Press, 1998, p. 265.
17. **papal countess:** When she received the title in 1939, Estelle Doheny was the first woman honored with this title in the state of California. It remains a very rare honor. At Mrs. Doheny's request, the title was used for only the most formal occasions. In 1931, Mr. and Mrs. Doheny were given the pontifical titles of Knight and Lady of the Ancient Equestrian Order of the Holy Sepulcher.
18. **new record price:** "Gutenberg Bible," *Times* (London), March 12, 1947.
19. **value of:** "Gutenberg Bible Bought for £22,000," *New York Times*, March 11, 1947.
20. **studios of the BBC:** Television broadcasts had resumed only one year earlier in June, after the station was taken off the air during World War II. "Gutenberg Bible Televised," *Maryborough Chronicle*, August 1, 1947, http://trove.nla.gov.au/ndp/del/article/147457215?searchTerm=gutenberg%20bible&searchLimits=.
    Regarding BBC's being back on air as of June 1946, see https://en.wikipedia.org/wiki/BBC_One.
21. **"remain in England":** "Gutenberg Bible Sold," *Yorkshire Post*, March 12, 1947; "Gutenberg Bible Sale" *Nottingham Evening Post*, March 11, 1947; "Sale of Gutenberg Bible," *Gloucestershire Echo*, March 11, 1947.
22. **"regret lost Gutenberg":** Telegram from A. S. W. Rosenbach to Mrs. Edward L. Doheny, March 11, 1947, time-stamped 9:41 a.m.
23. **"gloomy fog":** Rita Faulders, audio interview with Lucille Miller, August 15, 1984.
24. **"no idea who had it":** Rita Faulders, audio interview with Lucille Miller, August 15, 1984.
25. **"private hands":** Letter from A. S. W. Rosenbach to Mrs. Edward L. Doheny, March 12, 1947.
26. **"I purchased":** Letter from Ernest Maggs to Mrs. E. Doheny, March 26, 1947.
27. **"no quibbling":** Rita Faulders, audio interview with Lucille Miller, August 15, 1984.

28. **strictest confidence:** Letter from Estelle Doheny to Ernest Maggs, April 2, 1947.
29. **a family firm:** Frere, Philip Beaumont, *The Story of a Law Firm: Being the History of Frere, Cholmeley and Nicholsons, 1750 to 1950*, Published privately for Frere, Cholmeley and Nicholson, by B. T. Batsford, 1950.
30. **aristocratic pedigree:** Kermode, Frank, "Literary Upper Crust," book review, *New York Times*, December 19, 1999, https://archive.nytimes.com/www.nytimes.com/books/99/12/19/reviews/991219.19kermodt.html.

    Also see excerpt "Osbert Sitwell by Philip Zeigler, *New York Times* on the Web": https://nytimes.com/books/first/z/ziegler-sitwell.html.
31. **"found his friendship":** Ziegler, Philip, *Osbert Sitwell*, New York: A. Knopf, 1999, p. 374.

    Frere continues to handle other legal matters for the writer, including copyright litigation and charges of slander, and he steps in to help Osbert with a crazed fan by physically dissuading her from drowning herself in the Round Pond in Kensington Gardens.
32. **wide range of interests:** See the Bryher Papers, General Collection, Beinecke Rare Book and Manuscript Library, Yale University, GEM MSS97 Box 108.
33. **who had retired from active practice:** "Clerks' letter books,"AIM25, Archives in London and the M25 area, http://aim25.ac.uk/cgi-bin/vcdf/detail?coll_id=8789&inst_id=111&nv1=search&nv2=.
34. **law firm:** Frere, Philip Beaumont, *The Story of a Law Firm*, p. 16.

Chapter 7: The Countess and Her Gutenberg

1. **"mad price":** "Public Library Will Place on Exhibition First Gutenberg Bible to Arrive in America," *New York Times*, November 6, 1947. The Lenox Library is now part of the renowned New York Public Library.
2. **holiday exhibition:** "Scriptural Items Shown at Library," *New York Times*, December 1, 1947.
3. **President Harry S. Truman:** "Solemnity Marks Taking of Oaths," *Los Angeles Times*, January 21, 1949; "Biblical Verses Chose to Stress Peace Aims," *Los Angeles Times*, January 20, 1949, "Truman Ready to Take Oath, Defends Electoral System," *Los Angeles Times*, January 20, 1949.
4. **"repose of my soul":** Letter from Estelle Doheny to Father Flavin, undated, Archive of the Archdiocese of Los Angeles, Mission Hills, CA, Box 2.
5. **"finest Gutenberg Bibles":** Letter from David A. Randall to Miss Lucille Miller, May 23, 1950.
6. **to inspect the Bible:** Letter from Estelle Doheny to David Randall, June 7, 1950.
7. **$137,500:** Letter from David Randall to Robert O. Schad, August 11, 1950.

8. **"buy me a Gutenberg Bible":** Randall, David A., *Dukedom Large Enough*, New York: Random House, 1969, p. 115.

9. **four-page contract:** Letter from Estelle Doheny to General Theological Seminary, September 5, 1950.

10. **no one ever told:** Randall, David A., *Dukedom Large Enough*, New York: Random House, 1969, p. 116.

11. **Randall also claims:** David Randall to Dean Rose, September 24, 1962. Also see Randall, David A., *Dukedom Large Enough*, New York: Random House, 1969, p. 116.

12. **he's willing:** Christie, Manson & Woods International Inc., Estelle Doheny Collection from the Edward Laurence Doheny Memorial Library, St. John's Seminary, Camarillo, California, New York: Christie, Manson & Woods International, 1987–89, v. 1, p. 15.

13. **Sydney Cockerell:** Linenthal, Richard A. "Sydney Cockerell: bookseller in all but name" in *Transactions of the Cambridge Bibliographical Society*, volume 13 (2007), p. 383.

14. **"results you know":** Letter from David Randall to Estelle Doheny, January 24, 1951. Also see "News of Scribner Books and Authors," press release, February 5, 1951.

15. **"Not interested":** Telegram from Estelle Doheny to David Randall, June 3, 1953.

16. **$1.8 million:** "Gutenberg Bible Brings $1.8 Million," *New York Times*, March 9, 1978.

17. **grown her husband's fortune:** Edward Doheny's entire estate at the time of his death was appraised at only slightly over $9 million. The bulk of his assets had already been distributed to his heirs, and stock in his Pan American Petroleum and Transport Company had become greatly devalued during the Depression. Doheny's decision to bequeath his holdings prior to his death was fortuitous. In 1934, President Roosevelt initiated a rigorous inheritance tax.

      Estelle Doheny's estate at her death in 1958 was valued at roughly $37.5 million. When that number is added to the total sales from the dispersal of her book collection of $37.8 million, her fortune is calculated at roughly $75 million, an increase of 733 percent. See Davis, Margaret Leslie, *Dark Side of Fortune*, Berkeley: University of California Press, 1998, p. 276. Calculation is based on the Percentage Change Calculator at www.calculatorsoup.com.

18. **"imponderable coincidence":** Quote by dealer John Fleming, Reif, Rita, "Antiques," *New York Times*, January 15, 1978.

19. **book offered in March:** Sold for $1.8 million, this copy is now at the Gutenberg Museum in Mainz.

20. **world-record price:** Rief, Rita, "Gutenberg Bible Bought at Auction for $2 Million for Stuttgart Library," *New York Times*, April 8, 1978, and "University of Texas Pays $2.4 Million for Gutenberg," *New York Times*, June 10, 1978.

21. **"foundation stone":** Hamilton, Denise, "Curator Rekindles Early Chapter of Doheny Archives," *Los Angeles Times*, February 4, 1988

22. **"by not marrying":** Ibid.

Chapter 8: The Nuclear Bibliophiles

1. **nudged them out of their path:** Schwab, Richard N. "The History of the Book and the Proton Milliprobe: An Application of the PIXE Technique of Analysis," *Library Trends* (Summer 1987), p. 55.

2. **drill a hole:** Thomas A. Cahill, interview with the author, November 14–15, 2013, Sacramento, CA. Also see Cahill, Thomas A., "The UC Davis Gutenberg Project: Science in the Service of the Humanities," lecture, Pius XII Memorial Library, St. Louis University, September 28, 2009.

3. **slight changes:** Richard N. Schwab, interview with the author, November 14–15, 2013, Sacramento, CA.

4. **path-breaking insights:** Cahill, T. A., B. Kusko, and R. N. Schwab. "Analyses of Inks and Papers in Historical Documents through External PIXE Beam Techniques." *Nuclear Instruments and Methods* 181 (1981): 205–08.

5. **"much less than sunlight":** Cahill, T. A., B. H. Kusko, R. A. Eldred, and R. N. Schwab. "Gutenberg's Inks and Papers: Non-Destructive Compositional Analyses by Proton Milliprobe," *Archaeometry*, 26.1 (1984), p. 3.

6. **"carbon-based":** Thomas A. Cahill, interview with the author, Nov. 14–15, 2013, Sacramento, CA. Also see Schwab, Richard N., "The History of the Book and the Proton Milliprobe: An Application of the PIXE Technique of Analysis," *Library Trends* (Summer 1987): 53–84.

7. **a visionary:** McGill, Douglas C. "Adrian Wilson, 64, A Printing Teacher and Book Designer," *New York Times*, February 6, 1988.

8. **who would be willing:** Dr. Richard N. Schwab and Dr. Thomas A. Cahill, interview with the author, November 14–15, 2013, Sacramento, CA.

9. **whole apparatus:** Prior to the cyclotron testing, Charles Faulders made a trip to the lab at the University of California at Davis to check on the apparatus to hold the Bible. Faulders assisted Cahill and Schwab with modifications to better support and stabilize the heavy Bible during the tests. Faulders was part of the rotating team turning the pages of the Gutenberg Bible during the nonstop tests.

10. **a "she":** Rita Faulders, interview with the author, May 12, 2013, Camarillo, CA.

11. **plot out the chemical analysis:** Dr. Thomas A. Cahill, interview with the author. Also see Ing, Janet, *Johann Gutenberg and His Bible: A Historical Study*, New York: The Typophiles, 1988, pp. 86–88, 95–97.

12. **"These unique pages":** Schwab, Richard N. "The Gutenberg Meets the Cyclotron," November 2005, unpublished, courtesy of Richard N. Schwab. Also see

Schwab, Richard N.., Thomas A. Cahill, Bruce H. Kusko, and Daniel L. Wick, "Cyclotron Analysis of the Ink in the 42-Line Bible," *The Papers of the Bibliographical Society of America* 77, no. 3 (1983): 285–315. http://www.jstor.org/stable/24302918.

13. **distance between the Pole Stars:** There are occasional variations, but what's striking are the similarities. Richard N. Scwhab, interview with the author. Also see Schwab, Richard N., Thomas A. Cahill, Robert A. Eldred, Bruce H. Kusko, and Daniel L. Wick. "New Evidence on the Printing of the Gutenberg Bible: The Inks in the Doheny Copy," *The Papers of the Bibliographical Society of America* 79, no. 3 (1985): pp. 381–83. http://jstor.org/stable/24303664.

14. **Paul Schwenke:** Schwenke, Paul, *Johannes Gutenbergs zweiundvierzigzeilige Bibel: Erganzungsband zur Faksimile-Ausgabe*, Leipzig, 1923. Also see Schwab, Richard N., "An Ersatz Leaf in the Doheny Gutenberg Bible Volume I," *The Papers of the Bibliographical Society of America*, December 1987, p. 1 note 2.

15. **printed concurrently:** Schwab, Richard N., Thomas A. Cahill, Robert A. Eldred, Bruce H. Kusko, and Daniel L. Wick. "New Evidence on the Printing of the Gutenberg Bible: The Inks in the Doheny Copy," *The Papers of the Bibliographical Society of America* 79, no. 3 (1985): p. 387.

16. **detect changes:** Schwab, Richard N., "The History of the Book and the Proton Milliprobe: An Application of the PIXE Technique of Analysis," *Library Trends* (Summer 1987), p. 70.

17. **"almost hear":** Needham, Paul, "The Paper Supply of the Gutenberg Bible," *The Papers of the Bibliographical Society of America* 79, no. 3, 1985: 303–74. Richard N. Schwab and Thomas A. Cahill interview with the author, November 14–15, 2013, Sacramento, CA. Also see Schwab, Richard N., "Gutenberg Meets the Cyclotron," unpublished, 2005, with permission from Richard N. Schwab.

18. **"able to confirm":** Schwab, Richard N., "The History of the Book and the Proton Milliprobe," p. 70.

19. **"he took the ink secret with him":** Richard N. Schwab and Dr. Thomas A. Cahill, interview with the author.

20. **"conjugate pair of stubs":** Schwab, Richard N., "An Ersatz Leaf in the Doheny Gutenberg Bible Volume I," *The Papers of the Bibliographical Society of America*, December 1987, p. 480.

21. **compares it to other versions:** Ibid., p. 484.

22. **"followed his own inclination":** Ibid.

23. **refurbished atom smasher:** "Art Frauds Beware," *Popular Mechanics*, November 1982.

24. **Dead Sea Scrolls:** "Beaming in on the Past," *Time* magazine, March 10, 1986.

25. **"Few instruments of science":** "A Cyclotron's Story," *New York Times*, May 12, 1987.

26. **"sake of knowledge":** McColm, Del, "Gutenberg Bible Analysis Makes History," *Davis Enterprise*, April 16, 1982.

Chapter 9: The Unexpected Betrayal

1. **As Rita Faulders looks back:** Rita S. Faulders, *The Dissolution of the Estelle Doheny Collection*, St. John's Seminary, Camarillo, California, 1985–87, July 1994. Faulders writes in the report's foreword: "This report is my personal record of events during the years 1985–88, when The Estelle Doheny Collection was dissolved. I began writing the report shortly after the last auction, but because I had no clear idea what to do with it if finished I put the pages aside until recent months. . . . The facts written here are based on the office desk calendar I used as Curator of the Collection and notes made in my personal journal. . . . The reader may well detect some strong emotions on my part, and I make no defense or apology for that. I have the opportunity to say here what I could not say at the time. Before the sale was announced and while it was under way, I was told to say nothing to anyone."

2. **"choicest of the choice":** Ibid., p. 1.

3. **"poked into every corner":** Ibid., p. 2.

4. **in exchange for $6 million:** In the 1990s, journalist Judith Martel reported that proceeds from the sale of the Western Collection was in the $10 million range. According to a former archdiocesan employee, the money has never been fully accounted for. See Judith Martel, "Where Has All the Money Gone?" *The Mission*, March 1996.

5. **not to the seminary:** Chandler, Russell, and Sam Enriquez, "L.A. Archdiocese to Auction Off Its Gutenberg Bible," *Los Angeles Times*, February 28, 1987. "The price of the artworks and the name of the buyer were not revealed, but St. John's Seminary business manager James Hawkins said the seminary received no proceeds from the sale."

6. **"Didn't we tell you?":** Rita S. Faulders, *The Dissolution of the Estelle Doheny Collection*, St. John's Seminary, Camarillo, A, 1985–87, July 1994, p. 7.

7. **irrevocably breaking:** Last Will and Testament of Carrie Estelle Doheny, filed November5, 1958. Also see trust documents connected with the establishment of the Edward L. Doheny Jr. Memorial Library, papers of Rita Faulders.

8. **"non-compensatable":** Quoted by Robert O. Schad, "The Estelle Doheny Collection," *New Colophon III*, New York: Duschnes Crawford, Inc., 1950, p. 242. http://himesduniway.org/Doheny1.pdf.

9. **"exalt what is most noble":** *The Tidings*, May 1, 1981, Papers of Rita Faulders.

10. **"still remain on earth":** Letter from Richard N. Schwab to Rita Faulders, March 5, 1987.

11. **"Who would want to buy an old book":** Rita S. Faulders, *The Dissolution of the Estelle Doheny Collection*, p. 16.

12. **ten priests:** "L.A. Archdiocese Selling $20 Million in Art, Books," *Chicago Sun Times*, March 4, 1987.

13. **"Will you do all in your power":** "Building a Foundation for the Future, The Development of the Edward Laurence and Carrie Estelle Doheny Seminary Foundation, Its Purpose and Goals," privately printed brochure, Archdiocese of Los Angeles, 1987.
14. **some of the finest:** Schad, Robert O., "The Estelle Doheny Collection," *New Colophon III*, New York: Duschnes Crawford, Inc., 1950, p. 23.
15. **"riches of a thousand years":** Starr, Kevin, *Material Dreams*, p. 342.
16. **"monetary value":** Chandler, Russell, "Los Angeles Archdiocese's Treasures on Block: Scholars, Historians Grumble Over Sale of Doheny Collection," *Los Angeles Times*, March 7, 1987.
17. **"I personally would have contributed":** Ibid.
18. **"hypocrisy and be amazed":** "Sales from Doheny Library," letters to the *Times*, written by John Rilling, *Los Angeles Times*, March 20, 1987.
19. **"redeployment":** Letter from the Most Reverend Roger Mahony, Archbishop of Los Angeles to My Dear Friends, Office of the Archbishop, February 1987 accompanying the brochure "Building a Foundation for the Future, The Development of the Edward Laurence and Carrie Estelle Doheny Seminary Foundation, Its Purpose and Goals," privately printed, Archdiocese of Los Angeles, 1987. Also see: Chandler, Russell and Sam Enriquez, "L.A. Archdiocese to Auction Off Its Gutenberg Bible, *Los Angeles Times*, February 28, 1987.
20. **"another sad example":** Barker, Nicolas, *The Book Collector*, vol. 36, nos. 1–4, 1987. Also quoted in Rita S. Faulders, *The Dissolution of the Estelle Doheny Collection*, p. 26.
21. **"carry on the tradition":** *The Estelle Doheny Collection of the Edward Laurence Doheny Memorial Library*, St. John's Seminary, Camarillo, California (undated).
22. **"Dispersal of this collection":** Chandler, Russell, "Los Angeles Archdiocese's Treasures on Block: Scholars, Historians Grumble Over Sale of Doheny Collection." Also see Smith, Doug, "The Doheny's Sacred, Secular Treasure Trove Soon to be Lost," *Los Angeles Times*, March 7, 1987.
23. **"No, he was Lutheran":** Rita S. Faulders, *The Dissolution of the Estelle Doheny Collection*, p. 27.
24. **"intrinsically more valuable":** Martel, Judith, "Where Has All the Money Gone: Doheny Collection Sale," *Los Angeles Lay Catholic Mission*, March 1996.
25. **William Doheny Jr.:** Rita S. Faulders, *The Dissolution of the Estelle Doheny Collection*, p. 28.
26. **"dress rehearsals":** Conlon, Tom. "Doheny Collection Sale Leaves Void," *The Press-Courier*, March 8, 1987.
27. **John Fleming:** "John Fleming, A Book Dealer, Dies at Age 77," *New York Times*, December 21, 1987.
28. **"the greatest book and manuscript sale":** Reif, Rita, "Auctions," *New York Times*, March 13, 1987.

29. **"by implosion":** Rita S. Faulders, *The Dissolution of the Estelle Doheny Collection*, p. 29.

30. **sitting alone:** Rita Faulders, interview with the author.

31. **broadside folio:** Pope Alexander VI, *Copia de la bula del decreto y concession*. Broadside Folio. A unique printing of the "Bull of Demarcation," separating the New World into Spanish and Portugese Territories. See: *The Estelle Doheny Collection, Exhibition Handlist*, Christie, Manson & Woods International, 1987.

32. ***The Fall of Princes:*** Boccaccio, Giovanni, *The Fall of Princes*, translated by John Lydgate. London: Richard Pynson, 1494; See: *The Estelle Doheny Collection, Exhibition Handlist*, Christie, Manson & Woods International, 1987.

33. **manuscript essay by Mark Twain:** Twain, Mark, "The Work of Gutenberg," *Hartford Daily Courant*, June 27, 1900, p. 7, http://twainquotes.com/Gutenberg .html.

34. **"sharpest market downturn":** Bernhardt, Donald, and Marshall Eckblad, "Stock Market Crash of 1987," at Federal Reserve History, November 22, 2013, at http:// federalreservehistory.org/Events/DetailView/48.

35. **the final price:** $4.9 million–plus auction house commission of $490,000 for a total of $5.4million.

36. **seventy-five times what Estelle paid:** Number 45 will remain the most expensive book in the world for the next twelve years.

37. **"find another one":** Goldman, John J., and Eileen V. Quigley, "Gutenberg Bible Is Sold for Record $4.9 Million," *Los Angeles Times*, October 23, 1987.

38. **foremost American book collectors:** Christie, Manson & Woods International Inc., Estelle Doheny Collection from the Edward Laurence Doheny Memorial Library, St. John's Seminary, Camarillo, California, New York: Christie, Manson & Woods International, 1987–89, Christie's Catalog, v. 1, p. 15. Also see Shaffer, Ellen, "Reminiscences of a California Collector, Mrs. Edward Laurence Doheny, 1875–1958," *The Book Collector* 14 (1965): p. 49. Also see Conlon, Tom, "Doheny Collection Sale Leaves Void," *The Press-Courier*, March 8, 1987.

39. **"nothing permanent":** Hurtado, Albert L., "Professors and Tycoons: The Creation of Great Research Libraries on the American West," *Western Historical Quarterly*, vol. 41, no. 2, Summer 2010, pp. 149–69.

40. **"pulling out the books he wanted":** Rita S. Faulders, *The Dissolution of the Estelle Doheny Collection*, p. 31.

41. **"brought together by plan":** Website of the Archival Center at San Fernando Mission, at https://archivalcenter.org/archival-center-library/.

42. **gift beyond understanding:** Rita Faulders, interview with the author.

Chapter 10: The Virtual Gutenberg

1. **Japan's assets have surpassed:** "Japan Is Said to Be Richest," *New York Times*, August 22, 1989.

2. **nyuu ritchi:** Johnston, Eric. "Japan's Bubble Economy: Lessons from when the bubble burst," *Japan Times News*, January 6, 2009, https://japantimes.co .jp/news/2009/01/06/reference/lessons-from-when-the-bubble-burst/#.Wy U2dqczqUl.

3. **"flashy yen that struts":** O'Brien, Rodney, "Japanese Artists Find collectors Still Look Abroad," *New York Times*, July 3, 1988, http://nytimes.com/1988 /07/03/arts/art-japanese-artists-find-collectors-still-look-abroad.html.

4. **sunflower paintings:** Sterngold, James, "What Price Art? Ask Japanese Collectors," *New York Times*, January 8, 1990.

5. **"there would be no Maruzen":** See Maruzen Company Report: http://global documents.morningstar.com/documentlibrary/document/8ce92d1d5d1795e8 .msdoc/original.

6. **According to one account:** Man, p. 105.

7. **overlap between samurai instincts and the code of chivalry:** Toshi Takamiya, interview by Alan Macfarlane, October 19, 2009, at http://alanmacfarlane.com /DO/filmshow/takamiya_fast.htm.

8. **"always emphasized the importance":** *Middle English Texts in Transition: A Festschrift Dedicated to Toshiyuki Takamiya on His 70th Birthday*, edited by Simon Horobin and Linne R. Mooney, New edition, Boydell and Brewer, 2014, p. 298.

9. **"unimaginable":** Broadway, Bill, "The Digital Revelation: The Hand of Technology Brings Gutenberg to the Masses," *Washington Post*, July 12, 2003.

10. **"metaphysically profound":** Tričković, Divna, review of "Practical Methods in Digital Archiving of Rare Books—Examples from the HUMI Project," *Journal for Studies of Literature, Gender and Culture*, University of Belgrade, 2013.

11. **"opportunity for transcending":** *Middle English Texts in Transition*, Ibid., p. 301.

12. **methods and practices:** See Iwai, Shigeaki, "The Digitization of the Gutenberg Bible and other Historic Books," Keio University, http://pnclink.org/annual /annual2001/hk%20pdf/shigeaki%20iwai.pdf.

13. **one million hits:** "One Million Hits for the Gutenberg Bible," Presbyterian Record, May 1, 2002.

14. **"raison-d'être of the HUMI Project":** "HUMI Project," Appendix C, Keio University, March 25, 1998, http://wtec.org/loyola/digilibs/c_05.htm.

15. **without noticing:** Weingart, Scott B., "Do Historians Need Scientists?" *Scottbot* blog, February 11, 2014, http://scottbot.net/HIAL/index.html@p=40349 .html.

16. **complex system:** Needham, Paul, "Prints in the Early Printing Shops," *Studies in the History of Art*, vol. 75, Symposium Papers LII: The Woodcut in Fifteenth Century Europe, 2009, pp. 38–91.

17. **"not how it works":** Christie, Alix, "Was Gutenberg Really the Original Tech Disrupter?" *Financial Times*, December 4, 2014.

18. **Holy Bible:** Malkin, Sol. M., "Johann Gutenberg: 1400–1468," *Antiquarian Bookman*, November 18, 1950, p. 6.

19. **ten million books:** White, Eric Marshall, "The Gutenberg Bible at the Harry Ransom Center, Description and Analysis," University of Texas, p. 5.

20. **"Hardly an aspect of life":** Man, p. 2.

21. **"none of the glory":** Friedman, Robert, ed., *The LIFE Millennium: The 100 Most Important Events and People of the Past 1,000 Years*, New York: LIFE Books, 1998, p. 166.

22. **forever ended:** Richard N. Schwab, interview with the author.

23. **forty-ninth Gutenberg:** See https://global-geography.org/af/Geography/Europe /Germany/Pictures/Schleswig-Holstein_2/Gottorf_Castle_-_Rendsburgs_Fragment_of_the_Gutenberg_Bible_printed_14521454_in_Mainz.

24. **"spreading the Gospel":** Buffenstein, Alyssa, "8 Pages of Gutenberg Bible Expected to Fetch $700,000 at the Sotheby's New York," artnet, June 15, 2015, https://news.artnet.com/market/gutenberg-bible-sothebys-auction-307211. Also see Flood, Alison, "Fragment of Gutenberg Bible Expected to Top $500,000 at Auction," *The Guardian*, June 11, 2015, at https://theguardian.com/books/2015/jun/11 /fragment-of-gutenberg-bible-expected-half-million-dollars-auction-new -york; and Barry, Rebecca Rego, "Eight Pages of the Gutenberg Bible for Sale," *Fine Books* magazine, June 10, 2015, https://finebooksmagazine.com/fine_books _blog/2015/06/eight-pages-of-the-gutenberg-bible-for-sale.phtml.

25. **$100 million range:** Kim Pickard, founder of The Museum of Printing in Haverhill, MA, has suggested the $100 million price tag. See "World-class Collection: Museum of Printing Completes Move from North Andover to Haverhill," *Eagle-Tribune*, September 17, 2016.

26. **20,500-square-foot home:** Schmidt, Mackenzie, "The Most Expensive Home in Beverly Hills—Complete with a Cristal 'Vault' and Gold Rolls Royce—Just Hit the Market for $100 Million," People.com, May 4, 2017, http://people.com/home /the-most-expensive-home-in-beverly-hills-complete-with-a-cristal-vault-and -gold-rolls-royce-just-hit-the-market-for-100-million/.

27. **personal 757 jet:** Bishop, Jordan, "Donald Trump's $100 Million Private Jet Features Gold-Plated (Nearly) Everything," forbes.com, December 7, 2016, https://forbes.com/sites/bishopjordan/2016/12/07/donald-trump-private-jet -photos/.

Epilogue: Final Bows

1. "look like a Denny's": Martel, Judith, "Where Has All the Money Gone? Doheny Collection Sale," *Los Angeles Lay Catholic Mission*, March 1966, p. 1.

Bibliography

1. Folter, Roland, "The Gutenberg Bible in the Antiquarian Book Trade,"*Incunabula: Studies in Fifteenth-Century Printed Books Presented to Lotte Hellinga,* ed. Martin Davies, London: The British Library, 1999, pp. 348–49.

BIBLIOGRAPHY

Note Regarding Census of Known Gutenberg Bibles

According to scholar Roland Folter, "Of making B42 censuses there is no end." The first may have been the census recorded by Reverend Thomas Frognall Dibdin published in 1814. Folter was able to identify thirty-three more published before 1999. Folter's census may be considered the thirty-fourth.[1]

The numbers correlated to the various Gutenberg Bible's presented in this book are based on the survey of existing copies of the forty-two-line Gutenberg Bible undertaken by Ilona Hubay, *Die bekannten Exemplare der zweiundvierzig-zeiligen Bibel und ihre Besitzer* (1985).

In this seminal work, forty-seven copies, and their owners, were identified. Following its publication, two more copies were located in Russia and hence were not included in Hubay's census. Hubay's census was later extended in the online British Library's Incunabula Short Title Catalogue at http://bl.uk /catalogues/istc/index.html.

Books and Journals

Agata, Mari. "Stop-press Variants in the Gutenberg Bible: The First Report of the Collation." *The Papers of the Bibliographical Society of America* 97, no. 2 (2003): 139–65.

Amherst, Sybil. "Lord Amherst and His Library, The Story of a Great Book Lover." *Pall Mall Magazine* 42 (July to December 1908): 783–90.

Bonino, MaryAnn. *The Doheny Mansion, A Biography of a Home.* Los Angeles: Edizoni Casa Animata, 2008.

Carter, John and Nicholas Barker. *ABC for Book Collectors.* New Castle, DE: Oak Knoll Press, 2004.

Distad, Merrill. "William Amhurst Tyssen-Amherst, First Baron of Hackney, Country Gentleman, Collector, and Connoisseur, 1835–1909." Unpublished, Courtesy of Merrill Distad.

Duggan, Brian Patrick. *Saluki: The Desert Hound and the English Travelers Who Brought It to the West.* Jefferson: McFarland & Co., 2009.

Folter, Roland. "The Gutenberg Bible in the Antiquarian Book Trade." *Incunabula: Studies in Fifteenth-Century Printed Books Presented to Lotte Hellinga,* edited by Martin Davies, 271–351. London: The British Library, 1999.

Gambee, B. L. Review of *Gutenberg and the Master of the Playing Cards. The Journal of Library History (1966–1972)* 3 no. 1 (1968): 77–80. Retrieved from http://jstor.org/stable/25540081.

Goff, Frederick R. "Uncle Sam Has a Book." *The Quarterly Journal of the Library of Congress* 38.3 (1981): 122–33.

Handley, John L. *The Quiet Hero: The Story of C. W. Dyson Perrins 1864–1958.* Malvern: Aspect Design, 2010.

Hurtado, Albert L. "Professors and Tycoons: The Creation of Great Research Libraries in the American West." *Western Historical Quarterly* 41.2 (2010): 149–69.

Ikeda, Mayumi. "Two Gutenberg Bibles Used as Compositor's Exemplars." *The Papers of the Bibliographical Society of America* 106, no. 3 (2012): 357–72.

Ing, Janet. *Johann Gutenberg and His Bible: A Historical Study.* New York: Typophiles, 1988.

Kapr, Albert. *Johann Gutenberg: The Man and His Invention.* Aldershot: Scolar Press; Brookfield, VT: Ashgate Publishing, 1966.

Kusko, Bruce H., Thomas A. Cahill, Robert A. Eldred, and Richard N. Schwab. *Nuclear Instruments and Methods in Physics Research Section B: Beam Interactions with Materials and Atoms* 3, Issues 1–3 (April–May 1984): 689–94.

Landon, Richard. *A Long Way from the Armstrong Beer Parlour—A Life in Rare Books: Essays by Richard Landon*. Toronto: The Thomas Fisher Rare Book Library; New Castle, DE: Oak Knoll Press, 2014.

Lothrop, Gloria Ricci. "Strength Made Stronger: The Role of Women in Southern California Philanthropy." *Southern California Quarterly* 71.2/3 (1989): 143–94.

MacDonald, Gregory. "Recent Art Acquisitions in American Public Collections," *Art & Life* 11, no. 6 (December 1919): 342–45.

Mayo, H. "Newspapers and Bibliography: The Importance of Artifacts." *The Papers of the Bibliographical Society of America* 96, no. 4 (2002): 493–96. Retrieved from http://jstor.org/stable/24295640.

Needham, Paul. "The Compositor's Hand in the Gutenberg Bible." *The Papers of the Bibliographical Society of America* 77, no. 3 (1983): 341–71.

Needham, Paul. "The Compositor's Hand in the Gutenberg Bible: A Review of the Todd Thesis [Review of *The Gutenberg Bible: New Evidence of the Original Printing. The Third Hanes Lecture*]." *The Papers of the Bibliographical Society of America* 77, no. 3 (1983): 341–71. Retrieved from http://jstor.org/stable/24302922.

——. "Division of Copy in the Gutenberg Bible: Three Glosses on the Ink Evidence." *The Papers of the Bibliographical Society of America* 79, no. 3 (1985): 411–426.

——. "Gutenberg Bibles in Electronic Facsimile." *The Papers of the Bibliographical Society of America* 98, no. 3 (2004): 355–63.

——. "A Gutenberg Bible Used as Printer's Copy by Heinrich Eggestein in Strassburg." *Transactions of the Cambridge Bibliographical Society* 9 (1986): 36–75.

——. "The Paper Supply of the Gutenberg Bible." *The Papers of the Bibliographical Society of America* 79, no. 3 (1985): 303–74.

——. "Paul Schwenke and Gutenberg Scholarship: The German Contribution, 1885–1921." *The Papers of the Bibliographical Society of America* 84, no.3 (1990): 241–64. Retrieved from http://jstor.org/stable/24302983.

Oyens, Felix de Marez and Paul Needham. Review of *The Estelle Doheny Collection. Part I: Fifteenth-Century Books including the Gutenberg Bible, which will be sold on Thursday, October 22, 1987. The Papers of the Bibliographical Society of America* 81, no. 3 (1987): 376–77.

Pearson, David. *Books as History: The Importance of Books Beyond Their Texts.* London: The British Library; New Castle, DE: Oak Knoll Books, 2008.

Pelik, Rowena. *A. C. W. Dyson Perrins: A Brief Account of His Life, His Achievements, His Collections and Benefactions.* Worcester: Dyson Perrins Museum Trust, 1983.

Potten, E. and S. Tokunaga. Introduction: Incunabula on the Move: The Current State and Future Direction of Incunabula Studies. *Transactions of the Cambridge Bibliographical Society* 15, no. 1 (2012): 1–7. Retrieved from http://jstor.org/stable/24391714.

Randall, David A. "Dukedom Large Enough, Changing the Gutenberg Census." *The Papers of the Bibliographical Society of America* 56, no. 2 (1962): 157–74.

Reeds, K. Review of *Johann Gutenberg: The Man and His Invention. Technology and Culture* 40, no. 2 (1999): 403–404. Retrieved from http://jstor.org/stable/25147324.

Reichner, H. Review of *The Gutenberg Documents With translations of the texts into English, based with authority on the compilation by Dr. Karl Schorbach. By Douglas C. McMurtrie . . . The Papers of the Bibliographical Society of America* 35, no. 3 (1941): 219. Retrieved from http://jstor.org/stable/24297082.

Ricci, Seymour. *English Collectors of Books and Manuscripts (1530–1930) and Their Marks of Ownership.* New York: Cambridge University Press, 2010.

Sandon, Henry, *Royal Worcester Porcelain from 1862 to the Present Day,* London: Barrie & Jenkins, 1973.

Schwab, Richard et al. "Cyclotron Analysis of the Ink in the 42-line Bible." *The Papers of the Bibliographical Society of America* 77, no. 2 (1983): 285–315.

Schwab, Richard et al. "New Evidence on the Printing of the Gutenberg Bible: The Inks in the Doheny Copy." *The Papers of the Bibliographical Society of America* 79, no. 3 (1985): 375–410.

Schwab, Richard N. "An Ersatz Leaf in the Doheny Gutenberg Bible Volume I." *The Papers of the Bibliographical Society of America* 81, no. 4 (1987): 479–85.

Schwab, Richard N. et al. "Ink Patterns in the Gutenberg New Testament: The Proton Milliprobe Analysis of the Lilly Library Copy." *The Papers of the Bibliographical Society of America* 80, no. 3 (1986): 305–31.

Schwab, Richard N. "New Clues about Gutenberg in the Huntington 42-Line Bible: What the Margins Reveal." *Huntington Library Quarterly* 51 (1988): 176–209.

Schwab, Richard N. et al. "The Proton Milliprobe Ink Analysis of the Harvard B42, Volume II." *The Papers of the Bibliographical Society of America* 81, no. 4 (1987): 403–32.

Starr, Kevin. *Material Dreams, Southern California Through the 1920s,* New York: Oxford University Press, 1990.

———. "The Rise of Los Angeles as an American Bibliographical Center." Sacramento: California State Library Foundation, 1989.

Stoneman, W. P. Review of *Incunabula: Studies in Fifteenth-Century Printed Books Presented to Lotte Hellinga. The British Library Studies in the History of the Book. The Papers of the Bibliographical Society of America* 95, no. 1 (2001): 119–21. Retrieved from http://jstor.org/stable/24304723.

The Coming Sale of Part of the Robert Hoe Library. *The Lotus Magazine* 3, no. 2 (1911): 35–43.

The Gutenberg Bible, Catalogue of the Exhibition Held in the Princeton University Library, compiled by Mina R. Bryan and Howard C. Rice Jr. Princeton, New Jersey, 1960, p. 38.

Gutenberg: Man of the Millennium, From a Secret Enterprise to the First Media Revolution, Abridged version of the Catalogue of the exhibition Staged by the City of Mainz on the occasion of the sixth centenary of the birth of Johannes Gutenberg, City of Mainz, 2000.

White, Eric Marshall. "Gutenberg Bibles on the Move in England, 1789–1834." *Transactions of the Cambridge Bibliographical Society* 15, no. 1 (2012): 79–100.

Catalogs

Catalogue of Books and Manuscripts in the Estelle Doheny Collection, Ward Ritchie Press, Los Angeles, Vol. 1, 1940; Vol. 2, 1946; Vol. 3, 1955.

Catalogue of the Fine, Extensive and Valuable Library of the Rt. Hon. The Earl of Gosford, Puttick and Simpson, London 1884.

Catalogue of the Magnificent Library of Choice and Valuable Books & Manuscripts, The Property of The Rt. Hon. Lord Amherst of Hackney, Sotheby, Wilkinson & Hodge, Dryden Press: London, 1908.

Catalogue of the Magnificent Library, Principally of Early Printed and Early Illustrated Books, Formed by C. W. Dyson Perrins, Esq., Sotheby & Co., London, 1947.

The Estelle Doheny Collection Vols. 1–7, Christie's, New York, 1987.

Interviews and Private Archival Materials

"An Incomparable Volume of the Most Important of All Printed books," typed memo, Ernest Maggs to Estelle Doheny, 1950.

Monsignor Eugene Frilot interview, Glendale, CA, 2014.

Rita S. Faulders interviews, Camarillo, CA, 2012–2018.

Rita Faulders, oral history with Lucille Miller, August 15, 1984.

Thomas A. Cahill and Richard N. Schwab interviews, Sacramento, CA, 2013, 2015, 2016.

Libraries and Archives

Amherst Family Papers, Rose Lipman Library, London

British Library, London

The Bryher Papers, Beinecke Rare Book and Manuscript Library, Yale University, New Haven, CT

Digital Collections of Keio University Libraries, Tokyo

Edward L. Doheny Jr. Memorial Library, Archives, University of Southern California, Los Angeles

Estelle Doheny Collection, Archive of the Archdiocese of Los Angeles, Mission Hills, CA

Frank J. Hogan Scrapbooks, courtesy of Hogan & Hartson, LLP, Washington, DC

The Gosford Papers, Public Record Office of Northern Ireland (PRONI), Belfast, Ireland

Papers of David Anton Randall, Lilly Library Manuscript Collections, Indiana University, Bloomington

Papers of Henry W. O'Melveny, Huntington Library, San Marino, CA

Papers of Rita S. Faulders, Camarillo, CA

Thomas A. Cahill Papers, Crocker Historical and Archaeological Project [DOC MSS 67], 1981–2009, Saint Louis University Libraries Special Collections: Archives and Manuscripts

William Amhurst Tyssen Amherst Papers, Thomas Fisher Rare Book Library, University of Toronto

Websites and CD-ROMs

Digital Collections of Keio University Libraries, Gutenberg 42-line Bible, Keio University, Tokyo: http://dcollections.lib.keio.ac.jp/en/gutenberg /explanation

Dollar and pound ratios were examined using the calculators at https:// measuringworth.com/calculators/exchange/index.php.

Library of Congress (Octavo Edition), "The Gutenberg Bible"

Metropolitan Museum of Art: http://metmuseum.org/art/collection/search /544484

Oram, Richard W. "The Gutenberg Bible at the Harry Ransom Center: A General Introduction." *The Gutenberg Bible at the Harry Ransom Center*, Austin: University of Texas at Austin, 2004. CD-ROM.

INDEX